Broadcasting
in the Third World

Broadcasting in the Third World

Promise and Performance

ELIHU KATZ and GEORGE WEDELL

WITH

MICHAEL PILSWORTH AND DOV SHINAR

Harvard University Press
Cambridge, Massachusetts

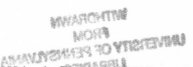

10 9 8 7 6 5 4 3
Printed in the United States of America

Library of Congress Cataloging in Publication Data
Katz, Elihu, 1926–
    Broadcasting in the Third World.
    Includes bibliographical references and index.
    1. Underdeveloped areas—Broadcasting. I. Wedell,
Eberhard George, joint author. II. Title.
HE8689.95.K37   384.55′4′091724   77-8282
ISBN 0-674-08341-5

Preface

The world in the 1970s is witnessing an important stage in the transfer of the electronic media of radio and television from the industrial countries of Europe and North America to the developing countries of the Third World. In the case of radio, the process is nearly complete. All the countries classified as developing by UNCTAD have now instituted some form of radio broadcasting. A few began as early as the 1920s, soon after the introduction of radio broadcasting in the West. Others began only recently. It was not until 1966 that Swaziland and Botswana introduced radio broadcasting. By now, however, the majority of people in the world live within reach of a domestic radio signal, however poor the quality of the signal in many areas, however remote the language of the medium from the vernacular of the listeners.

The introduction of television in the developing countries began much more recently. While many new and developing nations have adopted the new medium, television coverage is usually limited to the main urban centers and only rarely penetrates beyond their suburbs. So much remains to be decided, for good or ill, in television.

When we speak of transfer we are referring not to the transfer of technology alone but also to the transfer of sociocultural institutions with economic and political implications, institutions ready-packaged with organizational and program formats and even contents. Although the processes of transplantation vary widely, it seems to us that the problems raised in the various countries we have studied have a great deal in common. This shared pattern of problems that nations are encountering on the way to achieving the great hopes held out for the contribution of broadcasting to political, economic, social, and cultural development has attracted our attention. It is on these problems and hopes that our studies have been concentrated.

Social and educational planners, as well as academics in the 1950s and 1960s, regarded broadcasting as a possible panacea for many of the developmental problems of the Third World. Their views gained the support both of Western governments and of many international agencies. Indeed a process of mutual reinforcement led governments, multilateral aid agencies, and private enterprise to invest on a spectacular scale in order to speed the transfer of broadcasting from the West to the developing countries.

This volume is the result of almost three years of research into the ways in which broadcasting institutions have been transplanted and have taken root in the developing countries. We set out to study the promise held out for broadcasting both by the aid-givers and by the receiving nations themselves and to compare this promise with the performance of the broadcast media. However, we have not been concerned merely to document the existence of gaps between promise and performance. Both as students of broadcasting policy and as persons with practical experience of broadcasting, we are quite aware of the web of constraints—political, economic, and cultural—within which broadcasting operates. The emphasis of our study is on *process*, on the dynamics of accommodating the phenomenon of broadcasting and its institutional forms to the surroundings of a developing country for which it was not in the first instance designed. The reader, therefore, may find us more sympathetic to the problems of harnessing broadcasting to national development than are some of our colleagues.

We believe it is important to accept the urge for modernization. We also believe, however, that the agents of modernization—the broadcast media are a prime example—have side effects that were not anticipated, even though they occur with considerable regularity in country after country.

The broadcast media (and particularly television) in the developing countries are in general purveying a homogenized brand of popular culture, either copied or borrowed from broadcasting in the West. This uniformity may well advance the processes of modernization insofar as national sharing of images is concerned. It may also induce a standardized range of economic demands that may encourage mass-production techniques, but at the same time it is certainly destructive of indigenous political and cultural self-expression.

In our study we came across variations in the process of accommodation to local constraints. The mass media in the developing countries have gradually abandoned the element of autonomy from government control which was explicit in most models of broadcasting structure transferred from the West. Almost without exception, the media are by now in the direct or indirect service of the government of the day. There is not much room for dissent, however constructive, in the broadcasting services of developing countries. Ironically, there is not much room, either, for the inherited cultural values of the society.

The study on which this book is based was designed to be sufficiently comprehensive and representative to enable us to draw conclusions of some validity. It is based both on an extensive review of statistical and documentary data concerning broadcasting in ninety-one developing countries and on case studies in eleven of these.

The question of defining the developing countries arose early in our work. The various existing methods of classification all have weaknesses, and we finally elaborated the criteria (set out in Appendix B) based on a classification system developed by UNCTAD. There are, of course, more than ninety-one countries that may be classified as developing, but for the reasons given in the appendix, we have limited our selection of countries. The intensive case studies of broadcasting were carried out in Algeria, Brazil, Cyprus, Indonesia, Iran, Nigeria, Peru, Senegal, Singapore, Tanzania, and Thailand. The sample of countries that we studied in situ was drawn from a classification of our group of ninety-one developing countries along a six-category scale of socioeconomic development. We chose one or two countries from each category, taking account of their geographical location, colonial relationships, and level of media development. At least two members of the research team visited each of these countries. We interviewed broadcasters, members of government, and, where they existed, spokesmen of the opposition, as well as officials, cultural and educational leaders, and others. In each country, we enlisted the services of one or more associates to interpret and translate where necessary, to assist us in listening and viewing, to collect historical material, to assemble organizational charts and statistical material, and, in general, to ensure that we did not, through lack of knowledge of local conditions, omit essential elements of information.

We visited the countryside as well as the cities and spoke to ordinary listeners and viewers. Wherever we could, we participated in listening or viewing in teahouses, cafes, viewing centers, and schools and discussed with local inhabitants what we heard and saw. Among us we had command of English, French, Spanish, and Portuguese, and our associates helped wherever these languages were not sufficient. Our interviews were guided by a sixty-four-point checklist but were unstructured. Not every question was put to every interviewee, but care was taken to ask each question of a number of different respondents. Some of our most important information derives from this cross-checking.

We began with a predetermined list of the key persons and the types of people whom we wanted to meet, and we tried to be in touch with them in advance of our visits. We then built on these contacts on the spot, and many of our most useful interviews were provided by persons who were recommended to us by our initial interviewees or by our local associates. In almost every country we also met both present and former broadcasters and officials. Those who had been inside the system and, for one reason or another, had left often provided a critique of the system. Such information was cross-checked and used to complement the views of those currently in control of the system.

We did our best to develop an awareness of the local cultures. In addition to seeking out the obvious sources of information in and around government and broadcasting, we made it our business to talk with educators and, more generally, with those concerned with modernization on the one hand and with cultural continuity on the other. Occasionally we were fortunate to meet persons steeped in the traditions of their country who were able to assess the relationship of modernization and continuity. Through them, we attempted to analyze the functions and effects of the broadcast media in the changing society of each country.

It was not possible to conduct systematic surveys of audiences. We collected such material in the few cases in which the countries themselves had machinery to make it available. We hope the time will not be too far distant when we can reasonably expect the answers to questions that might have been asked had adequate audience-research machinery existed. What, for example, are the gratifications derived from viewing "Ironside" in Bangkok or from listening to American pop music in Nigeria? What is understood of "Peyton Place" or "Mission Impossible" in rural areas where electricity has only just arrived? Is the idealization of the American way of life really perceived by the viewers in a conscious way? What picture of the world does the imported staccato-style news format of radio and television bulletins present to the peasant farmer?

For some help with these, a mere sample of the questions in which we were interested, we drew also on the opinions of critics and newspapermen, on debates in the legislatures and in the press, and on other sources in each country. We gave special attention to the recruitment and training of workers for the broadcast media, their status in society, and the organization of their work. The provision, maintenance, and renewal of equipment was another problem that interested us, and, of course, the sources of the technology, the training, the organizational models, and the content of programs were matters of central concern.

Obviously, our study was undertaken in the course of a continuing process. We have not assessed definitively the gap between promise and performance. Our study could do no more than to identify particular points along a continuum of change. In the former colonial countries, our study in general took place a decade or more after independence. The early sense of celebration was well and truly over. We arrived, as it were, on the morning after.

Four themes characterized our encounters:

1. First, the growing self-awareness of popular movements and the need for governments to take account of them. In some countries governments have reacted by opening up the mass media; in most they have reacted by reinforcing their control of the mass media.

2. Second, the shift in economic strength among Third World countries. Algeria, Iran, Nigeria, and perhaps Peru are now able to rely on their oil revenues for a large proportion of their national means. Their neighbors, who lack oil or other scarce primary products, have become relatively poorer. The deployment of these resources has obvious implications for development and communication.

3. A call for more authentic self-expression. It was often emphasized to us that the media of mass communication are alienating people from their own cultural roots. Voices are being raised, demanding that the media serve not only the goals of national integration and economic development, but also the goals of cultural rediscovery and creativity. Some would go so far as to say that the doctrine of the free flow of information is damaging to their cultures.

4. Finally, the marginality of television to most developing countries, despite its intrusion into the life-style of capital cities. Planning for the use of this medium may yet be capable of direction, and our analysis and recommendations are addressed to that end.

The problem of ensuring that research is not out of date by the time it is published has concerned us throughout this study. We have endeavored to keep abreast of recent developments both in the developing countries themselves and in the relevant literature. However, it should be noted that our fieldwork in the eleven case-study countries began in September 1973 and ended in April 1975. Great changes have taken place in certain of the countries that we visited since our data were collected. There has been civil war in Cyprus, profound political reorganization in Nigeria, Peru, and Thailand, and minor changes have taken place in the broadcasting structures of Algeria and Brazil. We have not attempted the task of bringing the text up to date in regard to all these matters.

The study on which this book is based is the product of teamwork between the Department of Adult Education of the University of Manchester and the Communications Institute of the Hebrew University of Jerusalem. It was financially supported by the Ford Foundation whose grant was administered by the International Institute of Communications. We were much encouraged by the interest of Francis X. Sutton, deputy vice-president of the International Division of the Ford Foundation, Alessandro Silj, and David Davis. Lord Briggs, the chairman, and members of the IIC Projects Committee gave of their time to read and discuss our case studies and the final report. We are also grateful to the officials of the Institute who added the handling of our funds to their many other responsibilities.

We wish to acknowledge the assistance of Dr. Rita

Cruise O'Brien, who helped us with our case study of Senegal, and of Brian Nichol. Judith Whyte administered the collection of statistical and documentary data from the ninety-one countries in our study and prepared a bibliography of descriptive material on broadcasting in the developing countries. Stella Pilsworth annotated recent research material on broadcasting and national development and assisted in the preparation of tables. Cathryn Lanyon provided excellent secretarial support. The manuscript was typed by Hwee Sau Chun.

We benefited from the criticism and advice of many colleagues. In particular we wish to thank Peter Golding and Professor Jeremy Tunstall who commented on the manuscript in draft. Others who gave us advice and counsel include Arild Boman, Nicholas Bennett, Erskine Childers, Bert Cowlan, Eric Croston, Leslie Diamond, Professor Marco Antonio Rodrigues Dias, Wilson Dizard, K. Eapen, Alexander Eddington, Elizabeth Fox de Cardona, Dr. Estella Garland, F. Hakimzadeh, M. Haminhtu, B. Ivanovič, Lionel Izod, Peter Kent, Sir Charles Moses, Graham Mytton, Dr. Marcia Paredes, Richmond Postgate, Guy Scandlen, Richard Sherrington, Dr. Sirichai Sirikaya, Dr. Majid Tehranian, Jack Thompson, Michael Type, Johnny Wilkinson, and John Willings. We are grateful also to the staffs of the Institut Français de Presse, the Asian Mass Communication Research and Information Center, the Development Support Communications Unit of FAO, the UNESCO Mass Communication Documentation Centre, the International Press Institute, the BBC and IBA libraries, and the British Council.

In the countries that we studied in detail we are in the debt of the hundreds of broadcasters, government ministers and officials, educators, scholars, and ordinary listeners and viewers who took a lively interest in our work and were candid and informative in their conversations with us.

Contents

Tables

Part One

Promise

1

The Problem of Development and the Promise of Broadcasting

It is not surprising that the concepts of modernization and communication should have come to be connected. The mass media are among the chief symbols of modernity. The very words "mass communication" have a ring of newness. And, in fact, all the eleven new nations in which we conducted the case studies on which this book is based have introduced radio systems that, at varying levels of quality, cover their territories.[1] All of them have introduced television, albeit in many cases on little more than a symbolic scale.[2] Yet in spite of their affirmative actions in adopting broadcast media, the developing nations have invested little effort in the formulation of explicit policies for relating the media to development goals.

The goals themselves are well understood, and, for two decades at least, "development" has been accepted as the proper instrument for their achievement. New nations must be forged from tribal, regional, and ethnic groups; new political institutions must be created and given legitimacy and stability; economic growth must be fostered by increasing production and international trade; social conditions must be improved by reducing disease, increasing income per head, and improving educational standards; cultural homogeneity must be promoted by the rediscovery or creation of national symbols and art forms.

In our work we have come up against two sets of questions arising from these assumptions about the centrality of development. The first is the fundamental one. Is development on the scale and at the pace at which it is being attempted throughout the Third World either possible or desirable? Would it not be better to take a longer view than is envisaged in the development plans of most countries? Would it not be better to take a more selective view of what type of development is suitable? Is it evident that development as widely defined—that is, development toward the type of industrialized and urbanized society that is thought to have brought enviable benefits to the countries of Western Europe and North America—is what most countries of the Third World really need?

The second set of questions asks whether development is best served by government intervention on the massive, and often exclusive, scale on which it now takes place. It has been put to us that much development might be more effective, less wasteful, and closer to the needs of the people if governments restricted their intervention to those areas where activity on a national scale can be proved to be essential, or where considerations of homogeneity or national security require development to be undertaken by government itself. This argument, applied to broadcasting, leads to the question of whether state control and initiative are more conducive to broadcasting development than is local enterprise.

Both these sets of large questions are heavily loaded with sociopolitical import. In the course of our inquiries we have been interested to see that both sorts of questions are beginning to be asked in the developing countries. We have had these questions in mind in the writing of this book. We are also conscious that commentators on development problems who themselves come from relatively rich and stable countries need to guard against their bias toward gradualism and restraint.

The critique of the development process that has emerged in the 1970s tends to forget the situation of a quarter century ago. The people who now question whether certain of the goals of modernization are even worth striving for forget that after the Second World War the world was more optimistic about the prospects for the "take-off" of the economies of the new and developing nations and that the mass media came to be considered an important stimulant to this process. Social scientists wrote about the possible functions of the media in development and warned of possible dysfunctions. The specialized agencies of the United Nations and some of the major foundations took up these ideas and cooperated with governments to finance experiments in a variety of ways of using broadcasting for national development.

The acceptance of broadcasting has marched with other concomitants of development, such as geographical mobility. The poverty and inadequacy of the living conditions of large parts of the developing world have been such as to lead those suffering them to believe that conditions in other parts must be better. Thus has come about the migration from the village to the town, from rural areas to industrial areas, and from poor countries to richer countries. This mobility is sustained even where the evidence shows that, for the individual, migration may be hazardous and that the chances of real amelioration of living and working conditions are not high.

The acceptance of broadcasting also marches with the acceptance of modern types of education. The assumed, and in some ways actual, contribution to socioeconomic development that education is thought to have made in the developed countries of Europe and North America has been thought to be replicable in developing countries, if not for communities as a whole, then at least for the more fortunate of their members. Thus developing countries have pursued a transferred but largely unadapted model of education that has led neither the individual nor the community as a whole to the expected success, because the conditions that enabled education to contribute to the economic development of the

West are not present in large areas of the Third World today.

The acceptance of broadcasting, lastly, has marched alongside the transfer of political structures that, again, are thought to have given the peoples of the West the resilience and dynamism to achieve their present level of development. Thus the framework of representative government is introduced in the hope that it will engender a similar dynamism. But this framework is superimposed on a different tradition of government that may not place so high a value on resilience and dynamism.

Broadcasting has thus been one of a collection of transferred attitudes and institutions that in the countries of the West have been the effects of development, but that in the developing world have been regarded as among its causes. The causal process, however, has only rarely been elaborated, and the media have been introduced with only general statements of their hoped-for effects. In some countries, these statements are extremely vague; in others they are somewhat more explicit. The more explicit statements can be heard in those countries in which the broadcast media are unitary in structure and directly controlled by government (the predominant pattern in Asia and Africa), and the introduction of broadcasting, particularly television broadcasting, calls for the allocation of substantial public resources. Consequently, in these countries in particular the governments have had to formulate statements of policy in order to justify the allocation of such resources. But the aims set for broadcasting have been largely borrowed from Western Europe, where broadcasting, whether by radio or television, is formally expected to inform, educate, and entertain. Even where the expected promise of broadcasting has been articulated in the Third World, that articulation itself was imported with the technology of broadcasting.

The object of this chapter is to identify the promise that has come to be associated with the broadcast media in the minds of policymakers and political leaders in the new nations. We try to follow the emergence of the goals proposed for broadcasting, drawing on the sample of the eleven countries that we studied in detail. We find, naturally, that certain media policies are best understood against the background of events. Others are a response to the development of the media themselves, as much to the problems they have created as to those they have been expected to solve. In this context, we review writings of media theorists and researchers, some of whom have anticipated these problems. But our focus is on the promise of the media from the point of view of the developing countries. This allows us to assess the performance of the media according to criteria that the countries, not we, have chosen. Our focus covers three areas of development in which policymakers have most persistently expected the media to make a positive contribution: national integration, socioeconomic modernization, and cultural creativity.

MEDIA PROMISE IN THE ERA OF RADIO

In the 1930s and 1940s most of today's new and developing nations were not yet either new or developing. Radio was delivered to the colonial countries by the metropolitan powers and to the noncolonial countries either by farsighted entrepreneurs (as in Peru and Brazil) or by government-commercial alliances (as in Thailand). Some of the colonial countries received broadcasting later than others (Cyprus in 1948 and Tanzania in 1951, for example), but in all of those in our sample radio arrived prior to independence and was organized as a government system. Among the noncolonial countries, only Iran established a centralized broadcasting system, but this came quite late and probably reflects European influence.

The British and French governments in different ways saw in the transfer of radio broadcasting to the colonies an extension of their political and cultural influence. Apart from extending the reach of empire, the early policies and promises that guided radio development in the colonial countries included such objectives as the enlistment of loyalty, the promotion of tranquillity and unity, the preparation for autonomy, the achievement of modernization, and the encouragement of indigenous creativity. The developments evoked mixed reactions from the populations served. Some were pleased to be given access to the metropolitan culture; those linked with nascent movements for liberation, on the other hand, regarded the imperialist broadcasting services with suspicion and antipathy, although they were prepared to accept training by expatriate broadcasters in order to prepare themselves for the day when liberation would come. In Indonesia, for example, "cultural associations" working toward national liberation managed to make active use of the Dutch-established radio.

In the commercial broadcasting systems, represented in our sample by Peru, Brazil, and, in a modified form, Thailand, profit was the promise of broadcasting. But even in the countries adopting these systems there were early statements, particularly in Brazil, about the cultural importance of radio, and this theme has been echoed and reinforced in Brazilian policy statements on communication in recent years. The Brazilians were just as explicit about the mission of radio in the spread of Portuguese as was the metropolitan broadcasting to Algeria and Senegal that promoted the use of French. Going beyond nationalism, the introduction of radio in Brazil was accompanied by far-reaching predictions that the new medium might bring peace and harmony to the world. Although radio in Thailand is nominally under government or army control, nevertheless (apart from the government stations and the mandatory broadcasting of the official news bulletin by all stations), the proliferation of small-scale entrepreneurial radio there has a strong similarity to the South American pattern. In all three countries periodic attempts have been made to control or limit advertising, to constrain broadcasters, to extend coverage, to introduce government networks, to eliminate corruption, and to wrest influence and power from expatriate control. Some of these efforts have been more successful than others. But, on the whole, except for the institution of licensing systems for private stations, the era of radio has lacked a formulated policy for broadcasting, even when development planning began.

Not all private radio stations are commercial. The role of missionaries and other religious bodies in radio development is significant. In a number of countries—Peru is a good example—the religious missions perceived the promise of radio as an instrument of their efforts in evangelization and education. Several types of effort have been made to harness radio to the task of reducing illiteracy, reducing disease, and improving farming methods, as well as promoting Christianity. "Radio Voice of the Gospel," which broadcasts from Addis Ababa in Ethiopia, is an example of a religious station pursuing similar aims on an international scale.

In sum, the extension of empire, the making of profit, the rallying of independence forces, and missionary activity have been some of the different promises perceived in radio. In some of the British territories and occasionally elsewhere an explicit connection was made between the potential of radio and the needs of political, economic, and cultural development. This process of development envisaged independence only as a distant goal.

THE INTRODUCTION OF TELEVISION

The decision to introduce television in many countries more or less coincided with the beginnings of national socioeconomic planning. One might have expected a more development-oriented television broadcasting policy to have emerged from the conjunction of these events, but it did not. Even where the groundwork had been laid by the

colonial powers, it took several more years for policymakers, politicians, and broadcasters to recognize the need to
consider these relationships. Why the delay? Perhaps the
agenda of the new nations was too full to allow the implications of the medium for nation-building and development
to be considered. Perhaps the new leaders were satisfied
with the role played by radio in rallying the forces of national liberation and hoped that this role would incorporate
television. Perhaps development planning was too much
preoccupied with socioeconomic, and too little with cultural, considerations.

Television on a small scale was introduced in most countries in the late 1950s and early 1960s. Of the eleven nations
we studied in detail only three have explicitly connected its
introduction with development. The first television broadcasts in Peru and Senegal were educational experiments
inspired by UNESCO. The Peru experiment was rapidly
submerged and all but silenced by the largest entrepreneurs
in radio broadcasting who opened commercial stations in
Lima. In Senegal, President Senghor agreed to locate a
pilot educational television project in Dakar with the assistance of UNESCO. After the experiment shut down, its
equipment was used to advantage in 1972 in a French government-sponsored operation to broadcast the Olympic
Games direct from Munich. After a further delay a locally
transmitted television service has begun in Senegal, broadcasting for a few hours a day to the elite of Dakar.

The government of mainland Tanzania has resisted the
introduction of any television at all, insisting that the medium is too expensive and that Tanzania's radio coverage is
as yet too imperfect. In 1972, a small color television station
was opened in Zanzibar, the other partner of the United
Republic of Tanzania, which derives substantial foreign
exchange mainly from the export of cloves. It remains to be
seen whether opening this station will undermine the reso-
lute policy of President Nyerere. According to First Vice-

President Aboud Jumbe, who is the chief minister of Zanzibar, the emphasis of Zanzibar Television Service "is on education, and that we could best do through colour television." Speaking at an African symposium on color television jointly organized by the Zanzibar Ministry of Information and the government of West Germany, the vice-president explained that he and the Revolutionary Council meant education "in the widest meaning of the word, including instructional programming, vocational guidance, home education and the dissemination of healthy political ideas." [3]

In the majority of the developing countries, however, television was introduced for reasons extraneous to development. In some cases, it was introduced prior to independence by colonial governments. Television was introduced in Cyprus by the British, we were told, to help keep the people off the streets—as a tranquilizer, so to speak. A national television service was proposed by the British in Nigeria, but it is characteristic of Nigeria's problems that the Western Region, in association with one of Britain's independent television companies, beat the national service to the draw in 1959 by opening what was claimed to be the first television station in Africa.

Television was brought to Iran by the enterprising Iranian bottler of Pepsi-Cola, who also owned the franchise for the sale of RCA television sets. In Thailand, a consortium of the government Public Relations Department, the armed forces, and private enterprise joined to introduce Bangkok's first television station in 1954, soon after Japan and the Philippines had established theirs. Bangkok's was the first in continental Asia. By common consent of observers and participants in Thailand, it was the Thai fascination with gimmickry and the traditional value of *sanook* (fun) that explains the haste. As with the introduction of television in Senegal, Indonesia began television broadcasting in 1962 timed to the opening of a sporting event, the Asian Games.

These curious and haphazard episodes punctuate the development of television in the Third World. Sporting events have often been the immediate reason for linking up with satellite transmission.[4] Television coverage in Iran was extended in time to broadcast the coronation of the Empress Farah. After his coup in 1953 President Rojas of Colombia ordered the establishment of a television system in time to mark the first anniversary of his dictatorship.[5] More recently, President Idi Amin of Uganda installed color television equipment at a cost of $6 million for the meeting of the Organization of African Unity in Kampala. As it happened the equipment was also available in time for his most recent wedding in 1975. Color television was introduced in Thailand to coincide with the Miss Thailand beauty contest. These reasons are frivolous, and the frivolity is reinforced by the fact that the television services so introduced are confined very largely to the capitals and their suburbs, owing to the propagation characteristics of television signals. The extension of coverage is often a priority of governments, which then find the cost excessive. This is one of the constraints that cause promise to diverge from performance. In countries such as Peru, Algeria, or Brazil, where the urban centers are concentrated along the coast, transmission over vast areas inland or across mountains and deserts is especially difficult and expensive.

That is also the case in Thailand and in Iran, where high mountains block signals from the metropolis. Language is another constraint. While radio can afford to diversify languages through multiple channels or alternate programming hours, the very high cost of television production and transmission precludes the same solutions. The lack of electrification in the countryside is still, however, the main constraining factor.

But technical difficulties are not the sole explanation for the limited expansion of television. Also important is the fact that consumers live in cities. None of the broadcasting systems that we studied operated its television service without some advertising income. Moreover, receiving sets are expensive, costing more than a year's income for a farmer in many countries. As long as reception technology is considered to be the responsibility of the audience, the concentration of sets will therefore be where the cash income is concentrated, that is, in the cities. And the consumers, of course, are mainly the members of the urban professional and commercial classes and the government officials. They are also the politically active, who constitute the reference group within which leadership operates. The rural population which constitutes 70–90 percent of the population of most countries relies largely on subsistence farming and is in no position to articulate a demand for television or other government services. It is ironic that the target populations for development efforts are likely to be last in line to receive the electronic media.

Yet it is not only pure frivolity that sometimes blinds the leaders of these countries to the developmental potential of television. Indeed, almost everyone except a handful of media professionals (practitioners and researchers), certain agencies of social change (such as UNESCO), and some political leaders perceives television more as diverting than as informative or persuasive. That is the image of television in the West, notwithstanding that the social scientists and the agencies of change treat the media so seriously. Television, at its best, *is* entertaining, at least as much as it is informative. And entertainment may contribute as much as information to development, even though it is rarely used in that way.

Moreover, it "pays" to perceive television primarily in terms of entertainment. Governments that do so sleep more comfortably at night in the knowledge that television is unlikely to betray them. At best, it diverts people from their own problems and the problems of society. Even better, there are advertisers, both foreign and domestic, who are willing to pay to have the people diverted. This willingness is good for the income of the broadcasters, as well as for the people and their leaders. Moreover, an entertainment-based medium can be expected to keep away from delicate problems of government and politics in return for a free hand in other areas of programming. A medium conceived of in this role can be expected to be loyal to the powers that be.

Thus there is no reason to assume that the introduction of television is automatically equated with development by the leaders of the new and developing nations. Typically, it is introduced for a variety of other purposes: as an opiate of the people, as a symbol of nationhood, as a projector of the image of the leadership, as part of a national celebration, to transmit a sporting event, as a result of an attractive proposition by a foreign broadcasting company or set manufacturer, as a result of the educational prodding of UNESCO, or to meet the cosmopolitan expectations of big-city dwellers demanding the right to be entertained in the cosmopolitan manner. Though television has its share of prophets in the new nations, the introduction of television can be said to have diverted attention from the early formulations of the promise of radio.

COHERENT BROADCASTING POLICIES: SOME BEGINNINGS

The broadcast media, as we see, were not originally conceived of as major instruments of development policy. Even independence did not direct systematic attention to broadcasting for this purpose. And this is so even though the media are tightly controlled by governments. Their offices are patrolled by armed guards; they take care to present only approved news and precensored programs. A developmental goal underlies this, of course: the goal of national integration and loyalty to the center. But this goal is often pursued at the expense of other developmental goals and in the absence of a coherent national policy for the use of the media or for development as a whole. If there is a policy, it is a negative one: to prevent other messages from getting through. It appears, however, that many of the nations that achieved independence in the late 1950s and early 1960s have in recent years come to recognize the need to define the role that the broadcast media should play in national development.

In almost every one of the countries we studied, there seem to have been critical moments when the ruling groups began to take serious notice of broadcasting. A coup, a war, the threat of insurgency, a political struggle, a radical revision of cultural or economic policy—in short, a crisis or turning point of some kind—can be identified as having caused the leadership to look again at the development of broadcasting in the context of the development of the nation as a whole.

In Peru a revolutionary junta took charge in October 1968. For the first time in the coup-pocked history of modern Peru, the generals represented the lower classes. They wanted to expel the multinational companies as quickly as possible, to speed land reform and to improve transportation, to give workers policymaking and profit-sharing roles in industry and commerce, and to incorporate the Indians (46 percent of the population) socially and culturally into the mainstream of the society.

The media are part of the plan to achieve these ends. The Peruvian government has taken 51 percent of the shares of two television networks and arranged to program for them jointly. It has demanded 25 percent control of key radio stations and has replaced the editors of newspapers and assigned the papers to represent sectors of the population. The government also operates a fully state-owned radio and television network of its own, and it promises to extend coverage beyond the urban centers. A reversal of the ratio of imported to domestically produced television programs is represented by a call for 60 percent local production. A national communications policy group within the Central Office of Information is planning to revolutionize programming by giving access to groups heretofore unrepresented, by systematically combing the country for authentic folklore and art, by forging links with the national development agencies in the areas of agriculture, health, and literacy, and by a gradual shift of focus to national holidays and symbols based on indigenous tradition rather than European patterns.

Will these plans work? We don't know. We mention them here as an example of the link between a crisis and the growth of communications planning.

Similar links between broadcasting and a radical plan of socioeconomic reform may be found in other countries. The consolidation of power by the leadership group in each of these cases led to the formulation of ambitious development goals. And in each case, as in the case of Peru, the media were assigned a significant role in the plan.

In Thailand in 1973 academics and intellectuals staged a demonstration in Bangkok demanding that the military junta finally produce the draft constitution that had repeatedly been promised. The demonstration got out of hand and turned into a bloody assault on the students by the army and police. The king intervened personally but not soon enough to prevent the students from burning down several government buildings. These included the offices of the Public Relations Department, the provider of the news, which was said by the Bangkok newspapers to have lied repeatedly in defense of the army action during the course of the street fighting. The result was that the military government had to leave the country and civilian rule was restored. The event led to a realization on the part of the new government that the official news bulletin, transmitted by all stations twice a day, had lost its credibility. Consequently there was a new openness to proposals put forward some time earlier by a British Broadcasting Corporation expert that diverse views should be presented in the news, that public reactions to the news should be solicited from the man in the street, and that complaints against the government from, for example, farmers might be tolerated.

Compared to the Peruvian revolution the Bangkok demonstration was a relatively minor episode. It serves to show, however, that a crisis in government can call attention to the broadcast media and their function. In this case, serious reconsideration was given, at least for a while, to the proper role of the media in regard to the provision of news. The opposite result is, of course, equally possible in different circumstances.

Algeria, after the triumph of the Front de la Libération Nationale (FLN) in 1962, has proceeded by a process of trial and error as the needs of the country (as perceived by the leadership) have emerged. In the early 1970s, a policy of neotraditionalism was promulgated. Arabic was to take the place of French, and the indigenous cultural tradition was to be reexplored. Radio and television were to be used more intensively to raise the cultural level of the population by providing formal education for those who had been deprived of it or had dropped out and, above all, by introducing a more extensive provision of adult education. This change was due not to political crisis but to a growing recognition of the nation's ability to cast off inherited models in the fields of culture, economics, and international relations.

Cyprus underwent a sharp change in broadcasting policy in 1967, during the period after the constitutional arrangements made to link the two ethnic communities broke down in 1963 but before the island was torn asunder in 1974. It was a period during which the achievement of independence led each side to reinforce its own sociocultural position at the expense of the commonalities on which the constitution had been based. When English ceased to be enforced by the colonial power as the lingua franca, the

choice between Greek and Turkish as the medium of instruction and of communication became charged with even
greater political significance. The new leadership of broadcasting in this period began to shape a policy of indigenous
expression in the Greek tradition, for television was in the
hands of the Greeks, as was the more powerful of the two
radio stations, and to shift the balance of importation of
programs toward Greece and away from Britain. The
breakdown of such limited consensus in cultural policy as
had been written into the constitution was due to the failure
to recognize its importance when the island's constitution
was drafted. The search for identity was thought to have
been completed by the adoption of a dual Cypriot and either Greek or Turkish identity. This analysis proved too
optimistic.

Nigeria has also experienced the threat of disintegration
since the early sixties, and this is reflected in the development of its broadcasting system. The regions have kept
pulling away from the center and have thought radio and
television development important in the establishment of
their several identities. The multistate structure that replaced the former tripartite regional division threatened to
make the broadcasting situation even worse, as each of the
states strove to start its own television station. More and
more concern was expressed about the apparent inability of
the federal broadcast media to contribute to the process of
national integration in Nigeria.[6]

While Algeria is trying to move away from French culture, Senegal is trying to steer a course between the French
and the indigenous cultures. Preoccupation with this dilemma of identity is reflected in Senegalese broadcasting
policy. The policy reflects the government's growing
awareness of the interior of the country and its needs, as
well as the recognition that these have to be met in terms of
the local, rather than the former colonial, culture.

In this capsule review of some of the turning points in

planning for national development in politics, economics, and culture on the one hand and in broadcasting on the other, several things are evident. Broadcasting policy and, specifically, the introduction of television were not initially the result of well-thought-through development plans. The immediate motive for the introduction of television was, typically, extraneous to development goals, although at a deeper level its main function was to help to solve the problems of national integration. Development planning of a formal type was not usually begun until several years after independence, generally in the mid-sixties. During this period, the potential role of broadcasting for development began to be more carefully explored, often in a simplistic fashion. But the failure of many early experiments has led to more realistic exploration that is still continuing. At least as important as the role of broadcasting in political integration or economic development is the link of broadcasting with the shaping of a country's cultural identity; here is an area of development that is a subject of growing concern.

Indeed, in searching for patterns in our data, we have stumbled on much the same point that Clifford Geertz seems to be making when he says, "Now that there is a local state rather than a mere dream of one, the task of nationalist ideologizing radically changes. It no longer consists of stimulating popular alienation from a foreign-dominated political order, nor with orchestrating a mass celebration of that order's demise. It consists in defining, or trying to define, a collective subject to whom the actions of the state can be internally connected, in creating, or trying to create, an experiential 'we' from whose will the activities of government seem spontaneously to flow." [7]

Not all the countries we studied are struggling with a crisis of cultural identity, but some definitely are. More of them will do so as they begin to attain some success in political integration and economic modernization, for these achievements are by no means correlated with the establishment of identity. As modernization is achieved, the question, Who are we, who have done all this? [8] reemerges. If the answer is a return to tradition, as in the case of Algeria, for example, a conflict arises with the secularizing and cosmopolitan influences of modernization.

Peru and Iran are also struggling with this dilemma, each in its own way. Whether the mass media can cope with these three trends simultaneously, unifying the polity, spearheading modernization, and joining in the rediscovery of traditional roots, is a question to which we shall return. Most observers feel that the mass media can be only on the side of modernization.

THE PROMISE OF BROADCASTING: WHAT THE SOCIAL SCIENTISTS SAY

Geertz is not alone in perceiving the mass media as agents of what he calls "epochalism," moving with the present, rather than of "essentialism," holding an inherited course.[9] Indeed, students of communication and modernization have taken this view for some time.

Best known is the work of Daniel Lerner, who so much assumes the relationship that his definition of being modern includes exposure to the broadcast media.[10] This exposure, in turn, correlates in Lerner's data not only with holding modern opinions but also with holding opinions at all. Most important from Lerner's point of view is the role of the media in the development of "empathy," the ability to perceive and identify with the social, political, and technical needs of new-nationhood beyond the confines of experience in extended family and village. Thus radio-listening and newspaper-reading become the sociopsychological bricks of nation-building, the modern equivalent of the painful process of actual movement from countryside to city that characterized modernization in the West. The media, says Lerner, can convey a sense of what a government or a big city is about. They can also drive a wedge between the generations, leaving the village elders to brood over tradition while their sons, reinforced by the media, take the great leap forward.

Lerner's thesis has been challenged. Some studies have demonstrated that empathy is not greater among radio listeners than among nonlisteners. Nor are the media easily isolated as prime movers in modernizing attitudes.[11] Yet other studies, the most definitive of which is the painstaking comparative research of Alex Inkeles and David H. Smith, find exposure to the mass media correlated with almost any conceivable definition of modernization.[12] These authors insist, moreover, that the relationship is causal: the mass media demonstrably lead to modern attitudes and behavior after every other explanatory variable has been held constant.

Impressive as this evidence is, the case cannot, in the absence of longitudinal data, be considered closed. The Inkeles and Smith study does not follow people over time to see, for example, whether exposure to the mass media actually stimulates the feeling of efficacy, the idea that things are "up to me" and not only to God or chance.

By the same token, it remains to be demonstrated effectively that the broadcast media actually stimulate participation in the political process or increase identification with the state. Relevant data, some of them quite convincing, do exist, but the long-run causal effects of mass communication are, at least technically, still uncertain. Moreover, some would argue, as has James Mosel with respect to Thailand, that the message of the media is passivity and that, therefore, the media fit nicely into traditional contexts regardless of their manifest content.[13] Even further along this continuum are those theorists who argue that the dominant functions of the media are escape and the reinforcement of the legitimacy of things as they are.[14]

Rather better established is the connection between mass communication and modernizing practices. The change to new agricultural practices, the willingness to try recommended family-planning techniques, the struggle to overcome illiteracy have, to varying degrees, been promoted by campaigns in the mass media. Wilbur Schramm, translating Lerner from the political to the technical-economic realm of modernization, wrote a primer on this subject for developing countries.[15] Deep-rooted attitudes cannot easily be changed by exposure to the media alone. Instrumental practices of various kinds that do not conflict with traditions or beliefs may be quite responsive to change. To be genuinely effective, however, the broadcast media need to be reinforced by word of mouth, preferably through trusted friends or advisers, or by campaigns of personal intervention as practiced, for example, by literacy corps, health officers, agricultural extension agents, and community development officers. Everett M. Rogers, among others has elaborated this point.[16]

Some social scientists, then, have recommended mass communication to the attention of developing countries. They have identified ways in which the broadcast media may help, but have cautioned that the media should not be expected to do the whole job. They have been roundly criticized by colleagues who see development and modernization as the equivalent of westernization,[17] and westernization as tantamount to selling one's birthright for a mess of pottage. Arguing from a Marxist perspective, these theorists see broadcasting as an extension of Western capitalism, another expression of the imperialism that, so Lenin argued, is necessary to the survival of capitalism. They allege that broadcasting, in alliance with the local elite that it helps to establish and with the multinational corporations, becomes an agent of capitalism, promoting conspicuous consumption, individualist striving, class exploitation, and the other trappings of westernization. By motivating individuals to aspire to mobility and higher standards of living, the media, in programs as well as advertising, are creating the kind of consumer demand that maintains the dependence of the economies of the developing countries on the economies of the West. If the true goal of national liberation is to break the cycle of exchanging primary products for finished products, the media and the other agents of modernization are subverting that goal. Indeed, the very dependence on the importation of television programs and films reflects the unequal relationship. So does the dependence on foreign technology for transmission and production.

Another group of social critics focuses more narrowly on the message of the media. Partly because of the high proportion of imported programs, partly because of imitation, the dominant message of the media, they say, is consumption, violence, cupidity, and jealousy, and these values are alien to many traditional societies.[18] Nicholas Bennett argues more subtly that even schools and educational television, in their various manifestations, reinforce the idea that leaving home and farm is the only thing worth doing and that getting still another certificate or diploma is the aim of life.[19] Bennett does not blame the West for this; these ideas are very deeply rooted in some of the most classical of Asian cultures, and local media magnify them.

This second group of social scientists, who seriously question the ethics of the mass media and the alien values they transmit, take the manifest message of the media quite seriously and assume, at least under present circumstances, that most new and developing countries are incapable of producing an authentic message of their own (although Dallas Smythe holds out hope for China).[20] But we note that none of these scholars doubts the efficacy of the mass media. Indeed, the effect of this criticism is not, of course, to discredit the influence of broadcasting, but to deflect attention away from simple studies of *effect* to studies of the *content* of mass communications and to the imbalance of the communications flow from the metropolitan capitals of the West to the developing world.[21]

It is true, in fact, that the messages of the mass media everywhere are highly similar. The programs one sees on television in Bangkok are not much different from those one sees in Lima or in Tehran. This uniformity is curious, given the differing organizational structures that characterize the broadcasting systems of these countries and given the promise that is held out, by students of the media and national leaders alike, for the contribution of the broadcast media to authentic national development. Some, as has been shown, argue that the capitalist necessity for dominance determines the homogeneity of programs. Others, like ourselves, are more oriented toward functional explanations. For us, the question of what can be done about it, whether the media can be harnessed to, among other objectives, authentic cultural expression, is still open. We are not committed to the proposition that the media are capable only of sowing the seeds of cultural homogeneity and thus, ultimately, of dependence on the West and its trinkets. But we are aware that this is a danger. On the other hand, an attempt to seal frontiers against all news and influence from abroad seems to us both futile and dangerous. The identity crisis brought about in all countries by the mass media seems to us to deserve a better solution.

In any event, national leaders do not always believe the social scientists or take the advice of international agencies. Only a few developing nations accepted the excessively enthusiastic proposals of the 1960s for employing the broadcast media for educational, social, and economic development. An even more cautious, and perhaps more appropriate, attitude has developed in the 1970s. The media are now being incorporated into development planning by the leadership and their new generation of well-trained advisers as part of a more integrated, longer-term policy of socioeconomic change. That does not mean that these new plans will work, but that at least more serious attempts are being made.

The same sort of attitudinal change is evident in the field

of indigenous of self-expression. In the concern for authenticity that is sweeping the new nations, there is an awakening neotraditionalism. Intuitively, the media are identified with the forces of modernism and seen as agents of alienation. In this confrontation most social scientists are on the side of tradition, some of them, like us, finding themselves issuing warnings against imperialism in the field of communications. One cannot help feeling a certain sympathy with those people in the new nations who would harness the mass media to cultural continuity and development as well as to economic development.

In short, communications scholars have been advising development planners for some time to pay closer attention to the broadcast media. One group has paid rather more attention to the medium than to the message. They see the broadcast media as agents of modernization both at the level of individual attitudes and at the level of political institutions. Empirical research has tempered some of their more enthusiastic hypotheses, but there seems little question that the mass media have at least a share in the process of modernization.

A second group, no less committed to the efficacy of the media, have warned against their message. In their present form, this argument goes, the media are delivering alien images that are antithetical to the values of the developing societies and are doing a disservice to "authentic" development.

But the social scientists—both groups—are ahead of the planners. We find that the evolution of official interest in the role of broadcasting in development is still at an early stage.

THE PROMISE OF BROADCASTING: WHAT THE NATIONS SAY

If we are correct so far, in most new nations some time elapsed between the declaration of independence, or the first decisions to embark on a policy of development, and the explicit formulation of related goals for the media. We find much less evidence of such formulation than we had expected. Insofar as it exists most of it centers on the need to achieve national unity. We do not belittle this important use of the media. It reflects the first and paramount concern of most new nations. It finds expression in the takeover by government of the direction of the media in most of the countries we have studied. Efforts to extend the coverage of broadcasting are part of the same area of promise, as is the use of the media to promote national leaders.[22]

More recently, as development planning has begun to take more account of social factors, the link between broadcasting and modernization has become more explicit. It is at this point that proclamations of the media's promise, if not their performance, intersect with the ideas of the first generation of media researchers and with the practical experiments in the use of broadcasting for achieving literacy, birth control, higher agricultural yields, and so on.[23]

When the media are used for the communication of technical information to promote behavior change, certain new problems arise. It becomes apparent, for example, that the policies of introducing a national language and of covering the entire country, which serve the goal of national integration, are not well suited to the more local, familiar, and personal approach required for programs of modernization.

But even as policymakers take account of the goals of integration and modernization in their thinking and planning, the problem of cultural authenticity arises. As Geertz emphasizes, it is the very achievement of independence and a degree of unity that renders the question of cultural codes salient. The use of the media for national integration and for modernization has then to be reconciled with the much more difficult question of ensuring that the values implicit in the media programs are the values appropriate to these goals. National integration may be aided by calling the attention of the nation to whatever is being broadcast and by focusing that attention on the personalities of the leaders. Modernization aims may be achieved through broadcasting specialized programs for farmers, for particular ethnic groups, or for housewives, but the problem of creating or continuing a culture is something else. Attacking the problem through broadcasting involves a concern with entertainment, that aspect of broadcasting with which the broadcasters are most concerned and which policymakers tend to ignore. But the awareness that, whatever else they do, the media are transmitting culture, their own or somebody else's, has in recent years begun to exercise the new nations. In the early years, even where there was some attempt to formulate policy for the use of the media in political and technical development, there was little or no deliberate attempt to use the mass media to contribute to shaping a national identity. The realization that a shared culture has both intrinsic and instrumental implications for a nation has now focused attention on such matters as the proportion and relative popularity of imported television programs, the authenticity of home-made programs, the origin of the music broadcast on radio, the values implicit or explicit in entertainment programs, and the fate of the traditional arts.

These questions began to be asked in the fifties and sixties in one form or another by social anthropologists and social developers rather than by communications researchers, although they are perhaps implicit in Lerner's idea that the media make familiar a variety of roles beyond the immediate experience of the listener or viewer.[24] But they have come to be recognized as important by the policymakers in the course of the revolution of rising expectations that has exposed populations to the media and raised questions about the gap between local standards of living and those portrayed on film and television.

This range of questions has led to assertions that British, French, and, above all, American neocolonialism imposes cultural diets of "made-for-export" programs through a

combination of international marketing and diplomatic con-
niving. These assertions are, in part, a reflection of the
"morning after" mood of those new nations that were the
least discriminating in their adoption of the mass media.
These nations now complain, with justification, that their
cultures have been overwhelmed by "Peyton Place" and
"Hawaii Five-0." This recognition of the cultural problems
caused by the indiscriminate admission of alien values was
used by so-called radical social scientists in the 1960s as evidence to support the "conspiracy theory" concerning the
U.S. military-industrial complex, which they alleged to be
running (and ruining) the world. In this way the doctrine of
the free flow of information was attacked and to some extent discredited.

The developing nations themselves began to be more discriminating in their cultural imports, and we find in the
ways in which their goals have been formulated all three developmental themes to which we have referred: the political, the socioeconomic, and the cultural.

Consider the evolution of the goals of broadcasting in
Iran. Twenty-five years after the introduction of radio,
when the emphasis on the establishment of Iranian prestige
through overseas broadcasting seemed to overshadow even
the concern with national integration, the shah spoke explicitly of his hopes. Inaugurating National Iranian Television (NIT) in 1966, he spoke of integration, the stimulation
of cultural development, and widespread popular participation. High priority was given to the expansion of the
transmission networks. The priorities formulated by the
broadcasting authorities in connection with the Fourth National Development Plan (1968–1972) reflect a more tech-
nocratic and liberal bias. The first of the goals listed is "to
publicize national development affairs from their social, political, and economic points of view" and "to keep the public informed of current events." Strengthening national
unity and fostering culture, art, education, and entertain-

ment are lower on the list, reflecting, as might be expected, the bias of planners.

In Algerian broadcasting, on the other hand, cultural goals have been given great prominence and are at present pursued with at least as much vigor as social and economic ones. The new emphasis given to the Arabic language and to traditional Arabic culture derives from the wish to reduce dependence on the French language and culture and from the need to harness all citizens to the development process. The connection between cultural development and technical-economic development is made very clear in the Development Plan for 1970–1973:

> One of the essential conditions for the participation of all [citizens] in the building of the economy, particularly during the present period of intensive effort in this direction, is the broadcasting and the understanding by all concerned at all levels of the objectives that the nation has set itself. At the same time the raising of the cultural level [of the people], which depends in the first instance on the educational effort, is equally dependent on the activities of the broadcasting system and on giving as many citizens as possible access to the national cultural heritage.
>
> The infrastructure of the information media and the different means of artistic expression provide the main agents for the pursuit of these two objectives. In the field of radio and television, the objectives to be achieved are the extension of the transmission network, the increasing of Algerian program production, and the multiplication of links to make possible interregional and international program exchanges.[25]

In pursuit of these objects the proportion of domestically produced programming was sharply increased. Whereas in 1969 only 25 percent of the programs were locally produced, by 1973 the proportion had increased to 49 percent. Special attention was given to strengthening the links with the Maghreb and other Arab countries and to reducing dependence on France. It is interesting to note, however, that there is a good deal of resistance among intellectuals to any extremist policy of Arabization. Many of these persons, including some of the writers and producers who work for the broadcasting service, by no means want to be cut off from French culture and the access to the wider world that it gives them.

The determination to use broadcasting for the promotion of socialism and development among the people is also the explicit goal of broadcasting in Tanzania. The goal having been identified, the pursuit of it led to the takeover of radio by the government in 1965. As the minister of information has explained, "The duty of the service is to help and sometimes even to bring about a direct ideological and attitudinal revolution among the millions of Tanzanians, many of whom have no other means to get to know about the goals and priorities of our Party and Government." This duty applies both to the national and to the commercial channel: "The principal aim of our Commercial Service will be to establish a basis of bringing about a revolutionary attitude so that they appreciate and buy more of what are our own products so that the nation as a whole moves towards the central economic aim of self-reliance." [26]

The last, it might be added parenthetically, is one of the more original and perhaps achievable goals for a commercial service in the repertoire of goals we have surveyed. Cultural goals are by no means secondary in Tanzania, however. Above all, perhaps, stands the centrality of Swahili as the language of broadcasting, which brings the message of unity and identity to the hundreds of language groups in Tanzania. In a certain sense, the decision not to introduce television is also an expression of concern over the continuity of culture. Tanzania has resisted the temptation to install a television station in the capital city. The resistance is based not only on the reluctance to spend scarce resources or on the desire to avoid giving advantage to the big city but also on the assumption that television promotes such urban values as individualism and self-interest and that this effect would be damaging to the traditionally communal character of village life. As noted, television has now entered Zanzibar. In view of the firm policy against television on the mainland, it is not surprising that First Vice-President Aboud Jumbe went out of his way to justify this step by emphasizing both the themes of national unity and those of culture and entertainment.[27] Of unity he said, "We foster co-operation among neighbors, among members of the party at branch, ward and regional levels, and so unify the country and mobilise our people in a matter of one or two hours for nation building or defence."

Thailand and Indonesia also stress goals of political and cultural unity, but they are equally explicit about the role of broadcasting in counteracting enemies from without and within. Thus the first objectives of broadcasting are "(1) to promote national policy and common interests in the areas of politics, military affairs, economics and social welfare; (2) to promote the loyalty of the citizens to the country, the religion and the King; (3) to promote the unity and mutual co-operation of the army and citizens." Immediately following is the statement that the objectives of broadcasting are "(4) to invite citizens to retort to and oppose the enemy, including the doctrines which are dangerous to the security of the nation, and to encourage co-operation with friendly nations." [28]

The most forceful example of the link between development planning and broadcasting is to be observed in Peru. Following the coup of 1968, the military junta acted for the first time in the name of the lower classes and the indigenous population rather than the elite and the Europeans. It proclaimed a socialist policy of nationalization, rapid modernization, and the mobilization of the heretofore unintegrated majority for political participation. A transformation of cultural symbols, giving new centrality to the

Indians and underplaying Spanish influence, is an important element of the plan.

Describing the situation of broadcasting in Peru prior to the revolution, a senior government spokesman deplored the predominance of the profit motive and its consequences for broadcasting. Ownership had become concentrated in the hands of a few power groups; there was no incentive for educational broadcasting; broadcasting was concentrated in the main cities; and programming was dominated by advertising, which took up 37 percent of prime time. The major part of the programming was of foreign origin, thus making the media agents of ideological penetration and domination and imposing patterns and modes of living alien to Peruvian needs.

To eradicate these abuses and to harness the media to the revolutionary goals, a radical restructuring of broadcasting was proposed. The General Law of Telecommunication of 1971 decreed:

1. That all broadcasting services "for reasons of security and in order to serve as media of mass education" were to be placed under the control of the state (under the new Sistema Nacional de Información [SINADI], of which the Oficina Central de Información is the executive arm).

2. That television stations should function only as state-owned or state-associated organizations in which the state was to be guaranteed not less than 51 percent of the shares.

3. That commercial radio stations might function either as state-owned or as state-associated stations, with no less than a 25 percent participation by the state, or as private enterprise.

4. That nonprofit educational stations should operate only with the approval of the Ministry of Education.

5. That station ownership by one company be limited to a total of seven stations, with no more than one radio station and one television station in any one province.

6. That the proportion of locally produced programs should

be increased to 60 percent, and that locally produced programs should be produced by Peruvian nationals to the extent of 90 percent.

7. That all advertising be locally produced.
8. That advertising time be limited to 20 percent of broadcast output.
9. That all stations give one hour per day to the state for educational broadcasting.
10. That diverse views be given freedom of expression.
11. That all workers in telecommunications companies be organized as "industrial communities" in which management and profits would be shared with owners, as in the fishing, mining, and other industries.

The high-level planning group whose task it is to translate these general principles into practice wants to experiment with new forms of participatory television and to develop ways of encouraging both artistic and political involvement at the local and regional levels. They expect broadcasting to help in the fight against illiteracy, linguistic diversity, and regionalism in order to forge a shared national identity, a higher standard of living, and higher standards of social justice.

Disquiet over the cultural goals of broadcasting has also begun to be discussed in Nigeria, whose problem since independence has been to integrate the disparate regions and tribes that were combined for administrative purposes by Lord Lugard at the turn of the century. In recent years Nigerians have begun to ask fundamental questions about the functions and effects of broadcast entertainment. The director of programs at the Nigerian Broadcasting Corporation has noted ironically that the NBC is regularly producing programs about Nigerian culture called "Nigerian Sketches," "Nigerian Cavalcade," and so on. He has pointed out that it is hard to imagine the BBC labeling its programs in the same way as "British Music" or "British Plays." This need to identify Nigerian material shows, he

has argued, that the NBC has still not shed the last vestige
of colonial attitudes. There is still a common assumption,
he believes, that any programs relating to Nigerian culture
are somehow special and experimental: "I dare not preach
cultural isolation, for no culture can survive if it is perma-
nently isolated. I preach a Nigerian cultural pre-eminence
. . . [T]he quality of NBC's performance has unfortunately not been remarkable for a broadcasting organisation
maintained by the blood and sweat of ordinary Nigerians.
Efforts have been apologetic, sometimes condescending,
devoid of conviction and ideology, and completely insensi-
tive to the gathering storms of an inevitable deluge from the
muddy cultural waters of Europe and America." [29]

In Brazil, while pronouncements about the educational
and cultural implications of broadcasting have been rather
more explicit than in other countries, the reiteration of this
promise has of late been the subject of considerable government attention. In several recent declarations by the minister of communications, the broadcasters are admonished on
the one hand to remember their commitment to the nation's
economic development and on the other to desist from the
portrayal of alien cultural goals. Speaking to the Association of Broadcasters, Minister of Communications Quandt
de Oliveira declared that "the ministry . . . expects that
radio and television stations will fulfill their contractual and
legal obligations, their code of ethics, so as to reach increased cooperation for the achievement of goals compatible
with the efforts of a country to take off from underdevelopment to its deserved position in the world picture." [30]
A month or so later, the minister asserted that "commercial
television is imposing on the youngsters and children of our
country a culture that has nothing to do with Brazilian culture. Thus . . . instead of being a creative element in the
diffusion of Brazilian culture, television appears as a privi-
leged vehicle of cultural import, a basic factor in the de-
characterization of our creativity." [31]

PROMISE AND THE TRANSFORMATION
OF PROMISE

The examples we have given suggest that the identification of promise and goals in the developing countries changes over time both between countries and within countries. Certain regularities seem to emerge, however, and they are worth recording, even if the generalizations do not apply to all cases. We are talking here of the rhetoric of policymaking, not of the varieties of structure, control, or performance, although these have their regularities, too.

In the ideal case, the three types of policy concern—the integrative, the developmental, and the cultural—appear in sequence, almost as if there were a self-generating process moving policymakers to focus on each in turn. Realistically, however, they more often appear in different sequences in response to the pressures of external events. But they do not displace one another.

Typically, then, a new nation is concerned about its political integration. This concern, having first found expression in the colonial period, becomes paramount on independence. Control of the media is seen as essential for the achievement of the integration goals. Foreign ownership, control, or influence is ended and is replaced by an insistence on native-born managers and performers. The question of language is discussed in order to agree on a medium through which broadcasting can promote national unity. The effort to personify this unity means that much air time is devoted to broadcasts by the national leader. Efforts are made to extend coverage and lower the price of receivers, so that the largest possible number of citizens may be exposed to broadcasting.

The second phase of broadcasting policy emphasizes the role of broadcasting in social, economic, educational, and technical development. Typically, this phase is associated in a new nation with the formulation of a national development plan and, in an older nation, with an ideological revolution, which is followed by the formulation of such a plan. The media are in this phase seen as instruments of communication with both urban and rural populations concerning development goals, as major tools in the struggle against illiteracy, endemic disease, inefficient agricultural practices, and traditional attitudes toward work and achievement.

Often it is a reaction against the secular symbols of nationhood and the modernization of the institutions of education and work which brings about the debate on culture. It becomes clear at that stage that media policymaking has all but ignored the role of entertainment. Control of information has been established. Education has been intensified. But the rest of the programming, which constitutes by far the major part of the broadcast output, has been treated as though it were neutral, as politically and developmentally irrelevant. As a result, traditional culture, except for language in some cases, has not found its place in the broadcast media, while the Beatles and other pop stars on radio and "Ironside" and "Lucy" on television threaten to overtake the national heroes.

We have pointed out that the pursuit of the three goals may well contain elements of contradiction. Thus, the mass audience required for the achievement of the broad goal of national integration may be unnecessary for the specific purposes pursued in achieving socioeconomic modernization, just as the medium and content appropriate to the two purposes may vary. Even more likely, the goals of modernization and cultural continuity may conflict if the one emphasizes individualism, secularization, and material values while the other emphasizes collectivism, tradition, and spiritual values.

In chapters 5 and 6 we confront promise with performance. We ask whether, and how much, broadcasting has contributed to the achievement of these goals. We try to point out the conditions under which the media live up to the promise invested in them. We explore further the dilemma of the coexistence of the "epochalist" demands for modernization with the "essentialist" demands for authenticity. But before doing this it is necessary to review the ways in which broadcasting systems have become established in the developing countries.

Part Two

Process

2

Broadcasting Structures in the Developing Countries

That broadcasting is significant tends to be taken for granted by media experts and broadcasting professionals in any country. For example, a television expert is inclined, when asked about the significance of television, to think of the transmitter on the hill outside the capital, the more or less splendid office of the broadcasting organization, and the production facilities. All these are important. But the real significance of television depends on none of these things. It lies in the number and location of the receivers available for potential viewers. The same applies to radio. It is of interest to know that there are two or three parallel program services. But it is vital to know which of these, if any, can be received reliably outside the urban areas, how many people have suitable receivers, and what proportion of these sets are likely to be in working order and equipped with fully charged batteries.

Time and again in our country studies we have come across broadcasting systems that on paper looked comprehensive and effective, but a single spot check, whether of production, transmission, or reception facilities, has shown the system to be seriously defective. For this reason all statistics on broadcasting in the Third World should be treated with caution. This applies to the figures presented here. These are likely to overstate the position of broadcasting rather than the reverse. In this chapter, we set out the framework of broadcasting in the developing countries, as it appears from the group of ninety-one that we defined as developing.

ORGANIZATION

The organization of broadcasting in the developing countries reflects the prevailing political and social ideologies of each country (see Table A.1, Appendix A).

Broadcasting is everywhere subject to state legislation. The original justification for this control was technical. Available frequencies are a limited resource, and governments took the view that its utilization must be controlled in order to enable their countries to make the most effective use of the frequencies allocated to them by international agreement. However, in the developing countries government control of broadcasting usually involves much more than the allocation of broadcasting frequencies under license to broadcasting organizations. Political considerations have progressively caused control to extend to the content of services.

AFRICA

In Africa all the national broadcasting systems are not only government-controlled, but also government-operated.[1] In four countries, (Ghana, Malawi, Mauritius, and Nigeria), "autonomous" public corporations, modeled on the BBC, are formally independent of government in their day-to-day operations. It is clear, however, that this independence is largely notional and that the original BBC principles of public-service, as distinct from government, broadcasting have been adjusted to fit the less politically stable conditions of Africa. The structures of broadcasting in all but seven of the thirty-six African states in our study were established by a colonial power and largely reflect the metropolitan broadcasting structure.

All Africa's television services are controlled and operated by government primarily because of the high capital and recurrent costs involved in mounting a broadcasting operation on a European (as distinct from an American) model. No private companies or entrepreneurs in Africa have the resources necessary to mount such an operation. Although some foreign partners were involved in the initial stages of the growth of television in some countries (such as Nigeria), these withdrew after a few years when it was appreciated that the growth of a "market" (in terms of the sale of sets and transmission networks) would be a slow process. Most were content to recoup their capital costs and to retain longer-term advisory and consultancy relationships.

Asia

The organization of broadcasting in Asia is superficially similar to the pattern obtaining in Africa. Almost all the radio broadcasting services are operated directly by government, and certainly all are controlled by government. Where there is variation from the unitary pattern of broadcasting, it tends toward the American pattern of multi-operator commercial broadcasting. This is the case in the Philippines and, to a degree, in Indonesia, South Korea, Lebanon, and Thailand, where some broadcasting stations are operated on a commercial basis. However, these services are additional to national government broadcasting services. In all the other Asian countries, broadcasting is carried on by the government, in most cases directly through a government department. In Malaysia this is the Department of Broadcasting of the Ministry of Information. In five countries (Iran, Iraq, Cyprus, Korea, and Turkey) broadcasting is operated by a corporation or authority that, in formal terms, is independent of government. In practice, however, the governments concerned exercise a great deal of control, even over the day-to-day operation of the organizations. The key difference between broadcasting structures in Asia and those in Africa is rooted in the history of the colonial relationships and in the nature of Asian culture and society. Because of the more advanced state of their social institutions and the higher level of urban development, many Asian countries instituted radio broadcasting in the period between the two world wars, whereas in Africa most radio services were inaugurated during or after the Second World War. The transfer of institutional models (British, Dutch, and French) occurred earlier, and the acculturation process therefore also occurred earlier. Thus broadcasting structures in Asia tend by now to be less closely related to Western European models than is the case in Africa. Undoubtedly, the institutional structures in which broadcasting operates in Asia are not indigenous, but the more obvious aspects of transplantation are by now rarely noticed.

SOUTH AMERICA

The organization of broadcasting in South and Central America is radically different from that prevailing in Africa and Asia. Although there are not as many receivers per capita as in the United States, there are more radio and television stations. Over 5,000 radio stations operate in South and Central America. Brazil has almost 1,200 radio stations, over 90 percent of these being commercial stations. The typical South American broadcasting structure is succinctly described by Julian Hale: "Typically, governments throughout the central and southern part of the American continent own one or two stations themselves, or else demand time on specified commercial outlets at specified times. But the vast majority of radio stations are small-scale vehicles for jingles, pop songs, news, and local ads, fashioned on the North American model." [2]

In most cases the broadcasting system is now supervised, if not controlled, by the government, usually through a special department. For example, in Mexico the Telecommunications Department supervises the allocation of frequencies, and the Secretariat of Broadcasting supervises licensing arrangements for the stations. In some countries, such as Honduras, the government supervises all aspects of the system through the Telecommunications Department.

In the past, Latin American structures were largely based on the U.S. pattern: free enterprise being encouraged with minimum interference from government. This is not to say that governments did not have the power to interfere. But as long as the stations did not transgress the unwritten rules regarding criticism of government or editorializing they were left very much to their own devices.

Another feature of broadcasting in Latin America similar to the U.S. pattern is the grouping of large numbers of small independent radio stations into networks or associations. These networks are controlled by a few companies, which are generally owned by rich and powerful families. Large profits were easily made in radio in the early days, and families that had initially made their money in cattle, sugar, oil, and newspapers were well placed to establish radio networks. Because radio profits had been easily made, many radio entrepreneurs branched out into television when the time came. Television operating licenses tended to be granted to wealthy government supporters who would take a friendly attitude toward the politicians. Concentration of ownership is also a feature of television broadcasting, but in all South American countries governments are more involved in television than they are in radio. This is particularly true in Peru and Brazil, where governments are increasingly moving toward formulation of integrated communications policies.

CENTRAL AMERICA AND THE CARIBBEAN

Broadcasting structures in Central America and the Caribbean have generally followed this free-for-all pattern except in the former colonial territories, where the African/Asian pattern has predominated. In the formerly British islands, broadcasting is operated by corporate bodies modeled on the British pattern, although inevitably there is close supervision by governments. The strength of this postcolonial influence is illustrated by the fact that the colonial patterns persist even in the former colonial countries on the Central and South American mainland.

Table 2.1 sets out in summary form the variations of broadcasting structures. If one notes that even those public authorities whose legal structure is formally independent of government are largely government-controlled, it may be said that in about two-thirds of the ninety-one countries of the study the broadcasting systems are publicly financed and in about one-third of them there is a significant element of private-enterprise participation. The number of countries in which broadcasting is left entirely to private enterprise (Costa Rica, the Dominican Republic, Honduras, and Panama) is not significant.

FINANCE

The transfer of broadcasting in the form of systems and institutions rather than flexible concepts has meant that the financial structures of European and North American broadcasting also had to be adopted (see Table A.2). When the BBC was asked to help set up a broadcasting station in a developing country, the station was established on the BBC model, albeit scaled down to the assumed needs and resources of the country. Similarly, when the first of the 1,200 or so radio stations was launched in Brazil, the entrepreneurs concerned looked to North American models for financial guidance.

Thus the financial assumptions varied with the place from which the transfer was made. In general, even radio costs in the European national systems were comparatively high, and therefore the financial assumptions of the transferred model were relatively high. The South American radio stations were a good deal cheaper because of the lower-cost models from which they derived. In all cases radio broadcasts were, and remain, substantially cheaper than television broadcasts. The cost ratio between radio and television may be as high as 1:30 or more, given that

Table 2.1 Control and ownership of broadcasting systems in ninety-one countries, by number and percentage of countries in each area.

Form of broadcasting system	Africa	Asia	South America	Central America and the Caribbean	Oceania	Total
Public authority only	14 (34%)	5 (20%)	0	0	0	19 (21%)
Government agency only	22 (54%)	13 (52%)	0	1 (8%)	1 (100%)	37 (41%)
Private only	0	0	0	4 (31%)	0	4 (4%)
Public authority and private	3 (7%)	1 (4%)	0	2 (15%)	0	6 (7%)
Private and government agency	2 (5%)	6 (24%)	11 (100%) [a]	6 (46%)	0	25 (27%)
Totals	*41*	*25*	*11*	*13*	*1*	*91*

Source: See Appendix B.
a. The typical South American pattern includes a small number of government stations together with a large number of private stations.

television models also were imported from high-cost systems in Europe and North America.

Insofar as the creation of broadcasting institutions in the Third World became a matter for governments, therefore, relatively high-cost models tended to be adopted. Even high-cost radio stations were within the means of most developing countries. But the scale of expenditure required for television is of a different order, in terms both of capital and of operational expenditure. Since television remains a marginal medium in the majority of developing countries, the resources made available to it are limited. This restriction results in poor standards of production which, in turn, are not likely to make a strong case for increased resources.

Because of these financial problems, it is rarely the case that a broadcasting system in the developing countries is financed from only one source. In Africa, where most systems are mainly government-financed, broadcasting also relies to varying degrees on advertising revenue and on license fees. In South and Central America, where the systems are predominantly financed from advertising revenue, government support is also involved in most countries, although usually on a very small scale. In our sample of ninety-one countries only twelve (Guinea, Libya, Niger, Rwanda, Somalia, Togo, Zaire, South Vietnam, Yemen, Haiti, Costa Rica, and Cuba) finance their broadcasting systems from one source alone. All these systems are financed by government, except for those of Costa Rica and Haiti, which are entirely financed by revenue from advertising.

The degree of government financial involvement in broadcasting depends primarily on the structure of the system. Where the system is directly owned and controlled by the government, as, for example, in Libya, all expenditure is met from government sources. In cases such as this, broadcasting is usually operated by a government department, and the service is financed by normal budgetary provision. Where, however, the broadcasting service has a legal status separate from government (as, for example, in Ghana, where broadcasting is carried on by the Ghana Broadcasting Corporation), financial support is generally sought from other sources. Some countries, notably Laos (until 1974), rely on funding from foreign sources. Where this is unavailable or politically unacceptable, the public is charged for services. The income so provided may be collected in several ways.

Members of the public may be required to pay for the broadcasting service through some system of subscription. In this way everyone owning a receiving set contributes to the cost of operating the system. The commonest method of collecting the fees is by licensing all receivers and levying a license fee. In the United Kingdom this method is thought to provide the BBC the best guarantee of independence from both government and advertisers. Other ways of financing broadcasting include a tax on the sale of receivers. In Nigeria this tax is 100 percent of the retail price for television sets, but in other countries it more commonly is about 50 percent. In some countries (Malawi, for example), dealers who wish to sell receivers have to buy a license from the government. Finance from general tax revenue involves every taxpayer, whether he owns a set or not. As this method presupposes that access to broadcasting is universal, it is difficult to justify its introduction in the developing countries where audiences are still small. Wherever government supports broadcasting directly, this last method is in fact in operation, although it may not be stated in these terms. Another method that only indirectly affects the taxpayer is the sale of advertising.

As Table 2.2 shows, in seventy-nine countries in our sample the broadcasting system is financed by some combination of these methods. In thirty-one countries it is financed by a combination of government finance, license revenue, and commercial advertising revenue. Thirty-

Table 2.2 Financial structures of broadcasting systems in ninety-one countries, by area (in number and percentage of countries).

Source of revenue	Africa	Asia	South America	Central America and the Caribbean	Oceania	Total
License fees only	0	0	0	0	0	0
Commercial revenue only	0	0	0	2 (15%)	0	2 (2%)
Government only	7 (17%)	2 (8%)	0	1 (8%)	0	10 (11%)
License fees, commercial revenue, and government	19 (47%)	10 (40%)	1 (9%)	1 (8%)	0	31 (34%)
Commercial revenue and government	11 (27%)	6 (24%)	10 (91%)	9 (69%)	1 (100%)	37 (41%)
License fees and government	3 (7%)	2 (8%)	0	0	0	5 (5%)
Other mixed systems	1 (2%)	5 (20%)	0	0	0	6 (7%)
Totals	41	25	11	13	1	91

Source: See Appendix B.

seven countries do not operate license systems, but rely only on government support and advertising revenue. Only five operate a system supported by government and license fees alone. Countries that have introduced minor variations to these patterns include Ghana, where the system is financed by a combination of government support, commercial revenue, license fees, and also relay (wired distribution) service revenue; Upper Volta, which in addition to receiving support for broadcasting from its own government, commercial advertisers, and license fees also receives French government aid; Zambia, where finance is provided not only by government, commercial advertisers, and license fees, but also by foreign sources and other (unstated) sources in the form of grants; Afghanistan, where the system is financed by government and commercial advertisers and also by the imposition of an import tax on receiving sets and by grants from foreign countries, chiefly West Germany; and Egypt, where, in addition to the usual sources, revenue is obtained from a tax on the use of electricity.

The control of broadcasting budgets is obviously a very important aspect of the relationship between broadcasters and government. Government officials are quite likely to scrutinize individual items of expenditure and to suggest cuts or to interfere in the making of programming decisions. Where a licensing system is in operation the cost of collecting the license fee is often disproportionately large. (In the U.K. it is estimated that the licensing system costs $17 million per annum to operate.) [3] The high administrative costs of the organization charged with levying the fees and the widespread evasion in those developing countries where a license system is operated are contributing factors. Where evasion is endemic, the cost of enforcing the system may prove to be greater than the revenue obtained. For this reason some countries have dispensed with license fees, particularly for radio ownership. Slightly over half the African countries in our study still operate license systems;

this number compares with 48 percent of the Asian countries and a mere 8 percent of all the countries in South and Central America and the Caribbean.

Where a broadcasting system relies heavily on commercial advertising revenue, it is essential for the broadcasters to seek out the audience that the advertiser wants to reach. This audience is bound to be largely urban, with a moderate level of disposable cash income and access to radio or television receiving sets. Advertising thus contributes little impetus to expand the coverage area beyond the cities or to provide programs that will not attract a maximum audience.

Whereas in South America, Central America, and the Caribbean broadcasting is mainly commercial and is not dependent to a large extent on governments for financial support, this is rarely the case in Africa and Asia. These government-controlled broadcasting systems are not generally eager to become dependent on advertising as a source of revenue, lest such dependence reduce the effective control that government exercises over the broadcasting organization. It is also generally the case that the staff members of the government systems are civil servants. Morale and motivation tend to be low, and there is little incentive to attract or maintain advertising contracts. In Algeria, for example, advertising accounts for just 2 percent of revenue. The remainder is provided by government (55 percent) and license fees (42 percent). Similarly, in Senegal, where the broadcasting system is financed by government and advertising revenue, the latter source accounts for only 10 percent of the total income. In Indonesia advertising provides only 11 percent of revenue, with government providing 84 percent and license fees only 4 percent, owing to widespread evasion. In Iraq commercials account for only 10 percent of the total revenue, with 90 percent coming directly from government. As Sidney Head has noted, in the few countries where concerted efforts have been made to increase advertising income, billings have gone up severalfold.[4] However, as we have pointed out, it is impossible for a broadcasting service to be completely self-financing because of the need to transmit programs that are not commercially viable, such as services transmitting programs abroad, educational broadcasts, programs for rural areas, and government information programs.

Tanzania has developed an interesting combination of services that to some extent overcomes this problem. There are two channels: one is a public-service channel which, together with light music, entertainment, and advertisements, carries information, adult education programs, and rural broadcasts. The other is a commercial channel broadcasting popular music only during peak listening hours (early morning, lunchtime, and in the evening). In Algeria and Indonesia plans are in hand to introduce a second television channel for a national service, while the present channel, which at present is restricted to the highly populated areas, will become a metropolitan channel with commercials and European program formats.

TECHNOLOGY

There are three types of broadcasting technology: production, distribution, and reception (Table A.3). Production technology includes all equipment used in the production of material for broadcasting, such as studio equipment, lighting, cameras, control systems, and recording and editing equipment. Production equipment is expensive: typically, a color television camera costs between $80,000 and $100,000; a telecine (used for showing films on television), between $40,000 and $60,000; and a videotape recorder for recording color television programs on magnetic tape costs between $60,000 and $80,000. Radio production equipment is less costly. The technology used for distributing programs to the receiving sets is also expensive. Generally, the higher the power of a transmitter, the greater its cost;

consequently it is possible for radio transmitters to be more expensive than television transmitters. Reception technology is commonly regarded as being relatively inexpensive. Radio sets usually cost around $30 to $40, and television sets between $100 and $600, the price being largely dependent on whether the set receives in monochrome or color. However, when one considers that within a broadcasting system as a whole there may be many thousands and even millions of receiving sets, it is clear that the overall cost of reception technology is possibly even greater than that of production and distribution technology.

The key difference between production and distribution equipment on the one hand and reception equipment on the other is that reception equipment is less sophisticated and can be assembled, even if not entirely built, in a country that does not have a highly developed modern industrial sector. However, all but very few countries, such as India, have to import radio and television production and distribution equipment.

PRODUCTION

The main production equipment manufacturing companies are American (NBC International, ITT, RCA, Schlumberger, Ampex International), but there are also large companies in the United Kingdom (Thomson Television International, Pye-TVT, EMI, Marconi, Rank), France (TRT, Thomson-CSF), Germany (Fernseh, Siemens Telefunken), the Netherlands (Philips), and Japan (Nippon Electric Company).

It is in the area of television production technology that the developing countries have, by and large, been free to choose equipment from whichever company they thought offered the most suitable package. However, there are exceptions. The former French colonial territories of Africa have traditionally maintained close links with France, particularly with the French equipment manufacturer

Thomson-CSF, which specializes in television production equipment. The countries that were under British colonial rule have followed a more flexible policy. The radio equipment is predominantly of British manufacture, much of it having been supplied as part of the independence agreements. When these countries came to install television systems, many chose to buy equipment from other sources. The Nigerian Broadcasting Corporation, for example, which was completely equipped at its inception with British radio equipment, gave its television contract to NBC International, an American company.

As offers of equipment are in many cases part of the aid programs of developed countries, there is often a temptation to accept some equipment from one country and some from another without regard to the long-term problems caused by the reliance on a variety of manufacturers. The maintenance of an assortment of brands of equipment encounters severe difficulties. The ordering of spare parts cannot be efficiently organized. The training of technical and production staffs is a much heavier burden, as they have to become familiar with a variety of very different systems. In many cases the acceptance of such offers has provided only short-term benefits.

The pattern of the use of production equipment varies little because, although there are numerous manufacturers, the basic configurations and use-patterns of all broadcasting systems are similar. Radio production equipment is increasingly available in portable versions particularly suitable to a developing country. Since, however, habits of use were inculcated in more static days, few developing countries seem to make extensive use of this portable equipment. They remain largely dependent on studio facilities for their production work.

For television the obstacles to production outside the studio are greater: outside broadcast units are very expensive, as they require custom-built vehicles with sophisticated control systems and support facilities. Recent technological developments have enabled small portable television equipment initially developed in Japan to be upgraded to broadcast standards through the use of "time base correctors." As yet no developing countries have begun experimental use of these portable systems for broadcasting, but it is likely that in the next few years these innovations will revolutionize the pattern of television origination all over the world.

DISTRIBUTION

There are two means of distributing audio and video signals to receiving sets: wireless distribution by broadcasting signals from transmitters using the radio frequency spectrum, and wired distribution by electric wave-forms via cables or wires. Radio and television *broadcasting* involves the transmission of signals intended for general reception, while audio and video *communications* are directed to specific individual receiving stations.

Wired distribution methods are commonly used where for various reasons an "over air" signal will not provide adequate reception or where the density of the population renders it economic. This is the case in Manhattan in New York, where many television sets receive their programs from wired distribution systems because the large number of high-rise buildings deleteriously affect radio frequency broadcasts. In some developing countries—for example, in Ghana, Nigeria, Sierra Leone, Singapore, Malagasy, Togo, and Zaire—wired distribution services (or rediffusion services) were introduced as a means of providing low-cost receivers at the time before the "transistor revolution" when a radio receiver was a relatively expensive commodity. Rediffusion services require only that a loudspeaker box be attached to the cable, thus enabling the cost to the audience to be reduced to a minimum. In all such systems the "wired boxes" are rented from the organization responsible for the operation of the service.

However, the most commonly used means of program distribution is by broadcasting signals over the radio frequency spectrum. Several characteristics of radio frequency broadcasting are unique to those parts of the earth where the developing countries are situated, since the tropical zone of the earth causes signal propagation problems not found anywhere else.

Medium-frequency broadcasting is popular in the developing countries because relatively large areas can be covered with smaller transmitters, but medium-wave signals are affected by the interference problems peculiar to the tropical zones. Between September and February the signal strengths required to overcome the high levels of atmospheric noise are much greater than those required in other latitudes.

The traditional wave band for broadcasting in the developing countries has always been shortwave, which enables radio signals to be broadcast over long distances with relatively few transmitters. However, there are also problems with this means of broadcasting, as the variations in the ionosphere (which reflects shortwave broadcasts) in the tropical areas cause high levels of interference both from other stations and from natural sources that wreak havoc with shortwave broadcasts. Added to this, the shortwave frequencies are overused, often contrary to international agreements, causing unnecessarily high levels of interstation interference.

The VHF (very high frequency) bands are used for both radio and television broadcasting, whereas the UHF (ultra-high frequency) bands are used solely for television broadcasting. The propagation characteristics of VHF and UHF broadcasting depend on the geographical relief of an area and on the pattern of meteorological activity in the lower atmosphere. Signals are of two types: the direct wave is a line-of-sight wave that travels through the atmosphere, whereas the ground-reflected wave depends primarily on the terrain. In fact, the service area of VHF broadcasting is limited to line-of-sight coverage, although refraction in the atmosphere allows very limited coverage over the horizon. Because VHF reception is of a much higher quality than MF (medium frequency) or HF (high frequency) reception, there is widespread agreement that VHF radio will become much more important in the developing countries in the near future. The disadvantage of VHF is that a large number of transmitters are required; however, recent technical developments have made VHF transmission a more economically attractive proposition.

In summary, almost all the developing countries that we have studied face transmission problems that none of the developed countries have had to surmount. Tropospheric and ionospheric interference and poor ground conductivity combine to make coverage of the geographical areas of the developing countries almost impossible. Largely because ground conductivity has not been mapped in most developing countries, particularly in Africa, it has often been the case that transmitters have not provided anywhere near the planned coverage. In fact, because propagation characteristics are so bad, it is impossible to establish comprehensive coverage within international frequency allocations using medium-wave transmitters alone. As summarized in Table 2.3, short and medium wave broadcasting is predominant, but inevitably, most developing countries eventually will turn to FM (frequency modulation) broadcasting on the VHF bands.

Regarding the actual transmission equipment, the considerations outlined above have largely determined the types of transmitters that are in use. Transmission equipment, like production equipment, is manufactured in the developed countries and imported by the developing countries. The same problems arise over aid-tied equipment offers: in Indonesia, of a total of 126 government radio transmitters with a total power of 1,113 kw, 50 were supplied by

Table 2.3 Number and percentage of radio and television transmission facilities, by area.

Type of Transmitter	Africa	Asia	South America	Central America and the Caribbean	Oceania	Total
Radio						
Shortwave	201 (47%)	468 (34%)	794 (27%)	130 (10%)	0	1,593 (26%)
Medium-wave	202 (47%)	797 (58%)	1,994 (68%)	991 (73%)	1	3,985 (65%)
Long-wave	2 (0.5%)	2 (0.1%)	0	0	0	4 (n.s.)
FM	23 (5.5%)	109 (7.9%)	157 (5%)	239 (17%)	0	528 (9%)
Totals	*428 (100%)*	*1,376 (100%)*	*2,945 (100%)*	*1,360 (100%)*	*1 (100%)*	*6,106 (100%)*
Television	121	184	360	173	0	838

Source: See Appendix B.

a U.S. company, Gates; 24 by other U.S. suppliers (8 by TCA, 7 by Redifon, 6 by RCA, 1 by General Electric); 11 by the Dutch Philips company; 2 by Telefunken Germany; and 41 by other companies. This goes some way toward explaining why 80 percent of the transmitters are operating at less than 60 percent efficiency. This problem is by no means atypical.

RECEPTION

Without widespread ownership of receivers to receive the signals that are broadcast, the broadcasters are wasting their time. For their own peace of mind they must assume that someone "out there" is viewing or listening. But an examination of both policies and practices relating to the provision of reception equipment in the developing countries shows that little attention is paid to this aspect of distribution. It is ironic that in many countries millions of dollars have been invested in expensive production and transmission equipment without any comparable concern to ensure reception facilities. Not only is the provision of receivers left almost entirely to the private citizen, but also in a number of countries heavy taxes are levied on the purchase of sets. The level of cash income of the vast majority of the population outside the main urban centers being low, purchase of a radio receiver is rarely afforded and that of a television receiver is almost unheard of. Throughout Africa and Asia, and to a lesser extent in South and Central America, the figures for set ownership indicate that the penetration of the broadcast media is slow and that the level of ownership of receivers in use remains low (see Table A.4).

The significance of the figures on receivers in use in the developing countries becomes apparent when one considers the number of radio and television sets in Europe and North America (Table 2.4).

Table 2.4 Number of radio and television receivers in selected developed countries, per 1,000 population.

Country	Radio sets per 1,000 population	Television sets per 1,000 population
United States	1,813	530
United Kingdom	700	530
France	765	238
Germany (FDR)	334	302
USSR	200	200

Source: *World Radio TV Handbook*, 1975.

The figures for the developing countries, of course, hide significant differences between urban and rural areas. Since reception is best in urban areas and cash incomes are higher, radio and, where applicable, television receivers are concentrated in these areas. Thus the actual number of sets per thousand in the largely rural areas of the developing world is likely to be much lower than the country-by-country figures suggest.

The summary figures in Table 2.5 illustrate the significant differences between Africa and Asia on the one hand and the Americas on the other in the penetration of both radio and television. The ratio of television sets to radio sets per thousand is also interesting. Whereas in Africa the ratio is 1:7 and in Asia 1:5, in South America it is 1:3 and Central America and the Caribbean 1:3. Apart from the most obvious reasons for this imbalance—the absence of a television signal in many areas—two other factors account for the differences. Whereas a transistor radio uses small inexpensive dry-cell batteries, television sets have a much higher power requirement. This means that an outside power line must be used or, if this is not available, a generator or set of rechargeable lead-acid batteries is needed. As electrification rarely penetrates the rural areas of African and Asian countries it is extremely difficult to operate television receivers

Table 2.5 Number of radio and television receivers in ninety-one countries per 1,000 population, by area, 1977.

	Africa (41 countries)	Asia (25 countries)	South America (11 countries)	Central America and the Caribbean (13 countries)	Oceania (1 country)
Total population	369,475,000	1,244,731,000	223,061,000	107,056,000	153,000
Total number of radio sets	26,000,000	76,600,000	60,000,000	23,700,000	50,000
Total number of television sets	3,600,000	15,600,000	21,400,000	7,600,000	—
Radio sets per 1,000 population	70	62	268	222	327
Television sets per 1,000 population	10	13	96	71	—
Distribution of radio sets among the five areas (=100%)	14%	41%	32%	13%	0%
Distribution of television sets among the five areas (=100%)	8%	32%	44%	16%	—

Source: UNESCO, 1979.

even where a signal is available. The high cost of a television receiver, which may be several times the annual cash income of an African or Asian farmer, is the other obvious reason.

The reliability of receivers is also important. Modern transistor radios are reliable and can withstand most conditions of use. However, television sets are as yet relatively fragile and comparatively unreliable. Few are designed specifically to operate in the rigorous conditions of the tropics. Consequently the breakdown rate for television receivers is enormously greater than that for radio receivers. In the majority of countries there are few if any facilities for the repair and maintenance of television sets, so that when a part needs replacing or an adjustment has to be made the set is virtually useless. This problem highlights the difficulties that ensue when complex Western technology is exported ready-made without creating an adequate supporting infrastructure in the receiving countries.

Reception technology, like transmission technology, is predominantly imported from the developed countries. However, many developing countries are themselves now beginning to assemble radio and television receivers from components. This practice is bringing down the cost of receivers to levels equivalent to those in the developed countries. But progress is slow, and it is unlikely that really low-cost solutions will be found in the near future. The provision of adequate reception technology is likely to remain the weakest link in the broadcasting distribution systems of the developing countries for some time to come.

These, then, are the conditions under which broadcasting operates in the developing countries, where the constraints and pressures that affect broadcasting organizations throughout the West are greatly magnified. It is clear that the exportation of broadcasting structures and technology with little regard for the very different conditions of most Third World countries is still causing grave problems even after several decades of such experience. To illuminate further the present features and state of development of broadcasting in our group of ninety-one countries we now look to the past, to the colonial relationships and economic and political ties that have determined so many of the characteristics of broadcasting in the developing countries.

3

The Transfer
of Broadcasting

Having surveyed the state of broadcasting in our group of developing countries, we now turn to an analysis of the way in which this situation came about. Whereas Chapter 2 illustrated the relative homogeneity of broadcasting structures, an evolutionary analysis of broadcasting discloses a variety of strands deriving from the Western countries that have taken the lead in the exportation of broadcasting. Our case studies and the secondary source material show that most of the countries concerned have relied on models of broadcasting developed in the United States, France, the United Kingdom, or one of the other colonial nations of Europe that were able to influence or even dictate the pattern of broadcasting in their dependent territories or in those countries over which they exercised some influence.

The models adopted in Western countries were, of course, themselves designed in response to the particular circumstances obtaining at a particular point in each country's history. In the main their structures and characteristics reflect the preoccupations and objectives of the societies within which they were set at the time of their creation. The viscosity of structures in general and of broadcasting structures in particular accounts for the fact that the basic structures have subsequently been changed only in the face of substantial political or social upheavals.

The United States and Britain provide examples of such relatively static broadcasting systems. The North American model, consisting of a multiplicity of private institutions operating freely within widely set limits and subject to a minimal element of public control through the Federal Communications Commission, has changed little since its creation in the early days of broadcasting. It has withstood repeated efforts to bring it under more extensive public control and to inject into it a substantial public-service element, although the pressures in both these directions have not been without influence on the mode of operation of the American commerical broadcasting corporations, both at national and at local levels.

In the United Kingdom the public-service model designed in 1926 has survived with little change to the present day. The introduction of Independent Broadcasting in 1954, although injecting a self-financing element into the broadcasting system, did not affect the basic characteristics of the model. As one of us has demonstrated elsewhere, "One has only to put side by side the documents governing the conduct of the two British broadcasting organisations, the Charter and Licence of the BBC and the Television Acts under which the Independent Television Authority operates, in order to be struck forcibly by the essentially unitary character of the broadcasting system of the United Kingdom." [1]

In France the model of a state-controlled broadcasting system of a unitary type survived the Second World War and was in fact reinforced during the Fifth Republic under President de Gaulle. It was radically changed only in 1974 in response to the ever more insistent demand for a reduction of government control. The only manner in which it was thought that such a reduction could be brought about was by means of the radical dismantling of the highly centripetal structure of the Office de Radio-Télévision Française (ORTF) into six distinct and independent units, each responsible for only one part of the previously unified structure. The reorganized system has hardly been in operation long enough for a reliable judgment of it to be possible. Given the chronology of the establishment of broadcasting in the countries formerly under French rule, as well as the chronology of their achievement of independence, it is not surprising that the model they inherited was a highly centripetal one that is in many ways likely to suit their circumstances better than the reorganized model.

The reliance on these models of broadcasting in the developing countries may be most clearly identified in the structures of the broadcasting systems, that is, in the institutional and political arrangements under which the broadcasting systems operate. However, much more than the structural forms were transferred to the new nations in their quest for membership of the electronic age. Perhaps the factor that most determines the nature of broadcasting systems is technology. The importation of complex technology brings with it many associated constraints and needs: engineering and production staffs must often be trained in the country from which the equipment is imported; methods and systems of working are necessarily imported; and then there is the continuing dependence of the importing country on the exporting country for spare parts, continued training, and new generations of compatible equipment. The choice of a particular color system for television, for example, will determine the suppliers of most of the broadcasting equipment for many years.

When the institutional and technological aspects of the broadcasting system have been imported and a station begins to broadcast, the need arises for the production and importation of the content of the broadcasting service.

We deal with the transfer of each of these aspects of broadcasting below, but it is important to note a further, less tangible aspect. This is the aspect of a particular model of broadcasting that may be termed the implicit set of assumptions upon which the model is based. This set of assumptions will include norms, unwritten rules, styles of production, values, professional codes and expectations, beliefs, and attitudes. These factors may be less tangible than others, but they are no less important. They are transferred directly through training, socialization, and expectation, and indirectly as functions of the importation of structures, technologies, and content of broadcasting that originate in the advanced industrial nations.

The process of transfer took various forms, depending on the nature of the relationships between the exporting country and the importing country. Where there was a colonial relationship the transfer of the metropolitan model was almost complete. Where there was no colonial relationship the nature of the process of transfer was determined by economic, and perhaps political, expansionism on the part of the developed countries, dependence on the part of the developing states.

Certain features of the development of broadcasting systems are common to all the developing countries. There is always the initial phase that involves the transfer of a metropolitan model to the country concerned. This phase may extend over a long period of time, during which services established during the colonial period gradually expand until the achievement of independence, when they become nationally owned systems. The period may in fact be extremely short, as, for example, when a complete "turnkey" project is installed over a matter of months, as was recently the case in the Sultanate of Oman (installed by Pye-TVT in 1975).

The second phase involves efforts to adapt the broadcasting system to the societal, political, and economic context of the new country. In some countries the metropolitan model of broadcasting survived only a short time after independence; in others, where the political assumptions implicit in the model were more suited to the emergent political structures, the model survives more or less intact to this day.

It may be argued that there is also a third phase, although

its boundaries are not clearly differentiated. The perspective of the mid-seventies makes it possible to perceive the shift toward more homogeneous structures of broadcasting and away from the highly disparate pattern of development that marked the phases of transplantation and acculturation. The fading of the colonial connections and influences enables assumptions established in the colonial period to be called into question. One sees increasing uniformity but also a growing awareness that broadcasting problems might be better shared with neighbors and other developing countries than with the former colonial nations or strictly national or indigenous institutions.

The countries in our sample have been classified into five categories, according to the type of transfer (Table A.5): (1) those in which entrepreneurial initiative was responsible for the introduction of radio and television, operating under the American type of regulatory system; (2) those that followed the model developed in the United Kingdom; (3) those that were established on the French model; (4) those that were influenced by other European colonial countries; (5) those that developed a system made up of the strands of a variety of models.

While continuing to draw on the material provided by ninety-one countries, the more detailed aspects of this chapter derive from our eleven case studies. In analyzing the processes of transfer and institutionalization in each of the five categories, the case studies are employed illustratively.

TRANSFER TO INDEPENDENT COUNTRIES: THE U.S. MODEL

Those nations that either had never been colonized (for example, Iran and Thailand, with which we deal later in this chapter) or had been colonized by Spain and Portugal in the sixteenth and seventeenth centuries and had achieved independence in the early nineteenth century were free to choose their own broadcasting structures. One might have expected the former Spanish and Portuguese colonies in South and Central America and in the Pacific to be influenced by their former metropolitan powers. In fact, the absence of significant broadcasting developments in either Spain or Portugal, coupled with the pan-American links established since independence, caused them to be greatly influenced by the United States in the institutionalization of their broadcasting systems. The majority of the South American countries were already within the sphere of influence of the U.S. both politically and economically when broadcasting technology became commercially available. The South American countries were among the first after the U.S. to introduce radio broadcasting on a commercial basis. In 1922 Brazil, Argentina, and Chile opened their first radio stations. The Philippines followed suit in 1924, Cuba in 1925, Mexico in 1929, and by the end of the thirties radio broadcasting was well established in the main centers of population throughout Central and South America and the Philippines.

The regulatory structures adopted by the governments in these areas were almost identical to that developed in the United States, where the federal government, through the Federal Communications Commission, confines its control largely to the technical and juridicial aspects of the system, and where a large number of private radio stations operate on a commercial basis, their continued existence being dependent on the provision of a return on invested capital.

The early development of radio in Brazil was undertaken by clubs and societies that were poorly equipped and financed by members of recreational and cultural groups or by small-scale advertising. The broadcasting stations and radio receivers had to be licensed by the Department of Posts and Telegraphy in the Ministry of Transport and Public Works, which had itself acquired a transmitter from Western Electric and would broadcast daily the exchange rates of sugar and coffee, weather forecasts, poems, and music.

Radio broadcasting in Peru, however, rather than being established under cultural auspices, was from its inception a tinker's trade. Small stations were established by radio repair shops advertising their own services and by small family businesses. The stations were openly commercial in those early days, and government control was minimal.

As the Peruvian and Brazilian radio stations began to attract ever larger audiences, commercial concerns in other sectors of the economies of these countries began to invest capital. Newspaper chains diversified into radio stations, and even companies such as the Inca-Cola bottling company in Peru began to invest in them. Since in South and Central America businesses were often owned and operated by local oligarchies, the ownership of broadcasting also came to be concentrated in the hands of a few rich families and partnerships. Networks of radio stations were built up, the largest of which survive to this day.

After the Second World War television technology began to arrive, and the radio networks rapidly moved in to dominate the markets. The exporters, mainly American companies such as RCA, supplied equipment, organizational blueprints, and some basic training, especially in the technical operation of the system, together with programs. They did not usually provide capital investment and, because of local legislation, did not enter into formal partnerships. In fact, local entrepreneurs were the real initiators of television in most of these countries, although alliances with American organizations were significant.

The transfer of television, whether for political or commercial reasons, centered on the transfer of the technology alone with little integration of the system as a whole. As a result there were many problems over the availability of financial and human resources, the provision of adequate coverage and reception, the efficient utilization and maintenance of equipment, and the development of widely acceptable program policies.

The economics of broadcasting in the countries that adopted the American model were transformed with the introduction of television. Before television was introduced the development of small-scale local radio broadcasting had proved itself to be profitable, as demonstrated by the great proliferation of stations. The small scale of operations ensured that costs remained low, with the expenditure being fully covered by local advertising, which also provided moderate profits. The introduction of television radically altered this pattern. The vast majority of the population was economically inactive (in Brazil today, for example, this segment constitutes 70 percent of the total population), and thus the market was limited and the number of potential set-owners was low.

In addition, because of the high levels of both recurrent and capital expenditure that television requires, severe financial stringencies were necessary. Levels of staffing were reduced and local production standards were lowered. Many television stations closed down. Indeed, the bankruptcy of many stations and the subsequent trend toward the concentration of ownership in the hands of a few powerful groups, the restriction of television to large, relatively developed urban centers, and the ever-increasing amount of air time devoted to commercials were characteristic of television stations in these countries in the fifties. However, it is important to remember that in the early days of television broadcasting in these countries the state of development of production technology made it impossible to depend substantially on foreign programming. Those countries that introduced television before the advent of the videotape recorder (VTR) had to provide live programs, thus introducing at an early stage local production that encouraged creativity and cultural authenticity. Brazil produced all its programs locally for the first nine years of television, until telecine technology was introduced to the country in 1959. The first VTR was introduced in 1964.

Subsequent programming included much imported material (mainly American series), some local entertainment, and a great deal of advertising (as much as one-third of air time). Entertainment included the local *telenovelas*. The theme of the successful telenovela followed a pattern like this: "A poor but beautiful country girl comes to the big city, works as a maid in a rich household, is seduced, has an illegitimate baby, but prospers and opens a chic boutique or marries a millionaire playboy . . ." [2] Peru's own best-selling novela, *Simplemente Maria*, has been successfully exported to every Spanish-speaking market in the world. The other ingredient of South American television entertainment was the marathon variety show, adapted from radio. The news, too, featured baroque showmanship.

Thus the initial phase of the transfer of the U.S. model of broadcasting was marked by a proliferation of small commercial radio stations that were gradually forged into oligopolistic family empires. These same media interests introduced television, the progress of which was at first decidedly insecure but which finally, with the widespread adoption of videotaping and telecine, began to provide the profits that were expected on the basis of U.S. experience. By the mid-sixties the U.S. model of broadcasting was well established.

However, from this time on, governments in South and Central America began to assume a more directive role in their control of broadcasting. Radical changes were introduced in Brazil and Peru when they both experienced profound political upheaval in the mid-sixties. The Peruvian case is of particular interest since it features not only a rejection of the model transferred and developed before the 1968 revolution, but also an attempt to create an entirely new model better adapted to the goals of the government and to the conditions in the country.

Despite an active campaign led by the commercial owners of the broadcasting stations, who retained some freedom of action for three years after the revolution, the government moved in 1971 to take over the television service, to exert decisive influence in the field of radio, and to nationalize the telecommunications services operated until then by ITT, AT&T, the Swedish Ericsson Company, and a group of Swiss banks. The new law provided for the establishment of a joint television production company, Telecentro, which began operations in 1974. It produces programs for the two channels, which are owned jointly by the government and the former private owners. Since the two channels are supplied with programs through Telecentro, however, they are in effect controlled by government. The channels "buy" programs from Telecentro, paying the production center 60 per cent of their profits. As programming for the two channels is in the hands of the Telecentro board, there is not much left to the channels except to perform the technical function of transmission, seek advertising, and promote their programs. The channels may reject programs assigned to them, for reasons of morality or for technical flaws, but they have no direct recourse to outside producers. The channels, nominally, are competitors. While their programs are essentially similar, care is taken to give the viewer alternative choices. As fas as programming is concerned, in this two-channel system ownership, production, and programming are in the same hands. Of course, the Lima-based productions also continue to be delivered to provincial stations, which the government either owns or controls.

Radical changes were also introduced into the structure of Peruvian radio. The government has bought 25 percent of the shares of almost fifty radio stations. In addition, twenty-three stations of the bankrupt Cadena Nacional network have been entirely nationalized. Lima's defunct educational service on Channel 7 has been revived to become the basis of a state television network. The new network will parallel the two commercial networks by linking Channel 7 to the independent stations in the provinces. A new production company will be instituted within ENRAD (Empresa Nacional de Radiodifusión), the broadcasting arm of the Central Office of Information, which will program for all three networks. ENRAD will have new equipment supplied by Thomson Television International, originally intended for a production unit within the Ministry of Education, and will also receive French government aid. The state network of thirty-two radio stations will also be operated by ENRAD.

A greater degree of government involvement and centralization of the system is also characteristic of the structural changes instituted in Brazil. Law 236 of February 1967 documented these changes, which essentially adapted the 1963 Brazilian Code of Telecommunications to the views of the new government. The severity of the penalties for infringement of the law was increased, and the concentration of power by local and, particularly, foreign interests was also restricted. The law prohibited all types of foreign technical assistance that might permit "intervention or knowledge of the administrative life or the orientation of the broadcasting organization" and limited the number of stations that might be owned by a commercial organization. The most important structural change that followed was the establishment in 1968 of a Ministry of Communications, which drastically diminished the power of the various agencies working in the regulation of broadcasting to whom the private organizations had had easier access and over whom they had been influential. Changes in the regulation of radio broadcasting in 1973 were designed to reduce the high level of interference between medium-wave stations in the commercially promising areas and to increase coverage in other areas, particularly the Amazonas. Abandoning its former policy of acquiescing to the pressures of the commercial operators, the government took the initiative and forced commercial operators to conform.

Other governments in South and Central America also began to take a more active role in improving their national communication systems. While production remained largely the responsibility of private operators, the provision of national microwave systems was undertaken by governments. In 1965, for example, Brazil established a national communications agency, EMBRATEL, and in 1967 embarked on the installation of a nationwide microwave system. The Brazilian government has recently announced a plan to establish its own radio and television network, Radiobras, to eliminate the shortcomings of commercial broadcasting in supplying broadcasting services to all regions of the country and to coordinate the efforts of educational stations. Although this plan has increased the anxiety over nationalization among the private operators, officials in Brasília and Rio have declared that their intention is to supplement the existing structure rather than to compete with it.

All the South American governments and most of those in Central America that originally adopted the U.S. model have now inaugurated their own broadcasting stations and are becoming increasingly involved in the control and even ownership of the bigger private networks. Thus it is possible to perceive the movement toward the pattern of broadcasting prevalent in most of the other areas of the developing world, where governments control or own all the broadcasting outlets. It should be added, however, that because of the large number of private stations that continue to operate in South and Central America and because of the politically "harmless" nature of their output, the intervention by governments in their operations is as yet relatively limited.

TRANSFER TO DEPENDENT TERRITORIES:
THE BRITISH MODEL

The development of broadcasting in the former British colonies and protectorates was, paradoxically, a function of three mutually incompatible policies: the transfer of structures of broadcasting modeled on the British Broadcasting Corporation, the extension of BBC services to British expatriates in the colonies, and the development of local broadcasting services by colonial administrations.

The first steps taken in the transfer of British models of broadcasting were connected with the extension of BBC services throughout the then British Empire. A special BBC service, the BBC Empire Service, relayed news and music to the British expatriate communities. In Nigeria, for example, radio broadcasting was available through relays of the Empire Service for almost twenty years, from 1932 to 1951. In addition, a few hours of programming per week originated locally. Radio sets were still relatively expensive in the thirties, and in Ghana and Nigeria wired distribution services were introduced. Signals from the U.K. were received over air on shortwave and then rebroadcast through the cable network to small loudspeaker boxes. These wired boxes, as they were known, were rented for a few cents a week, thereby avoiding the need for large outlay on a shortwave radio receiver.

Another solution to the problem of the cost of receiving sets was the development of a very simple designed receiver, commonly known as a "saucepan special." This set was very widely sold in Kenya, where radio broadcasting for the large settler community began in 1927.

Programs for the indigenous audiences began in Nigeria in 1939, when the first brief programs featuring Nigerian artists were produced locally and broadcast under the auspices of the Public Relations Office (later to become the Ministry of Information and Culture). Although most British colonies had some form of broadcasting by the mid-thirties there was still no coherent policy for harmonizing the services organized by the various colonial administrations.

The British government, realizing that the piecemeal development of radio broadcasting in the colonies would lead to problems, set up a committee under Lord Plymouth which was asked to "consider and recommend what steps could usefully be taken to accelerate the provision of broadcasting services in the Colonies and to co-ordinate such services with the work of the British Broadcasting Corporation." [3]

The committee, reporting in 1936, recognized that the Empire Service relays could not serve the indigenous needs of the colonies. They felt that colonial broadcasting services should provide a means for education and enlightenment in addition to providing entertainment. The committee "strongly recommended that, wherever possible, broadcasting services should be developed in the colonial territories as a public service by the governments concerned. On the question of control, they came out against individual companies . . . [but] recognised that in certain dependencies it would, in the long run, be embarrassing for the governments to be responsible for all programmes broadcast, but suggested that in the case of most dependencies the government would have to be the controlling body. They did not, however, rule out an organisation on the lines of BBC, which they described as a 'semi-autonomous body responsible to the government.' " [4]

The Second World War provided further impetus for the development of broadcasting in the colonies. Where British colonial territories were actually involved in the war (for example, Singapore and Burma), the existing broadcasting services were of course taken over by the occupying forces. After the war the British government reintroduced its own services, in the cases of Burma and Singapore under the aegis of the British army. In the case of Africa, broadcasting transmissions were increased to those territories where it was thought important to provide information about the progress of the war.

After the war, radio broadcasting soon became relatively well established. By 1948 there were 12,000 radio sets in Nigeria, in addition to 8,000 wired boxes. Programs were broadcast for eighteen hours a day, of which seventeen hours were relayed from the BBC Empire Service.

Where broadcasting had not developed before the war in response to the demands of expatriate British settlers, it was introduced shortly afterward. There were few settlers in Tanzania (then Tanganyika, a United Nations trust territory administered by the U.K.), and radio broadcasting was not introduced until 1951 as part of an experimental scheme based on the recommendations of a BBC expert. The scheme, which received a grant of about $30,000 from the Colonial Development and Welfare Fund, was intended "to provide experience in the production of local programmes for a native audience." [5] The equipment was very basic and coverage was minimal. Known as the Dar es Salaam Broadcasting Station, it transmitted for one hour per week in Swahili, with the program repeated twice. When a more powerful shortwave transmitter was installed and the station had become more highly developed, it was renamed the Tanganyika Broadcasting Service, still technically under British government control. The audience grew relatively rapidly, and by 1960 it was estimated that 72,000 receivers were in use.[6]

This colonial service model was adopted in all the British colonies and dependencies, and in fifteen of the twenty-five such countries in our group this model was never radically changed.

In the remainder of the countries the concept of a public-service corporation modeled on the BBC usually supplanted the colonial-service model in the course of the approach to independence. In all such cases BBC staff members were either assigned for fairly long periods or were sent on short training missions to oversee the progress of incorporation. The usual policy was to fill senior executive, technical, and production positions with expatriates whose job it was to ensure that the broadcasting system was functioning "correctly." They were also responsible for selecting and training local staff members who were groomed for the jobs that would be made available when the expatriate staff left. In the British colonial territories, expatriate staff members came almost entirely from the BBC and were attached for two-year tours of duty: "Between 1950 and 1962 nearly 60 BBC staff were seconded to the NBC . . . the objective . . . [being] the complete Nigerianization of all departments as rapidly as possible." [7] A limited number of local staff people were sent to England for training by the BBC. In the early years the trainees merely sat in on standard BBC training courses; it was not until 1966 that the BBC began to run specialized courses for overseas students.

The Nigerian Broadcasting Corporation was the first broadcasting corporation to be established in the British colonial territories. As such, it was a prototype of this kind of transfer of structures. A booklet issued to mark the tenth anniversary of the NBC states: "The original governmental proposal saw NBC as a duplicate of the BBC with a national organisation and regional branches. The regional wings were to be guaranteed, within the broad lines of the Corporation's policy, a considerable amount of regional autonomy in deciding programme content." [8]

The mode of government provided for an independent board of governors, broadly reflective, as in the U.K., of the various sectors in the life of the nation. The only departure from the British pattern was that the director-general and the acting secretary to the corporation were made ex-officio members of the board. The director-general was head of the hierarchy that has continued to the present day, with divisions for administration, secretariat, accounts, engineering, news, external broadcasting, and programs.

Central administration and heads of divisions were located in the capital, Lagos, with counterparts in the three provincial capitals.

Thus were concepts of broadcasting fashioned in Britain between the two wars transferred to the British colonies in the throes of emergent nationalism. The contradictions inherent in this situation rapidly came to the surface as independence approached. The Western democratic notions of multiparty democracy on which the public-service model was based faded rapidly as political instability and military takeovers shook the former colonies. The autonomy of the broadcasting corporations crumbled everywhere.

Broadcasting in Tanzania (then Tanganyika) functioned between 1960 and 1965 within such a framework of contradictions. On the one hand the Tanganyika Broadcasting Corporation adopted the BBC ethos, emphasizing public service, impartiality, and autonomy; on the other, the corporation included among its goals the provision of information, education, and entertainment in accordance with the national interests of Tanganyika. Although no drastic change was introduced during the first five years of the operation of the corporation, it was finally nationalized in 1965 and became a department of the Ministry of Information and Tourism. Explaining the decision in the National Assembly the then minister of information, Mr. Wakil, said, "In a two-party state like Britain the opposition party fears the control of radio falling into the hands of the governing party. Tanzania is a one-party socialist state and it is the intention of TANU, Afro-Shirazi, and the government to use the radio for informing the public of the social and political progress of their country. For every Tanzanian, the parties and the government are institutions aiming at social reforms and there can be no question of radio misleading the people." [9]

As a result the corporation was dissolved, and the radio service was incorporated into the Ministry of Information and Tourism, which was renamed the Ministry of Information, Broadcasting, and Tourism. The policy of the broadcasting service is now determined by the Mass Media Committee of the TANU party, over which the minister of information and broadcasting presides. This committee consists of four members of the Central Committee of the party together with the editor of the government and party newspapers, the director of radio, the editor of radio news, and the principal secretary of the Ministry of Information, Broadcasting, and Tourism.

The inauguration of television broadcasting in the British colonies coincided in large measure with independence, except in those countries such as India and Pakistan which had been independent for some time before television became available in the late fifties and early sixties. In some countries television was introduced for overtly political reasons.

In Cyprus, television was introduced in 1957 by the British colonial government at the height of the EOKA rebellion. In fact, the first (British) director of radio noted that television was brought to Cyprus in order to "keep people off the streets." [10] Identical circumstances of communal unrest surrounded the introduction of television in Singapore in 1963.

In Nigeria television was introduced in 1959 by the Western Region government which accepted an offer made by Overseas Rediffusion Ltd. (a U.K. company) to establish a fully fledged service, including equipment, manpower, and programs, to be financed by advertising, so that the regional government could have a channel of expression independent from the federal NBC service.

The pattern was repeated later by the Northern State, which in 1961 entered into a similar partnership with Granada and EMI of England, and even by NBC in 1962, which, in reaction to the introduction of television by the regional governments, signed an agreement with an American company, NBC International.

The problems associated with the introduction of television into these countries were complex. Given that the demands of television in terms of technology, know-how, and finance were greater than those of radio, the process of transfer involved much more reliance on foreign aid. Poor local conditions associated with terrain, electrification, climate, staffing, and finance all loomed much larger in the case of television. Commercial involvement by overseas partners was short-lived, further contributing to the reliance on state subsidy and, eventually, state control and ownership.

Nigeria provides a case history of the search for structures that are compatible with the local circumstances of a newly independent country. Even before the advent of independence in 1960, it became apparent that the substantial autonomy from government of the Nigerian Broadcasting Corporation was unrealistic. The demands of a government needing to assert its authority over a country of 50 million people of diverse ethnic, linguistic, and cultural characteristics, between 70 and 80 percent of whom were illiterate, made closer controls of broadcasting inevitable. On the other hand, NBC failed to supply a policy that fully catered to the diverse regional interests resulting from the three-way division (West, East, North) of the country. This failure encouraged the institution of independent regional stations by the then three regional governments, leading the federal Ministry of Information in 1961 to ". . . amend the Nigerian Broadcasting Ordinance to enable the Minister responsible for Broadcasting to give general and specific directions to the Corporation on matters of policy or matters appearing to the Minister to be of public interest and also to enable him, after consultation with the appropriate regional Boards, to make recommendations to the Governor-

General in Council as to the appointment of all members of the Corporation . . ." [11] The amendment also included provision for "the members of the regional Boards to be similarly appointed by the Governor-General in Council on the recommendation of the Minister." [12]

The private companies very soon realized the limitations of the Nigerian market and were subject to heavy losses. This led in later years to financial intervention by the regional governments in order to keep the services alive, culminating with the private companies selling all their shares to the regional governments and withdrawing.

Similar patterns of events recurred throughout the former British colonial territories, always with the same result: the assumption of control of broadcasting by the ruling group, often military, in each country. There are today, of course, differences between states in the extent to which they proclaim in formal terms that their broadcasting corporations have some degree of autonomy from government. Informally, however, the pattern is consistent: state control, state financing, and sometimes straightforward state ownership (as in Tanzania).

TRANSFER TO DEPENDENT TERRITORIES: THE FRENCH MODEL

The French model of broadcasting is based on the notion of state control of a unitary broadcasting structure. In other respects the French model embodied in Radiodiffusion Télévision Française (RTF, 1959–1964) and later in the (formally) more autonomous Office de Radio-Télévision Française (ORTF, 1964–1974) is similar to the British colonial service model. As such it is perhaps not surprising that the French model of broadcasting has proved remarkably stable in the former French colonial territories.

The development of broadcasting in the French colonies was in many ways similar to the early British pattern of relayed metropolitan services aimed primarily at expatriate settlers and the local elite in the urban areas. The French colonial pattern regarded the more evolved colonies, such as Algeria, as *départements* of the metropolitan republic. In West Africa, the urban areas along the coast were regarded as parts of France. Known as *communes de plein exercice*, they had the right to elect deputies to the French Assembly, while the interior regions were administered in a largely regulatory manner by colonial officers.

Thus although radio broadcasting began locally in Algeria in 1925, in 1937 the metropolitan radio service (known as France Cinq, the fifth channel) was extended to cover Algeria. Programs were relayed directly from Paris for twenty-five years, until independence in 1962.

The colonial radio service in West Africa, Radio Afrique Occidentale Française, was based in Senegal but also served Mali, Mauritania, Chad, Dahomey, Gabon, Guinea, and the Ivory Coast until these countries gained independence in 1960.

In the French territories considerable emphasis was placed on training at RTF, and later at ORTF, in Paris for local staff members who were expected to fill senior positions. The first French agency responsible for broadcasting systems in the colonies was the Société de Radiodiffusion de la France d'Outre-mer (SORAFOM). In the first year of its existence it trained three hundred African broadcasters at its training center in Paris, Studio-Ecole de Maisons Lafitte. Staffs from developing countries were trained by actually operating a small radio station that broadcast programs to Paris. SORAFOM evolved into the Office de Coopération Radiophonique (OCORA) in 1962, which proceeded to develop SORAFOM's plans for the introduction and rapid expansion of television in the newly independent territories.

In all French colonies except Algeria, television was introduced some years after independence. In Algeria the war of independence erupted in 1954; two years later television was introduced in response to demands from the *colons*. At considerable expense a tropospheric relay system was installed in 1958, which enabled programs to be transmitted directly from France to Algeria. Only fifteen minutes of programming per day originated from the studios in Algiers at this time.

OCORA, the French government body responsible after 1962 for encouraging the development of radio and television in the colonies, was superseded in 1964 by the ORTF's Département des Affaires Extérieures et Coopération (DAEC). This department offered consultation and advice to the newly independent countries where the French government wished to maintain its influence. The French television equipment company Thomson-CSF was also heavily involved in the transfer of television systems to the former French colonies.

The introduction of television was much discussed in Senegal around the time of independence in 1960. In 1962 the president eventually gave his approval. Work began on the conversion of the station of Radio Senegal, offices were extended, and technicians and producers were sent to France for training at ORTF. At the same time UNESCO was considering setting up "a pilot centre for the production and testing of audio-visual materials and equipment for adult education, including literacy." [13] The project was to be established in a country in which television had already been introduced so that costs could be reduced. When no such country indicated an interest, the Senegalese delegation succeeded in persuading UNESCO to locate the project in their country, even though television broadcasting had still not begun. During the negotiations the Senegalese economy weakened, and President Senghor vetoed any further expenditure on television. Despite this blow UNESCO and the government finally reached agreement on the establishment of an experimental television service that would use the equipment and expertise already available, the total cost of $48,000 to be shared equally. It soon became apparent that this sum was inadequate, but after grants had been received from the United Nations Development Program (UNDP) and the French government, the television station was inaugurated at the end of 1964. The audience was strictly limited as the .05 kw transmitter employed had a range of only 30 kilometers. A variety of experiments in broadcasting for adult education was carried out.[14] In 1970, these funds were exhausted and the station closed down.

Although a number of senior politicians and broadcasting officials (including the director-general, who labeled television "a jewel for the tired and spent bourgeoisie") [15] were opposed to the reintroduction of television, in 1972, after a satellite ground station had been installed in Senegal, it became possible for television coverage of the Munich Olympic Games to be transmitted live and in color. President Senghor came under intense pressure from the elite in Dakar and from the French television equipment manufacturer Thomson-CSF to reintroduce television broadcasting for the period of the games. Thomson-CSF even undertook to install a system free of charge on a trial basis and to supply a number of receiving sets for community reception in Dakar. At this, President Senghor succumbed and the system was installed. The elite of Dakar ordered sets by air freight, and ORTF supplied free programs and films to fill in the gaps between sporting events. After the games it was impossible to close down television broadcasts because of pressure on the government from those who had bought sets, and so television was formally attached to Radio Senegal and a new structure was introduced, formalized in 1973. In fact, the Senegalese government adopted the ORTF structure and the new organization was called the Office de Radiodiffusion Télévision Sénégalaise (ORTS). In formal terms this administrative structure is identical with that of ORTF.

A similarly direct transfer of the French model occurred in Algeria. Although the country had gained its independence only after eight years of armed struggle and a very bitter withdrawal by the French *colons*, the model of broadcasting established was identical in formal terms to that of RTF. RTF became the ORTF in 1964, and Radio-Télévision Algériene adopted the new French model in 1967. In essence, the transformation from government agency to public authority in both France and Algeria was necessitated by the introduction of advertising. The introduction of the *Office* model in other French colonies derives from the same need to provide a structure that does not contravene established commercial practices. The adoption of this structure should not, however, be taken as an indication of a relaxation of state control. The autonomy of broadcasting in all the former French colonies is restricted to day-to-day management.

The strong metropolitan influence that for many years determined that programs were broadcast in French has recently been undermined by the development of nonaligned policies by most African states. In Algeria and Senegal, for example, it is now official policy to rely much less on French-language programs, particularly where broadcasting reaches beyond the urban centers. Similarly, equipment contracts are beginning to go to Eastern European, Japanese, and American companies rather than to the French concerns that have until recently enjoyed a monopoly. However, the exportation under very attractive terms of the French SECAM color television system has ensured that Thomson-CSF continues to be awarded the television contracts.

In summary then, although the French model is still intact in the structural sense, some of the assumptions implicit in it are now being questioned: the predominance of the French language; the reliance on the metropolitan culture; and the dependence on French business concerns for financial, technical, and administrative expertise. As we have indicated there are still areas where the French connection determines policies, but the signs are that multilateral relationships with a range of developed countries are undermining the hegemonic position that France formerly enjoyed.

TRANSFER TO DEPENDENT TERRITORIES: OTHER MODELS

Three other European states, Belgium, Spain, and the Netherlands, introduced broadcasting to the territories in which they had established colonial administrations. It is clear, though, that none of these states entered into arrangements for the transfer of models of broadcasting on the scale of Britain or France.

The Dutch model of broadcasting is pluralist to the point of fragmentation. The allocation of air time to the major cultural and political associations and the extension of access to any organized groups of citizens determines that the pluralism which has long been a feature of Dutch society is maintained. This pattern of broadcasting also developed in the Netherlands East Indies, now Indonesia.

Radio broadcasting in Indonesia began under the Dutch administration in 1924. A corporate structure, the Netherlands Indies Radio Broadcasting Corporation (NIROM) supervised the proliferating broadcasting stations by licensing private operators in addition to operating its own radio service and levying license fees for receivers.

In 1937, the private stations operated by local Indonesians established a nonprofit association "dedicated to the promotion of national culture and the development of spiritual and physical well-being of the Indonesian community by way of radio programmes." [16] In 1940 the colonial administration recognized the association and transferred to it the Netherlands Indies Radio Broadcasting Corporation's right to broadcast indigenous programming.

With the Japanese invasion in 1942 the development of indigenous broadcasting structures was temporarily slowed. On the cessation of hostilities in 1945 President Sukarno, who had declared the country to be independent in spite of Dutch government opposition, inaugurated Radio Republic Indonesia (RRI). RRI's broadcasts assumed great importance during the four-year armed struggle for independence from Dutch rule. It remains within the Department of Information to this day and is responsible for Indonesia's national radio and television broadcasting. However, remnants of the Dutch model still persist: the Department of Information issues licenses to some 700 small radio stations, both amateur and commercial, which operate throughout the 3,000 mile archipelago.

The Belgian colonies of Burundi and Rwanda were so underdeveloped that even radio broadcasting was not introduced until the early sixties when they achieved independence. In the case of the other former Belgian territory, Zaire, radio broadcasting has always been the responsibility of a government department, both before and after independence. Thus in the case of the Belgian colonies the technology of broadcasting was tranferred from the metropolitan power, but there was little concern over the transfer of institutional structures.

Similarly, the former Spanish territory of Equatorial Guinea was and still is backward in the development of its broadcasting system. The state-controlled model of broadcasting adopted in Spain was transferred with little alteration to this tiny African colony (population 310,000 in 1974), where the complexities of colonial administration were minimal.

Thus the transfer of definitive models to colonial states was substantially a concern of Britain and France alone. However, it would be wrong to think that all developing countries were subject to the processes of institutional transfer that we have outlined thus far. Certain countries have sought solutions to the problems of the institutionalization of broadcasting within their own cultures and traditions. Although a modern institutional form such as a broadcasting system is obviously not indigenous to developing societies, among those countries that were not subject to colonization in recent time a number have not relied on foreign forms to the same degree as have other nations. We now turn to an analysis of these systems.

TRANSFER: HYBRID MODELS IN INDEPENDENT COUNTRIES

In the countries that have never been colonized and where there were already highly developed urban centers before the introduction of the broadcast media, the tendency to rely on foreign institutional broadcasting forms has been more limited.

In Iran and Thailand, for example, the broadcasting structures were adapted from the outset to local conditions. The Iranian radio service was from 1940 to 1958 only a small department in the Ministry of Posts, Telephones, and Telegraphs and the prime minister's office. In 1958 it achieved increased independence when a General Department of Publications and Radio was established under the supervision of the prime minister's office. In 1964, a new Ministry of Information was created which incorporated the radio services within its framework.

From its inception in 1931, radio broadcasting in Thailand was controlled by the government and operated both by the Office of Publicity (later to change its name to the Public Relations Department) in the prime minister's office and by the armed forces. All of the stations functioned de facto along the lines of American commercial broadcasting. The difference was in the nature of entrepreneurship, for all stations have always been controlled by the government. Frequencies were allocated to regional commanders of the armed forces, who gave over the actual operation of the station to a business manager, often Chinese, who could proceed to sell spot advertisements and programs for sponsorship. Revenue from the enterprise would then be shared with the local commander.

Broadcasting in Thailand was from the outset a consumer-oriented operation designed primarily to give profit to station owners in the first place and pleasure to the audience in the second. Programs included music (mainly Western but also Thai), soap opera, and variety shows.

Equipment was imported indiscriminately from companies that, while offering advice and technical assistance, did not hesitate to supply facilities that were technically incompatible with those already installed. The problem of the variety of standards was further aggravated by the indiscriminate use of radio frequencies and the uncontrolled expansion of stations. This crowding of the spectrum encouraged anarchy and made it almost impossible to coordinate the use of the airwaves. To this day nobody seems to know the exact number of radio stations in Thailand (estimated to be between 200 and 300), and often several stations share the same frequency in the same geographical area.

In addition, the technical assistance extended to these countries in general by Western countries provided for the training of local engineers and technicians in the installation and operation of the equipment without placing adequate emphasis on maintenance and preventive practices. This omission proved eventually to have severe consequences and resulted in expensive adjustments at later stages.

The Thai government eventually became concerned over these problems, and during the early development of broadcasting tried to introduce a greater degree of structure into the almost chaotic system. The Radio Broadcasting Act of 1965, issued to supplement the Radio Communications Act of 1955, provided for radio-station-licensing procedures to be operated by the Public Relations

Department. An interministerial Committee of Radio
Broadcasting and Communications, set up in 1962, decided
in 1966 to abolish all commercial advertising, a decision
that is apparently still on the books but ceased to be effective in 1969. "Regulations Governing Official Radio Broadcasts" were issued in 1968 in draft form, defining goals and
establishing norms for the regulation of program content
and personnel.

Of the independent countries that adopted hybrid models, the first to introduce television were Thailand (1954)
and Iran (1958). All the other such countries that introduced television did not do so until the middle and late
sixties.

The incorporated Thai Television Company was created
by legislation in 1953 to operate the first television channel.
It was controlled by the Public Relations Department
(which owned 55 percent of the stock), with other national
entities as shareholders, including the Lottery Bureau, the
Thai Tobacco Monopoly, the three armed services, and the
Department of Industrial Workshops. This new organization was followed by the establishment of army-owned stations, including the first color service (circa 1963), to enable
the armed forces, as one informant put it, "to explain to the
public how they have been spending their budget."

As has been pointed out, when television began in the fifties videotaping facilities were still not available. In Thailand, where television broadcasting commenced in 1954,
much of the early programming was therefore live and,
consequently, authentic in content if not in form.

The early days of television in Thailand were marked by
an interest in using the new medium for presenting traditional arts, and experiments were made with shadow plays,
puppet theaters, and folk plays. At first the United States
Information Agency provided film for the new Thai television channel: "Firestone Hour" concerts; "The World
through Stamps," "Industry on Parade," and the like, but,

as in Brazil, the bulk of the programming was local: only about 30 percent was imported for the four-day-a-week schedule that lasted for three or four years.

The introduction of commercial connections to United States markets began in Thailand in 1956. After protracted negotiations a "country price" was established which reflected the Thai negotiators' view that the price should fit the size and potential of the audience and the Americans' interest in Thailand as the first television country in Asia. The final price agreed on was only fifty dollars per hour. Screen Gems (then MCA) began providing filmed serials and series such as "The Lone Ranger," "Monte Cristo," "Wagon Train," and "Private Eye," in addition to feature films that gradually started to attract an audience.

Television was introduced in Iran when Iradj Sabet, a Harvard graduate and heir to an aristocratic family, who was the agent for Pepsi-Cola and RCA in Iran, used his contacts in the royal court to obtain permission to establish an American-model station, Television of Iran. However, this endeavor proved to be incompatible with the prevailing political circumstances in Iran. After several years of operation, pressures toward the nationalization of television started to build up, particularly after the establishment of a government-owned station, National Iranian Television (NIT).

NIT challenged the Television of Iran (TVI) over its philosophy of broadcasting and its program content. NIT initially broadcast intellectual European programs, some of them provided free of charge by ORTF, together with German, British, and Japanese imports as well as Iranian programs. By contrast, Television of Iran, with more experience and a definite mass orientation, broadcast more entertainment programs, mainly MGM films and NBC series, with little local production (only half an hour per week out of about forty hours was devoted to a traditional music program produced by the Ministry of Culture). NIT failed in its attempt to overcome the popularity of TVI's programming; a survey carried out by the University of Tehran in 1968 indicated a clear preference by viewers for TVI (as high as 70 percent). These survey results were explained in terms of the audience's being habituated to American serials, to the fact that the 525-line standard used by TVI was compatible with the majority of the receivers while NIT broadcast on the 625-line standard, and also to the fact that TVI broadcast six hours daily while NIT broadcast only three. Eventually however TVI was nationalized (in 1969), thus providing NIT with two channels. The content was popularized by the program planners of the new 625-line station in order to encourage the audience to buy sets that operated on that standard, and the program quality of the former TVI (still operating on the 525-line standard) was improved. Within a short period, NIT was broadcasting a program pattern similar to TVI's.

In 1972 a new body, National Iranian Radio and Television (NIRT) was formed to centralize all the activities regarding the establishment, management, and operation of radio and television centers and also to prepare and broadcast radio and television programs.

The structure of NIRT is not based directly on any other model of broadcasting. It is the outcome of a study commissioned from the Industrial Management Institute in Tehran in 1970, designed to provide organizational solutions to the problems of the integration of radio and television and of the expansion of broadcasting services, which required that a large number of production and transmission centers be established and their operation coordinated. NIRT has experimented with the creation of a system of internal competition by replacing the usual vertical hierarchy with a horizontal "divisional" structure based upon semiindependent units or groups.

Iran's oil wealth has permitted the government to endow NIRT with astronomic sums relative to those available in other countries. However, whether money alone is sufficient to solve problems connected with the implementation of such goals as the increase of local production and the expansion of facilities for transmission, production, and reception is still questionable.

In Thailand the structure of television did not change at all during the 1960s and early 1970s, with the distribution of "spheres of influence" between the Public Relations Department and the armed forces remaining intact, at least until 1973.

In October 1973, as we have already mentioned, demonstrating students demanded constitutional reforms and the restoration of civil rights and set fire to the building of the Public Relations Department, which had been broadcasting blatantly distorted news about the outbursts of violence between the police and the students. The government was deposed and structural changes in the broadcasting system were introduced. The new prime minister appointed his deputy "to take charge of the country's radio and mass media policy in view of past mistakes and future holding of general elections which require massive education of the public in the workings of democracy." [17]

An attempt was made to decommercialize radio broadcasting; a more stringent procedure for franchising stations has been introduced, although its effectiveness is yet to be tested; efforts are being made to reduce, or at least not to further inflate, the number of stations; the goals of broadcasting have been given some shape. However, the overall situation is still chaotic.

The other independent countries in this group introduced television later, mostly in the mid-sixties, and benefited from the outset from the availability of videotape recording and, in some cases, the introduction of cheaper color television technology. These technical advantages made it easier to rely on imported programs. In Ethiopia, for example, over 85 percent of programs are imported, mainly from the U.K. and the U.S.

Libya, Iraq, Jordan, Syria, the Yemen Arab Republic, and the People's Democratic Republic of Yemen operate broadcasting systems that have been government-owned and operated from their inception and that are unitary in structure. There were, of course, links with metropolitan powers; Jordan still retains some British advisers, and the BBC has always maintained close links with the Jordanian television service. Egypt and Syria bought RCA equipment and involved American program advisers in the early development of their broadcasting systems. A British company introduced television to Iraq in order to promote the sales of receivers.[18]

We have outlined the prevailing patterns in the history of the institutionalization of broadcasting in all the developing countries. Internally there is increasing government intervention in those countries where broadcasting is not already government owned and operated. Externally in almost all countries the former colonial relationships have yielded progressively to more open systems of relationships with a variety of developed countries.

4

The Interaction of Broadcasting and Established Institutions

Broadcasting, as an institution, is being incorporated into the body politic of the new nations. This process of mutual accommodation raises questions. How, for example, has the educational system or the economic system reacted to the new institution? How has broadcasting been affected by the established agencies? What mandate is provided for broadcasting, implicitly or explicitly, by the political or economic power structures? What price, in allegiance, money, or performance, must the broadcasting system, whether nationalized or operating by free enterprise, pay for its franchise? And reciprocally, what pressures does broadcasting, as an institution, exert on the preexistent institutions? Does it affect their performance? And, if so, how? These questions are ones of institutional interaction.

As we have shown, European or North American models were copied in the introduction of broadcasting systems in the developing countries, either because the then colonial power regarded this procedure as axiomatic or because these models were regarded as the only ways in which a modern communication system could be structured. Over the years, however, the inheritors of these models have asserted their own judgments. These have often led them to modify the organization of broadcasting and to accommodate the inherited models to the needs of the new nations, as perceived by those exercising power. We shall consider this process of accommodation first in relation to the political power structure, then to the economic, educational, and cultural institutions.

BROADCASTING AND THE POLITICAL POWER STRUCTURE

The relationship of broadcasting to any political power structure is bound to be ambivalent. Given the assumed influence of the broadcast media on public opinion and attitude formation, governments everywhere, sensitive to public opinion and public attitudes toward themselves, tend to believe the media to be largely responsible.

In France, and to a more severe extent in Soviet Russia and China, attitudes toward the media have been consistent, if directive. The Anglo-American tradition, on the other hand, lays stress on the principle of freedom of expression, and particularly freedom of the press. In Britain and the United States freedom of expression has been a major sociopolitical principle since the Protestant Reformation of the sixteenth century, even though governments have more often honored this principle in the breach than in the observance. In relation to the development of broadcasting in the twentieth century they have often tended to take the view that there is some justification for public control because there is not the same free access to the raw material of broadcasting—broadcast frequencies—as there is to newsprint, the raw material of the press. This view has led the mainstream tradition of broadcasting to lay stress on public, as distinct from government, control and on the freedom of the broadcasters from direct government interference. Insofar as such freedom has been achieved and maintained, it has been done in one of two ways.

The North American tradition of free enterprise in the mass communications field has been able to flourish largely because the size of the continent allows for competition on the air without the same degree of co-channel interference as in European countries. Thus broadcasting is treated like any other service industry. Entrepreneurs are free, subject to minimal statutory restrictions, to establish and operate broadcasting stations in accordance with commercial criteria of demand and supply. As long as they observe the law of the land they are free to broadcast what they like, and material critical of the government of the day is expected to be part of the output. Since the available airwaves allow a variety of outlets, it is assumed that expressions of opinion on different channels will either cancel each other out or, being offered to only a limited section of the population, will not constitute a serious danger to the country's political framework.

The maintenance of freedom of expression in British broadcasting has been the subject of a more deliberate act of policy. This policy, designed in 1926 for a single-channel radio operation, aimed to render this channel independent not only of political but also of commercial pressures. Hence the emphasis on public, as distinct from private, enterprise and on control in the interests of "the people" as distinct from those of the government. The instruments used to achieve such independence have been, on the one hand, a controlling board of governors for the broadcasting service, whose members are intended to be broadly representative of the variety of interests in the country without being politically tied, and, on the other hand, the reliance on broadcast license fees paid by the users of radios or television receivers rather than on advertising revenue. It has become clear since Independent Broadcasting was introduced that the first instrument is regarded as more important than the second. It is thought (at least by wide sections of the community) that advertising revenue can legitimately be used to finance a broadcasting service as long as that service is under firm public control.

The extension of broadcasting has, as already indicated, tended to encourage the new nations to follow the practice of the metropolitan power. French colonies tended to adopt the French pattern; British colonies, that practiced in the United Kingdom. The North American pattern has tended to find its way into Latin America and into such parts of the Pacific and Southeast Asia as were not under the direct influence of one of the European powers.

Whether by colonial government or by commercial entrepreneurs, metropolitan structures were transferred to Africa, Asia, and Latin America with little regard, other than in terms of scale, to indigenous development. Even now one senses the influence of metropolitan traditions and practices in many broadcasting stations of the developing world. The brass plates in Broadcasting House, Lagos, indicate that the officials of the Nigerian Broadcasting Corporation have the same titles as their colleagues at Broadcasting House, London. The intellectual approach to their work of the officials of Radio-Télévision Algérienne is from the same stable as that of their colleagues working for the now dismembered Office de Radio-Télévision Française. The broadcasting patterns in large parts of South America bear the stamp of U.S. models, if not of U.S. entrepreneurs.

This literal transfer of institutions and practices has had certain positive results. It has set standards of quality and of professional performance that have been recognized as normative, even if it has not often been possible to achieve them. It has provided working relationships for broadcasters from the new nations with their more experienced colleagues from the metropolitan countries, which have often been useful. But the main influence has been inhibiting, since the existence of metropolitan models has prevented the development of norms more closely related to the wholly different sociopolitical circumstances in the developing countries. The failure to bring a more analytical and imaginative approach to the design of relevant broadcasting models has caused unnecessary difficulty and instability for most broadcasting organizations in the nation-building process.

Whereas in most European and North American countries the broadcasting organizations were established in countries with well-tried representative political systems, the establishment of broadcasting organizations in the new nations often preceded the establishment of similar systems, or was effectively concurrent with them. This meant that the concept of public control could not be related to the concept of representative government or of democratic institutions.

Reliance on the size and freedom of the marketplace was effective in South America, where private enterprise existed in most towns on the scale necessary for undertaking modern radio operations. The more enterprising of these operations expanded into networks and attracted outside investment to branch out into television. In Africa and to some extent in Asia, it was idle to think of the transfer of the norms of independence and impartiality inherent in the metropolitan models. When the models were applied, the independence of the broadcasting organizations soon became little more than a formality. In practice, government decided to control the broadcasting organization because cadres of independent citizens who had the necessary experience and were acceptable to government did not exist. Where, as in South America, the initiative was left to commercial enterprises, the element of competition tended to be limited because only a few indigenous firms were capable of mounting the capital investment and expertise necessary to launch a broadcasting operation. Many smaller territories had to seek such entrepreneurs and administrators outside the country, usually in the metropolitan nation, thus perpetuating external control of a vital instrument of national development.

Again, the populations of most countries from which the

model structures were derived were predominantly literate and had already acquired extensive experience with the role of a mass medium through the existence of newspapers. Few of the countries into which broadcasting was introduced had either of these qualifications. The majority of the population might well be illiterate, the scale of newspaper circulation minimal and largely confined to the elite in the capital. Mobility of information was likely to be confined to what could be transmitted by word of mouth from one village to another. The traditional patterns of life in many developing countries had been under strain for a generation as a result of the accelerated pace of change resulting from the impact of modernization.

The introduction into this situation of an alien medium of information has added further strains that we can recognize, but about the effects of which we as yet know little. Neither the authorities of the country concerned, who were anxious to speed the process of modernization, nor those of the country from which the model was exported, paid adequate attention to the possible side effects of such strains.

As a result the new broadcasting systems have come under a variety of strains: political, technical, cultural, and sociopsychological. In this section we are concerned particularly with the political aspects of these strains. From our studies it emerges that the model that has succumbed to these strains soonest has been the most ambitious in terms of sociopolitical maturity. The British liberal-humanist model, which assumed that governments in the developing countries could at this stage of their development sustain a broadcasting structure outside their immediate control, has proved to be unworkable, at least in the early years of national development. In country after country where the British model was established, the freedom of broadcasting systems as perceived in the metropolitan country has turned out to be incompatible with the objectives of government. Even where the endemic tendency of politicians toward self-perpetuation has been resisted, the model of a broadcasting service independent of government control has been found to be unacceptable by those in power. The absence of other means of communicating effectively with their populations as a whole has caused governments to take over the broadcasting service. The need, or assumed need, for a period of stability uninterrupted by political opposition in which to achieve the legitimation of their regimes has caused them to discourage the expression of dissent or criticism on the air. The need to shorten lines of command has tempted them to appoint like-minded friends in preference to experienced professionals to the responsible positions in the broadcasting organizations.

The pre-1974 French model has proved to be closer to the ethos of governments in the francophone parts of Africa. (In the successor states to French Indochina, events have led to a loosening of the French connection, although the broadcasting structures retain some French characteristics.) Thus, in the former French colonies in Africa the adaptation of the broadcasting institutions to the political needs of predominantly one-party states has been easier. The issue of acculturation has tended rather to be concentrated on the use of the French language. Both in Algeria and in Senegal, where we carried out case studies, the tension between the wish of the intellectuals to continue to use French (together with all that this means in cultural terms) and the wish of the politicians to reinforce the indigenous languages (Arabic in Algeria and, to a lesser extent, Wolof in Senegal,) has been a major political problem posed by the existence of a broadcasting service. The need to establish the countries' intellectual emancipation from France, as well as the need to establish a base for an autonomous national culture, is thought to require the establishment of a national language other than French. We shall return to the problem of language when we deal more specifically with the role of the broadcasting system in relation to the national cultures of the new nations.

The American model for many years after its introduction in the 1920s encountered little opposition in those countries, mainly in Latin America and to some extent in Southeast Asia, in which it had been applied. In the 1930s governments, such as Brazil's, began to introduce legislation to regulate broadcasting. But commercially based radio systems developed with little government intervention. This appears to have been the case largely because governments did not object to the prerequisite for the success of this model: its operation only in those areas with sufficient commercial potential to attract advertising revenue. In Brazil and Peru, among our case studies, serious attention began to be given to the needs of the interior of the country in broadcasting terms only in the 1960s. In Peru this attention recently led to greater government involvement in broadcasting activities, largely displacing the existing commercial enterprises. In Brazil there are substantial plans to extend television coverage beyond the 35 percent or so of the population living along the coast and in the prosperous southern part of the country, but few signs of the implementation of these plans. Increasingly, however, the freedom of private-enterprise broadcasting in these countries has become conditional upon noninterference in the political affairs of the country, if not upon uncritical support of the government in power. To that extent the American model also has been modified in the course of its application to the developing countries.

As indicated in Chapter 3 the process of political acculturation of the broadcasting structures imported into the Third World has been taking place in two stages. The first stage has been the development of the service, largely in the image of its metropolitan godparent; the second, the reorganization of the service so as to meet the needs and wishes of the government in power and of related pressure groups. But even in the process of acculturation, media structures have continued to impart the influences that they themselves have also exerted on the liberal democracies of the West. For example, Western observers note with concern that the rulers of many developing countries attempt to govern by means of radio or television. They address their people over the heads of their representative assemblies and their ministers and civil servants. The example of the dialogues between villagers and rural experts in the *Dissoo* programs of Senegal is of interest in this connection. These enable President Senghor to claim to represent the interests of the ordinary people over against the bureaucracy. Other leaders use broadcasting in similar ways. But although the tendency for broadcasting to enable leaders to outflank the normal organs of government has been moderated in the West by the well-entrenched and powerful governmental structures, the trend toward direct confrontation is there. It has been followed for many years, from President Roosevelt's "fireside chats" to the broadcasts to the French nation by President de Gaulle and the ministerial broadcasts for which special rules have been made outside the normal framework of the party-political broadcasts in Britain.

This illustration of the two-way movement of influence between broadcasting and the political structures if anything emphasizes the dangers arising from the assumption of control of the broadcasting media by those holding the reins of political power.

Even allowing for the problems of national development, and even distinguishing between the essential elements in a striving for unitary control and the unjustified muzzling of independent thought and expression, there are strong grounds for believing that there is much unjustified control, and that this is bound to defeat the objectives of national development in the medium term.

The assumption of full control over the broadcasting services is usually but one aspect of the abandonment of multiparty government. As Sir Arthur Lewis has pointed out, the European multiparty systems deriving from the development of a class structure peculiar to Europe are not necessarily appropriate to countries in which society is classless but arranged according to tribal structures.[1] The argument for the one-party state deriving from this structure has been made persuasively by Julius Nyerere, the president of Tanzania.[2] What is the role of the broadcasting organization in such a structure? Clearly it needs to reflect the essential unity of the country, but this does not always preclude constructive criticism from within, just as there is room for argument about controversial issues within the single-party structure.

The transmission of opinions that may differ from those of the leaders of a one-party state is not the only problem with which such broadcasting systems have to contend. Their even greater problem is to contain the cult of the personality of the leading politician, the promotion of which is often expected of them. Again, the need should be acknowledged for the personality of the new leader of a new country to be so projected that the population come to recognize him and to transfer to him the loyalties that formerly bound them to their local chiefs and leaders. But the absence of accepted arrangements for the peaceful achievement of a change of leadership induces in that leadership a fear of change and tends to encourage it to demand a magnification of the personality of the leader in an attempt to stave off change. For the achievement of the objective of nation-building, however, it is probably one of the more important tasks of broadcasters to project the personality of the national leader in a way that will reinforce his authority and yet prevent the creation of a larger-than-life image that will inhibit a change of leadership as and when this becomes necessary. At present it still tends to be necessary for those seeking to change the leadership to do so by means of a military coup, preferably carried out while the leader is out of the country.

Another difficulty of accommodation that the broadcasting system in a new country tends to face is the image of its own country that it is required to present to the outside world. Most countries have at least some external broadcasting intended to impress on their immediate neighbors and the worldwide audience the country's achievements. Since, in fact, foreign government monitors and other observers tend to regard the external broadcasting service as the official projection of government views and policies, even when this is not the case, the role of the broadcasting service as an instrument of the country's foreign policy is reinforced. The resources devoted to external broadcasting may be out of proportion to the resources available for the major purpose of the organization, that is, to contribute to the national development process. In certain countries, notably Tanzania, the volume of external broadcasting is deliberately expanded in order to support liberation movements in other countries of Southern Africa.

A last aspect of the political acculturation process that has to be discussed is in many ways the most important. It concerns the control of transmission coverage priorities by governments. Broadcasting is expensive. Hence few governments can afford to provide complete coverage of their countries in both sound and vision at the present time. This leads them to concentrate coverage in those areas where it is likely to bring the greatest political return in the short term, usually in the capital and in politically sensitive areas such as borders and areas with language problems. Thus all too often the capital and its immediate hinterland are well served by both radio and television services, whereas the rural areas where the developmental need is greatest remain deprived. Few governments have as yet established communications priorities that are related realistically to the development process in this sense. Among the exceptions are mainland Tanzania and Sri Lanka. Unlike the majority of their neighbors both countries are determined not to launch television as a service confined to the capital and absorbing a disproportionate share of the national resources devoted to mass communications. They have also resisted the introduction of television as a commercial enterprise by expatriate operators. This decision has been facilitated by the relatively unsophisticated life-style of the majority of their citizens and because the decision forms part of a broader, clearly defined policy aimed at national self-reliance.

In sum, the dominant role played by governments in the interaction between broadcasting structures and the political institutions of the developing countries is a fact of life. It is clear that none of the imported models has proved entirely acceptable to those exercising political power. It may be that the concept of a broadcasting service with an autonomous sense of responsibility to the national community that it exists to serve may become more acceptable as governments find their own positions becoming more secure. In the meantime broadcasters will continue to experience tension between their professional norms, which have been shaped by Western models and, often, by training in Europe or North America, and the practical relationship of dependence on the political systems within which they are working. The norms of balance that are inherent in the established broadcasting systems of the West tend to be abandoned for the time being.

Broadcasters also find themselves called upon to play their part in the creation of new national myths and events. They are required to adjust their news values to the events that government regards as important. Finally, as already indicated, they have the task of projecting the personality of the leader in a way that will attract and retain the maximum commitment on the part of the largest part of the population. In those countries where the broadcasting organizations are private enterprise institutions, these concessions form part of the conditions of obtaining a franchise. But the position of all broadcasters, whatever the auspices under which they work, is largely similar.

ECONOMIC IMPLICATIONS OF BROADCASTING

The launching of a broadcasting system introduces into the economy of a country a variety of needs that have to be met if the system is to develop. There is the need for equipment of three types: transmission, reception, and production. There is the need for trained manpower for management, engineering, and program production. In those countries where broadcasting systems are to be paid for wholly or in part by advertising revenue there is, in addition, the need for conditions that will attract such revenue, and for the sales, public relations, and advertising staffs to handle this side of the broadcasting organization's activities. In the majority of developing countries the whole range of these goods and services has initially to be imported since few, if any, are available locally.

TECHNOLOGY

The technological refinement of even basic equipment for the production, transmission, and reception of radio and television programs requires research and development resources available only in highly industrialized countries. Hence it was inevitable that the early broadcasting equipment development should have taken place in the United States and in Europe. This being so, the development of broadcasting services constitutes an attractive proposition to two types of external entrepreneurs. The first are the multinational corporations that are constantly in need of new areas for profitable investment. The second (who may or may not be identical with the first) are the manufacturers of broadcasting and ancillary equipment who are anxious to find new outlets for their goods and services. In recent years the development of design and production capability in Japan has effectively broken the oligopoly of a handful of firms that between the end of the Second World War and the mid-1960s dominated the market. RCA, Schlumberger, EMI, Philips, Pye, Telefunken, Siemens, Thomson-CSF, and Fernseh have now to compete with Shibaden and Nippon Electric. Although it may well be that in parts of Asia (notably India) and of Latin America productive capacity for transmission and production equipment will develop, the developed countries are likely to retain the major share of the market for some time to come.

The possession of technological know-how and production capacity put the former metropolitan countries into a strong position for the supply of their products to the countries under their influence.[3] This influence continued well into the independence period. It is only in recent years that countries like Tanzania, Senegal, Indonesia, and Peru have broken away from their metropolitan suppliers and gone out into the world marketplace. This breaking of the traditional economic links has enabled countries without colonial connections to compete. (It is one of the ironies of history that the Federal Republic of Germany is now benefiting greatly in economic terms from the fact that Germany was deprived of her colonies at the end of the First World War.) Today companies in Germany, Czechoslavakia, Japan, the Netherlands, and elsewhere are rapidly catching up with the positions held by American, British, and French firms, particularly if they are able to ensure a more reliable supply of spare parts and a more satisfactory after-sales service.

Thus the introduction of broadcasting institutions, and particularly of television, has had two effects. It has added a substantial burden to the foreign-exchange resources that the developing countries have to raise. And it has made them dependent on a small group of industrialized countries capable of providing the advanced technology required for broadcasting services. Only a few developing countries have so far attempted to break out of this dependence. India is the main example. Everything connected with the Indian Satellite Instructional Television Experiment (SITE), except the communications satellite itself, has been produced in India. Although there is little room in communications engineering for the application of the principles of intermediate technology, the Indian experiments need to be carefully evaluated. For example, the antennae for reception of the satellite signal in the villages have been constructed from chicken wire; their reliability needs to be assessed. Similarly, a combination of low-level training for local monitors with mobile repair units staffed by qualified technicians was thought to offer a reasonable promise of reliability for the television service even in rural areas.[4] No reliable assessment of the experiment is as yet available.

The position is somewhat different in the field of radio and television receiver production. Although the majority of television receivers used in most countries are still imported, a number of countries now produce radio receivers on a large scale, often under license. In Tanzania and Peru, for example, Philips subsidiaries are active. In Tanzania, in addition, a Japanese firm produces radios and makes batteries, as well as maintaining mobile repair units. In Algeria local production facilities at present account for half the output of television receivers. The nationalized monopoly for the manufacture of electrical equipment, SONELEC, is shortly hoping to open another factory to increase the proportion of locally produced receivers.

In all countries, however, the difficulties of the maintenance and repair of broadcast receiving instruments exceed those of production. Although transistorized radio receivers are sufficiently robust to withstand the rigors of use in rural communities, the lack of batteries is often an obstacle to the continuous use of receivers. In one African country we were told by the broadcasting organization that at any one time about 40 percent of the nation's radio receivers were out of use for this or other reasons.

In the case of television receivers the provision of a power supply is of course the crucial obstacle to the reception of signals in the rural areas. Thus the introduction of television accentuates a demand for rural electrification and the capital investment and recurrent expenditure that this implies. Here again the type of technology required renders developing countries largely dependent on the supply of equipment and expertise from the developed countries. Where, as in most countries, choices have to be made between rural electrification and rural water schemes, between building power stations and building hospitals, and between all these and the extension of television, it is arguable that the last of these should be low on the list of priorities. The fact that all expenditure on infrastructure is dependent on the ability of the country concerned to produce enough surplus revenue or to attract enough foreign aid should reinforce the disincentive to engage in "luxury" investment. Although the place of broadcasting in the hierarchy of needs of most countries is realistically low, in some countries priorities are distorted by considerations of the prestige that the possession of a broadcasting system will confer on the country. There are exaggerated assumptions about the usefulness of the system in creating and maintaining a united population willing to pursue the goals set for it by the government. There is also unscrupulous salesmanship on the part of foreign entrepreneurs anxious to sell expensive and complicated equipment irrespective of its immediate usefulness to the country concerned. It is likely that the disappointing results of much of the mass communications development in many countries will result in a more sober assessment of the relative usefulness of broadcasting and prevent a repetition of the mistakes often made ten or fifteen years ago in the first flush of independence.

MANPOWER

The second area of need that is disclosed as soon as the decision is taken to launch a broadcasting system is the demand for suitably qualified manpower. As already indicated, a demand is created for a managerial staff, for engineers and technicians, and for production and creative staff. If, moreover, a broadcasting system is to reflect the aspirations of its country it is desirable that the staffing should as soon as possible be met by local manpower resources.

The management cadres are important, not only for the effective running of the organization, but also because of the political sensitivity of the management decisions made in a broadcasting organization. For this latter reason it is not unknown for persons to be appointed to management posts in broadcasting whose political reliability exceeds their managerial competence. Although the results of such unsuitable appointments are often serious, the political nature of the appointments may well make it more difficult to rectify the mistakes. Subordinates are reluctant to criticize, since criticism might be interpreted as a judgment of the political stance of the manager rather than of his managerial ability and thus might endanger the critic's own position. This hesitation tends to compound management problems and to produce a declining spiral of efficiency that becomes increasingly difficult to reverse. The creation of a well-trained and competent cadre of managers is therefore problematic. Granted that appointments will be made that have the confidence of the appointing body, the new type of management situation also requires adequate preservice and in-service training. A broadcasting organization is a complex institution that demands a good understanding of the nature of communications technology, as well as an understanding of a group of people—actors, musicians, writers, producers—who tend to be individualistic and idiosyncratic. Its leadership involves responsibility for a communications instrument that is thought to have a major influence on opinion and attitude formation in the country. All these functions demand both strength of character and great political awareness. Thus the training needs are highly specialized and cannot easily be provided within a country where no precedents are available for guidance.

The training of engineers and technicians, although in many ways the most complicated, can usually be provided with much less difficulty. The demand for communications engineering skills throughout the world is such that there is no shortage of institutions to which staff can be sent for training. At the lower levels, moreover, the scale of local demand for technicians is such as to justify the inclusion of training facilities in the local technical college or university. A problem that arises wherever training facilities are provided is the failure to develop the imagination of trainees and to encourage the development of techniques of improvization and problem-solving. Engineers and technicians are then turned out who are competent as long as all spare parts are available, but who are helpless in their absence. Simple skills, such as the operation of metal-working lathes, which would enable them to make spare parts themselves are too often omitted.

There remains the training of the creative staff of a broadcasting institution. Here we have to distinguish between the encouragement of creative talent that already exists and that can be drawn into relationship with a broadcasting station on a free-lance basis and the training of production staff: cameramen, floor managers, lighting experts, script editors, directors, sound technicians, and producers. The former problem is largely dependent on the scale of the broadcasting operation. In the cases we have studied this ranges from organizations in countries in which virtually no creative artists or performers are professional, in the sense of deriving a livelihood from their activities, to organizations in countries with substantial cadres of professional artists and performers.

The recruitment and training of production staff is an aspect of the work of the broadcasting organization, the importance of which is often underrated. The jobs created by broadcasting constitute a significant enlargement of the category of professional communicators. Besides increasing the demand for journalists they provide one of the few outlets other than the teaching profession for graduates in the humanities and hence are significant in the context of human resource development of the country. Depending on the status accorded them, jobs in a broadcasting organization tend to be regarded either as the pinnacle of achievement or as a stepping-stone to more lucrative jobs. In those countries where broadcasting staff positions are equated with fairly low-level posts in the public service, the latter evaluation tends to obtain. Better quality in staffing is obtained where the status of broadcasters is given greater regard and where staff members are treated as professional men and women.

Training of production staffs tends to be undertaken mainly on the job. This is sensible as long as provision is made for periods of continuing education away from the job. As in most European countries, training at present tends to concentrate on the technical aspects of the job and to ignore the need for an understanding of the social philosophy and psychology related to the work, which all broadcasters need in order to make responsible judgments. The need for a social-science base for the training of production staff members is only slowly beginning to be recognized. The lack of broadcasting experience in many developing countries causes them to rely on training outside the country. Much of this training is useful, particularly in providing contact with fellow professionals in other countries. There is, however, a continuing tendency to regard the technical facilities available during training in a more highly developed broadcasting situation as the norm, and for trainees to return unable to use creatively the more limited resources available at home. We observed the depressive effect of an external training course that did not relate the scale of its operations to the resources and circumstances of the trainees involved. Here again cooperative arrangements between a number of developing countries with similar resources could do much to increase the relevance and utility of such training.

The effect that the creation of a broadcasting station has on the composition of the professional elite of a developing country is likely to be felt far beyond the confines of the broadcasting service. A new broadcasting organization provides employment for a portion of the growing cadre of qualified men and women. It also injects into the sociocultural life (of the capital, at least) a group of people whose professional concern is with culture in its broadcast sense. It creates new purchasing power and adds to that part of the population that can be expected to be articulate about issues of national interest. All these factors, although small in themselves, combine to change the profile of metropolitan life in the new nations.

ADVERTISING

The third group of effects of the introduction of broadcasting is felt in those countries where broadcasting systems derive all or part of their income from advertising revenue. Advertising in fact plays some part in the financial structure of broadcasting in all the countries that we have studied, widely differing though their socioeconomic structures and orientations were. The degree of dependence on advertising in our sample ranges from that of a country like Brazil, where the main television services are, on the American model, financed entirely by advertising revenue, to that of a country like Tanzania, where the advertising carried by one of the government's radio services not only is intended to raise revenue but also is justified as a means of accustoming the population to the growing range of indigenous consumer goods that the country's processing and manufacturing industries produce.

Advertising of goods and services presupposes the existence of purchasing power on a sufficiently large scale to make the advertising worthwhile. Advertising on a national channel, whether radio or television, presupposes the existence of a broadcasting network large enough to reach a significant proportion of likely buyers. It also presupposes a distribution network able to supply the goods and services advertised in all areas that the advertisements are likely to reach.

When one considers the sustained objections to reliance on advertising revenue that have long formed part of the European tradition of broadcasting, it is surprising that advertising should so soon have come to be accepted as a standard ingredient of the broadcasting scene in the developing countries, even in those where European models were firmly established. We were particularly interested to observe that the traditional European view of the incompatibility of public-service broadcasting and advertising has been abandoned without much argument, even in a country so firmly wedded to its own brand of socialism as Tanzania. It seems that advertising on the broadcasting services is seen in the developing world more as part of the process of economic modernization and the enlargement of the traditional concept of the market, than as an issue affecting broadcasting policy. The developing countries seem to have leapfrogged a stage in the movement toward the acceptability of the advertising industry in Europe, if not of that in North America. Having accepted the principle of advertising as part of the modernization process, they have little hesitation about the use of advertising on the broadcasting media. Yet few of the countries have any clearly defined control system for either the content or the form that the advertising takes. There is usually some censorship at a superficial level, aimed at the more obvious abuses. Little attention is given, however, to such matters as regulating the relationships between the client, the advertising agent, and the producer of the program in order to prevent corruption; to the penumbral effects of advertising on raising expectations that cannot be fulfilled; or to the indirect effect that reliance on advertising revenue has on the extension of coverage.

The acceptance of advertising involves, of course, the acceptance of all its accompanying service industries, such as advertising agencies, public relations firms, and sales staffs. Here again the creation of new opportunities for employment is important for the economy, however arguable the utility of the advertising process itself. Not only do the broadcasting organizations have their advertising sales and production departments, but a whole range of satellite activities grows up around them. Not the least of these are the market-research firms that usually provide the only form of audience research undertaken. It is inevitable but unfortunate that the larger impact of the broadcast services rarely forms the major interest of this type of research, so that the broadcasters may well learn what the effect of a particular series of aspirin advertisements has been, but cannot afford to find out the impact of a literacy campaign.

EDUCATIONAL BROADCASTING

The area with which broadcasting has in the last two decades come to be most closely identified in the nation-building process is education. The reasons for this are perhaps not as simple as they seem. There is, of course, a direct link between the creation of a communications system that can reach out to the population of a country on a scale previously unheard of and the use of such a system for educating the population in ways thought useful by governments. But the large-scale investment in experiments in the field of educational broadcasting of all kinds made in the 1950s and 1960s was also caused by the enthusiasm for all types of new educational technology engendered in the *developed* countries during those decades. This enthusiasm derived its impetus on the one hand from the wish to modernize traditional educational methods and on the other from the hope that less labor-intensive teaching methods might help to reduce the unit cost of education at a time of massive expansion of educational opportunities throughout Europe and North America.

Both these hopes were recognized as applicable, *a fortiori*, to the less-developed countries in which educational expansion was regarded as the key to national development on all fronts and in which educational resources were a great deal more scarce than in Europe or North America. Hence the many experiments in educational broadcasting, some sponsored by UNESCO, UNDP, and the World Bank, others under multilateral aid agreements, and others by developed countries, notably France, Germany, the United Kingdom, and the United States, under bilateral agreements. The best documented of these projects took place in the Ivory Coast, Niger, Senegal, American Samoa, and El Salvador. Other projects such as the proposed educational use of the Algerian and Indonesian communications satellites, which require an inordinate lead time, are not yet operational. Less ambitious projects, such as the proposed integrated media project in Thailand, are only at the stage of feasibility studies.

In the meantime the difficulties encountered with more sophisticated educational media projects in European North America, such as the former National Educational Television service in the United States, the Open University and the Television Service of the Inner London Education Authority in the United Kingdom, and the "Telekolleg" in Germany, have begun to raise doubts about the cost effectiveness of such ventures. The difficulties encountered suggest that the use of such systems in developing countries is also likely to prove debatable. When it becomes available, the full analysis of the Indian satellite experiment of 1975–76 will be of value in making this assessment.

Before examining in greater detail the very real problems in this field it may be useful to make a distinction between the intensive and the extensive uses of broadcasting for education. This distinction is important because the effectiveness of educational broadcasting of the extensive type appears to be much greater. Extensive educational broadcasting includes all types of programming that are intended in one way or another to encourage greater understanding or a change of attitude among sections of the general audience. Thus extensive education includes much material classified under "information" and some, whether intentionally or not, classified under "entertainment," as well as the whole range of informal educational broadcasting largely addressed to adults. Most of the extensive educational broadcasting of this kind is intended for reception in the home rather than in the context of organized listening or viewing groups. It requires little or no preparation on the part of the viewer, and it proceeds without multimedia support. There is, of course, some extensive education involving group listening, often with multimedia support, which has been very successful. It is arguable that programs of this sort verge on the intensive type of educational broadcasting since they rely for their success on local organization and on consistent listening or viewing over a period. It may therefore be best to consider wholly intensive and wholly extensive broadcasting as being polarized at the extremes of a continuum, at various points along which one might plot different types of educational programming.

The majority of the projects referred to have been concentrated at the intensive end of the continuum. They have been attempts to harness radio or television or both to the formal educational system as it goes on in the schools of the country concerned. In this type of operation the need to deliver specific program material at a specific time on a stated day to classes of pupils in a particular grade in all schools of a given educational system has caused immense logistic difficulties. Even in the developed countries these difficulties can be overcome only by means of a highly developed coordinating structure working with considerable resources. In countries where the educational systems are at best patchy and where the resources of the systems are already under considerable strain, the diversion of a considerable part of the resources to broadcasting can be justified only if significantly better results are likely to be achieved. Only rarely has this been the case up to the present.

In country after country reports indicate that brave hopes pinned on the results of the introduction of educational broadcasting have been disappointed, for two main reasons. The first is the problem of ensuring adequate and reliable reception. Here a cumulative process of elimination appears to operate. The provision of a usable signal over a wide enough area to make broadcasting worthwhile is difficult. For television this has, to our knowledge, been achieved only in strictly urban areas and has usually been confined to a country's capital city. Since the schools of the capital city tend already to be those best provided with buildings, teachers, and educational resources, they do not justify the diversion of scarce financial resources to the running of a television service. This is an example of the extent to which political and other pressures distort the proper distribution of national resources.

Radio coverage is more extensive and more reliable. In the judgment of the UNESCO commission presided over by M. Edgar Faure which reported in 1972, "Radio is the only advanced communications technique which has found its proper place in the developing countries . . . Yet it seems to us that insufficient use is made of this virtually universal method of distribution. People often seem to have been deterred by the reputedly greater efficiency of other media which, however, have the major defect . . . of being unable to hope for such widespread distribution . . . for a long time to come. The very low cost and adequate reliability in all climates of miniature transistor radios mean that radio broadcasting should more and more be recognised as a particularly suitable medium for educational purposes." [5] But even with radio, coverage has to be matched by adequate reception, and it is clear that even with transistor sets it is not always possible to ensure this. Moreover, the dearth of the most basic equipment in so many schools in most countries raises the question of whether a radio receiver can or should be afforded until the basic requirements of intermediate educational technology have been met. It is difficult to argue for radio when schools do not have any blackboards and chalk, or desks, or writing materials, or textbooks. Even where radio receivers are available, many of them appear to be frequently unuseable, either because of mechanical failure or because of a lack of batteries. In Nigeria, a country where educational broadcasting was introduced as early as 1953, only 3,900 primary schools and about 750 secondary schools were registered as listening in 1971. Of these it was estimated that 50 percent were not in fact using the broadcasts because the receiver was out of order or because of poor reception or because the teachers had not received the support materials. [6]

Even where reliable reception can be counted on, the use of educational broadcasts is by no means assured. The second reason for the disappointing results in many places where educational broadcasting of an intensive kind has been launched is poor program production. Although teachers in the classroom may be enthusiastic about the introduction of a new teaching aid, they will continue to use it only if it makes a substantial addition to their own knowledge, skills, or resources. Thus radio programs have to be of a high quality if teachers in the schools are to go to the trouble of building them into their teaching schedules. The Nigerian experience again illustrates the disappointing results. Late in 1959 the Nigerian Broadcasting Corporation asked the Ford Foundation to help in the establishment of a Federal Schools Broadcasting Service in Ibadan. The foundation provided $250,000 to launch the service and agreed to maintain it for eighteen months. During this initial period over five hundred programs were recorded for stock. The poor quality of much of this material, coupled with the lack of support from the regional ministries of education, meant that much of this investment, together with expenditures incurred during a more expensive second phase, was wasted.

A similar disappointment attended a much smaller educational television experiment conducted by UNESCO and the government of Senegal, with assistance from Canada, France, and the UNDP. Following an agreement between UNESCO and the government of Senegal in December 1963 to establish an experimental educational station covering the city of Dakar, a series of programs was transmitted beginning in 1964. The most significant of these were programs addressed to women who were gathered in "tele-clubs" in various parts of the city. Programs mainly dealing with hygiene, nutrition, and housekeeping were transmitted daily. They were followed by discussion in the clubs. The multimedia experiment was studied to assess the attitude change that could be achieved by this method.[7] The project lasted for five years. During the whole of this period only five hundred participants were enrolled. A second project, conducted between 1966 and 1968, used television for the application of new methods of literacy teaching. Neither of these projects has been repeated, nor does either appear to have made any significant impact on the development of the use of television in Senegal since then.[8]

The feasibility study carried out in Thailand by a UNESCO team for the use of broadcasting for education illustrates similar problems of transmission, reception, production, and coordination. In view of the present haphazard provision of educational programs by different stations at different times on different subjects, as well as the lack of liaison with potential users of such programs, the study report sees no alternative to the addition of yet another network to the many already existing in the country. It recommends a new AM radio network under the control of the Ministry of Education. The plan is based on elaborate schemes for linking broadcasts with educational centers in the villages and regional centers. Given the inability of the Thai government to assert any coordinating role over the existing broadcasting arrangements it seems doubtful whether the logistic preconditions for the success of the proposed scheme exist.

Problems both of coverage and of program production seem to be among the difficulties encountered in the development of intensive educational broadcasting in Brazil. In 1967 the government was for linking and rationalizing such activities as had until then been carried out sporadically in the more developed parts of the country, particularly through radio. With a great deal of help from the UN and bilateral aid agencies a substantial number of stations were either newly built or were newly equipped for educational work, most of it being transmitted by closed circuit. The first open-circuit educational station was Televisão Universitária de Pernambuco, started in 1968. This had both intensive and extensive objectives, being concerned to support cultural and artistic development through programs for home reception and to foster educational improvement of specific population groups through courses addressed to organized groups of students.

Educational broadcasting operations were also launched during the late 1960s in the states of Amazonas, Rio Grande do Sul, Paraná, São Paulo, Guanabara, Bahia, Rio Grande do Norte, Ceará, and Minas Gerais. In addition, a number of federal agencies began to operate educational television, such as the National Commission on Space Activities (INPE) and the Superintendency for the Development of the Northeast (SUDENE), where there are large poverty-stricken areas. But the role of government in coordinating and setting priorities in the development seems to have been ineffective.[9] As early as 1970 the journal *Visão* pointed out that between 1968 and 1970 the country had spent over $3 million on educational television (ETV) equipment and a similar sum on buildings and on production.[10] In 1970 $2 million more was to be spent on additional transmission facilities, some of them covering areas already covered by existing stations. An official report in 1973 mentioned the import of forty closed-circuit systems that had to be kept in their crates for more than a year because there were no plans for their use. The lack of integrated planning is also demonstrated by the fact that the Ministry of Communications reserved a hundred channels for educational television of which only forty had been allocated by 1970, and these were allocated without rational criteria. Thus relatively small towns such as Fortaleza and Goiània were given channels while Rio de Janeiro was not included in the allocation. Unsatisfactory reception, lack of standardized equipment, and poor maintenance all contributed to the logistic problems, which are examples of those that have vitiated educational broadcasting development throughout the Third World. In the issue of *Visão* quoted earlier, the assessment of the situation was summed up: "What has been and is being done in the country in the area of educational radio and television (with rare and notable exceptions) may be defined without fear as an antipedagogic synthesis as regards content and as a carnival of more or less pretentious dilettantism as regards technique and creative solutions." In 1972 the government established PRONTEL, the National Program for Educational Television, linked with the Ministry of Education and Culture in order to coordinate program production, technical orientation, the establishment of ETV production and transmission centers, and evaluation procedures. PRONTEL issued in December 1973 a National Plan for Educational Technology. It remains to be seen whether the confused and misdirected efforts of the multitude of separate educational broadcasting operations prove to be susceptible to effective harmonization.

These illustrations could be repeated from all parts of the developing world. It is evident therefore that in only a decade the brave hopes expressed by pioneers such as Wilbur Schramm have come to grief. Writing in 1963 Dr. Schramm claimed that "to a country where highly trained teachers are scarce [the mass media] offer the opportunity to share its best teachers widely. Where few teachers are trained to teach certain subjects, these media offer the hope that those subjects can be taught even before qualified teachers become available. Where projectors and films are scarce, television can serve as a 'big projector' for hundreds of schools at the same time. And where schools are not yet available or for people who, for one reason or another can not go to school, radio and television can offer some educational opportunity without schools." [11] Why has this claim proved to be wholly unrealistic? Does this mean that the role of educational broadcasting as part of the development role of broadcasting services is valueless? In the paragraphs that follow we set out the analysis that we derive from our case studies and our knowledge of the field in general.

THE FUTURE OF EDUCATIONAL BROADCASTING

There is no question that broadcasting both in sound and vision will increasingly be an ingredient of the daily life of the citizens of all developing countries. Given this expectation, the extensive type of educational broadcasting to which we have already referred is bound to take place through informational and entertainment programs as well as through programs with a specific didactic objective. It is therefore not a matter of whether the extensive educational role of broadcasting will continue and expand, but rather of how it will develop.

As regards intensive educational broadcasting, the question of its future is more doubtful. Quite apart from the economic and structural difficulties to which attention has already been drawn, two significant trends may well combine at some time in the future to render anachronistic the broadcasting of open-circuit educational programs to large numbers of schools across a country at the same time on the same day. The first is the trend toward a greater individualization of the learning process. It is coming to be recognized that people learn at different speeds, that they learn better if they can order and pace their learning to some extent themselves, and that this requires more rather than less flexibility in the arrangement of classwork. Although the economics of education will continue to demand the organization of pupils in standardized groups, particularly in developing countries, the need for maximum flexibility will reduce the tolerance of both teachers and pupils of externally determined timetables and subject matter.

The second significant trend is the advance in educational technology that enables it to meet the demand for individualization and flexibility. Audio and video cassettes, teaching machines, programmed-learning texts, overhead projectors and film loops, portapack television cameras, and portable transistorized monitors are all much more flexible for educational use than the program transmitted from a central point at a particular time. It is unlikely that many schools in low-income countries will be able to afford much of the new educational technology for some time to come. But insofar as any resources at all are available for audio-visual aids, educational authorities are increasingly likely to consider the available alternatives, both in terms of their educational usefulness and in terms of their cost effectiveness, before committing themselves. And it is by no means to be expected that they will wish to put all their money into educational broadcasting.

Much will depend on the relationship between the broadcasting authorities and educational bodies. Richmond Postgate reinforces the analysis given above of the logistic difficulties attending the successful running of intensive broadcasting education: "Failures are very common at interfaces. Most new schemes have many interfaces. For instance, a successful school broadcasting radio service involves a producer, teacher, inspector, headmaster, a maintenance system, a local supplier of batteries, a reasonable engineering system to produce a signal, a producer of acceptable support material, a distribution system, an effective feedback system, a personnel training system, and an organisation that sustains, harmonises and finances all these items." [12]

Postgate goes on to ask how many educational broadcasting schemes take account in their planning of the need to coordinate all these agencies and participants. In our experience very few do so. Educational broadcasting tends to be introduced on the initiative either of the broadcasting organization or of an external funding body that has decided that educational broadcasting must be useful to developing countries. We have already referred to some examples of this kind of ill-prepared intervention. Other factors also play a part. For example, where the initiative comes from either of these sources external to itself, the local ministry of education is unlikely to feel committed to making a success of the scheme. And if that ministry is not so committed, the scheme cannot succeed. It will lack energetic support from headquarters, and this lack of enthusiasm will filter through the administrators to the schools. The educational systems of most developing countries are highly centripetal. Advancement for the teacher at the base of the pyramid depends on his standing with his ministry, and this in turn is determined by his compliance with the orthodoxies current in that ministry. There is as yet little, if any, professional or intellectual autonomy among the grass-roots educators in Third World countries.

Ministry of education support cannot be guaranteed even when the educational authorities are drawn into consultation at the early stage of the design of an educational broadcasting system. The literal transfer of institutions from metropolitan countries to their former colonial territories, which has caused such problems in the field of broadcasting, has been applied wholesale to the transfer of education systems. And because education is seen as the major route to advancement, there has been little incentive to question the applicability of the educational systems of the metropolitan countries to the real needs of the country concerned. Educational systems have been resistant to change, and the cooperation required to make a success of a joint operation between a broadcasting organization and a ministry of education has often been lacking.

The problem of establishing a clear policy for the intensive educational use of broadcasting is, moreover, in all countries aggravated by the crisis of confidence to which education systems as a whole throughout the world are subject at the present time, largely as a result of their resistance to change. The nature of the crisis is identified differently by different students of educational development. In the United States, Philip H. Coombs identifies it mainly as a crisis of escalating costs; [13] in Mexico, Ivan Illich blames the institutionalization and professionalization of what should be an open and dynamic system; [14] Julius Nyerere of Tanzania sees it as the failure of the school to relate to the community around it; [15] W. Senteza Kajubi of Uganda, as the divisive character of the school in creating a small, powerful elite and an impotent majority; [16] and Paulo Freire of Brazil argues that education needs to become "the action and reflection of men upon their world in order to transform it." [17] These are only some of the views preoccupying perceptive workers in the field. Their difficulty is that education, besides being the largest item in the recurrent expenditure budgets of many developing countries, is also coming to be of interest to many other sectors of a country's life: the rural economy, the manufacturing and service sectors, the political system and cultural development. The traditional structures of educational administration cover only a limited part of this area, largely confined to school-based education. As education has spilled over into other sectors, other ministries have come to have a vested interest in their own educational activities and the traditional predominance of school-based educators is threatened. This threat to their predominance does not derive only from the diversification of public interest in education. It is reinforced by the fact that it is in the nonschool areas of education, such as broadcasting, community development, industrial training, and civic and political formation, that much of the innovative work in the field of education is being done today. These sectors also attract a growing share of national expenditure on education. In a country outside our sample where one of us carried out intensive fieldwork recently it was found that one-third of direct educational expenditure was incurred by the ministries of agriculture and fisheries, health, community development, posts and telecommunications, information, youth, and defense.[18] It is possible that the proportion in other countries is even greater.

In such a situation it is not surprising that a ministry of education finds itself on the defensive and lacking in enthusiasm for greater sharing of responsibility for educational matters with anyone else. Its natural conservatism is reinforced, and the institutional viscosity of a large-spending department, with probably the largest number of local agents of any government agency of intervention, resists change.

Thus the problems that tend to arise between those responsible for broadcasting and those responsible for education in the narrow sense are no more than one aspect of the much more widespread crisis of confidence among traditional educators. Nonetheless the blame is not all on one side.

The excessive claims that tended to be made for educational broadcasting in its early stages have not been helpful: the claim, for example, that educational television would eliminate the need for teachers, as in the experiment in American Samoa. As Lionel Elvin reminded the Commonwealth Education Conference in Jamaica in 1974 (in virtually the only reference to educational technology during the conference), "I don't think we are going to save a penny in cash by the use of audio-visual aids . . . I am told that the evidence of American Samoa is conclusive on this. They spent an incredible amount of dollars. They closed the teachers' colleges because they felt sure that the gadgets would do instead of the teachers. And it's not worked out. They are splendid aids: you often get better quality teaching than you would get otherwise, and therefore better learning, but they are no substitute in cash terms for teachers." [19] In fact the argument is more sophisticated than that: "Instead of merely attempting to recruit and train an ever-increasing number of teachers whose tasks will become increasingly complex, why not analyse the various educational functions with a view to redistributing the various human and material resources available wherever, in the educational system, their potential can be most fully utilised? This implies the acceptance on the one part that, instead of continuing to let the machine do only what the *teacher* cannot do, we should ask ourselves what it is the teacher should do that the *machine* cannot do." [20] But this argument has so far proved too sophisticated for most developed countries, let alone for countries where the basic educational problems are literacy and numeracy and where manpower is plentiful. Broadcasters would do well to take account of it, however, in their development of intensive educational broadcasting.

The extensive educational role of broadcasting is, as already indicated, much less disputed. Its proponents tend to be people less burdened by educational orthodoxies than many conventional educators. Whether one is undertaking health education by radio, or agricultural extension work, or political education, one is concerned in the main to influence adult citizens in matters that they recognize as important and to which they bring their own experience of life. Although listening groups, and to a much lesser extent viewing groups, and other multimedia approaches are used for much of the best extensive education by radio and television, all is not lost if the other media fail. The program can still go on, be listened to in the home, and in this way influence citizens in the desired direction.

The example already cited of the educational television experiments in Senegal indicates the extent to which extensive education forms a justification, in political terms, for the introduction of television itself. Similarly, in Tanzania, the extensive educational role of radio constitutes the major contribution made by Tanzania to the development use of the medium. It consists of multimedia campaigns addressed to adults and focusing on specific national issues thought to be susceptible to attitude change. The campaigns were begun in 1969 as part of the shift of emphasis toward the use of adult education in support of the national development process. They have been largely planned and supervised by the Institute of Adult Education which is a national institution financed by the Ministry of Education.

The 1969 project was aimed at encouraging people throughout the country to study the second five-year development plan. Its title, "To Plan Is to Choose," indicates its purpose. The concept of planning, of thinking ahead in order to modify circumstances in a desired manner, needs to be carefully explained in a society that has for too long been the object of natural forces and of external factors over which it has had little or no control. The project was planned in the form of a series of radio programs supported by written material for use by local discussion groups. In the event about 250 groups are said to have taken part, a figure that confirms the difficulty of ensuring the success of a multimedia exercise of this kind, even where reasonable logistic support is available.

Later projects have been undertaken to stimulate participation in the elections of 1970 ("The Choice Is Yours"), to mark the tenth anniversary of independence ("A Time for Rejoicing") in 1971, and to increase public awareness of what makes for good health in 1973. As the evaluation report on this last series recounts, "After discussion with various ministries, organisations and individuals about what subject might be suitable and what support might be available nationally, the subject of health education was decided upon. The reasoning for this . . . centered around the fact that the growing number of hospitals and dispensaries are able to provide better but still far from adequate curative medical facilities. Furthermore, though the incidence of some of the most dreaded diseases, such as leprosy and smallpox, has been reduced to manageable proportions in Tanzania, there remain those less dramatic diseases which probably constitute the most serious handicap to human happiness and the social and economic development of the country."[21] By this time the format of educational campaigns had greatly enlarged their impact. The report does not include figures for the number of study groups following the program, but the fact that training courses were arranged for 75,000 group leaders gives some indication of the scale of the campaign. The evaluation in this case adduced evidence that the campaign had had a significant effect on the preventive aspects of public health, such as the building of latrines, the elimination of breeding grounds for mosquitoes, and the cleaning of the compounds surrounding living quarters.

The role of radio in a campaign of this kind is both formal and functional. The functional element consists in providing a central core of information throughout the study period and to ensure that even those (usually the majority) who do not attend study groups pick up at least some of the information provided. The formal role is no less important. The use of radio confers on a campaign of this kind an element of national status that it is not otherwise easy to attain. Where mass education campaigns are concerned, this status is very important.

Campaigns such as these Tanzanian projects require, besides a common language, a high degree of integrative planning and cooperation between the agencies concerned. Where, as in Iran, such cooperation is lacking, the extensive development work of the broadcasting organization is wasted. Similarly, although foreign consultants in extension services and communications have been invited to Iran under the auspices of the Ministry of Information, the polite noncooperation between the ministry and NIRT has so far prevented the recommendations of the experts from being implemented.

It may be that plans now being laid will improve the usefulness of NIRT in the field of educational broadcasting. The "free university" project that is planned for 1977 as a multimedia system using broadcasting and correspondence study is intended to contribute to meeting the demand for higher education, particularly in subjects such as agriculture, produce and consumers' cooperatives, administration, health education, and teacher training. Similarly the proposal for an educational satellite by means of which centralized and coordinated elementary education is to be provided throughout the country may strengthen the contribution that NIRT makes to the development process.

In the light of these examples, we return to the question, Is there a future for educational broadcasting? In our view the use of broadcasting for intensive educational purposes, that is, for in-school or intrainstitutional use, is justified only where the need for enrichment or direct instruction can be clearly established and where more flexible and economical means of achieving the same objective are not available. Thus any project of this kind should be preceded by a rigorous task analysis and cost-benefit study. If such an analysis and study indicate that the effort is worthwhile, three criteria should be satisfied before the project is allowed to go ahead: (1) The relationship of educational and broadcasting expertise should be clearly established; (2) transmission and reception conditions should be such that at least 75 percent of the schools or institutions affected are capable of a good standard of reception; and (3) adequate funds and other resources should be available to ensure that the potentialities of the medium, be it radio or television, are fully exploited.

Similar criteria should apply to the use of broadcasting for extensive education. Since here the size of the target audiences is likely to be of a quite different order of magnitude it should be easier to satisfy the cost-benefit criterion. On the other hand the suitability of other media, such as the press, may well be a limiting factor. The relationship with other agencies responsible for similar extension work is also an important consideration. Unlike the intensive approach, where the local collaborator is clearly defined as the class teacher or other institutional official, the extensive program has to rely on the agricultural extension worker, the health educator, the local village headman, or another community leader to ensure adequate reception conditions and follow-up activities. If all these conditions are met, radio and television can clearly provide an important instrument for extensive education.

CULTURAL IMPLICATIONS OF BROADCASTING

THE NATIONAL CULTURE

We have already alluded to the impact on the culture patterns of the developing countries made by the introduction of broadcasting. The impact is of course little different from the impact that the introduction of broadcasting made on those countries in which radio and television were invented. And yet those countries were better prepared in that their internal communications were more highly developed than those of many Third World countries. Road and rail communications, newspapers circulating beyond the immediate neighborhood of their place of publication, an awareness on the part of the citizens of their national as well as their local identities, all had prepared the ground for the arrival of radio as a medium by which the same message could be heard throughout a country. Radio in turn prepared the way for television, the introduction of which was a slower process than that of radio owing to the more limited coverage of television signals. So it came about that the demand for television in most countries actually preceded its provision, indicating a preparedness for the new medium on the part of the population.

In the majority of the developing countries included in our sample the introduction of broadcasting was concurrent with the introduction of a whole range of modernizing activities. As Adam Curle has pointed out, "Until the end of the Second World War, no one was particularly concerned with the backward nations. Many of them were under colonial rule and the rest of the world could safely assign responsibility to the colonial powers. The majority of the poorer independent countries were too remote to excite much interest. But the uneasy years of peace following 1945 forced upon the wealthier lands some recognition of the poor ones . . . The leisurely pre-war plans for emancipation have been brushed aside . . . Almost overnight . . . the balance of power assumed a totally new character . . . Technical advances matched political changes in their radical swiftness . . . but the haste in which we have flung ourselves into the tasks of development has given us little chance of thinking seriously about some crucial issues." [22] Certainly little thinking has gone into the effects of the introduction of broadcasting on the culture patterns of most developing countries.

Of course the rate of impact has varied from country to country. In countries such as Brazil, Peru, Iran, and Thailand, where development was left largely to private enterprise, the impact was made where a profit might be expected. Thus the small radio stations established in the 1930s in Peru were often set up by radio repairmen advertising their own services or as a small family business selling radio sets or soliciting advertisements. The program of these stations consisted of pirated records, newspapers read aloud, and what one of our informants described as "innocent entertainment." Their impact on the culture of the community was limited both in extent and in content. In French West Africa a wholly different mode of development was adopted during the colonial period. Radio Afrique Occidentale Française had stations in Brazzaville, Cap Vert, and St. Louis which covered large parts of the French colonies in the region. The output of the stations was an extension of French cultural policy; little or no attempt was made to use them for the autonomous development of the populations living in their coverage areas. Most of the programming, in any case, was in French, so that it was of interest only to the French expatriate communities along the coast and to the small indigenous elite educated in French-language schools.

In some other countries, Indonesia, Nigeria, Cyprus, for example, there has been a marked effort by the newly independent governments, through their ministries of culture, to influence the media. They were seen, at least in the early stages, as important vehicles for the promotion of indigenous arts, local languages, and regional cultures. In these countries the wish either to break loose from a colonial culture or to recreate a forgotten culture was often a part of the independence "package" promised by independence movements led by people who were particularly sensitive to the need for the revival of indigenous culture.

Indonesia is a particularly interesting example. The development of radio broadcasting was important in the growth of the cultural self-consciousness of the Indonesian nationalists which, in turn, determined the strength of the independence movement. Scope for such a development was provided by the structure of Indonesian radio. The Netherlands Indies Radio Administration supervised the broadcasting system and licensed private operators as well as operating its own system. This made it possible for private Indonesian stations in 1937 to establish a nonprofit association "dedicated to the promotion of national culture and the development of spiritual and physical well-being of the Indonesian community by means of radio programmes." [23] In 1940 the colonial administration recognized the association, and during the Japanese occupation it was encouraged to develop broadcasting competence among Indonesians as part of the policy of strengthening anti-Dutch forces in the country. As a result the character of the broadcasting system that was established when independence came was more indigenous than in most other countries at that stage.

These three examples illustrate the varied nature of the cultural impact of the broadcasting services. They show that there is not a simple distinction between commercial stations that have no explicit cultural objectives and the public-service stations that do have such an objective. Nor is it reasonable to suppose that the presence or absence of such a stated objective actually determined the actual impact of the broadcasts. It is likely that, even in their early stages, the small local stations of the Peruvian towns made a difference in the awareness of the outside world among their listeners.

The deliberate decision to use the broadcast media for national cultural development is in most countries fairly recent. In Latin America it dates from the rise of the populist movements in the late 1960s, although government-sponsored films were in use long before then; in francophone Africa, from the decision to replace French cultural dominance by a similarly determined propagation of the indigenous culture; in anglophone Africa, from a similar motive, albeit without the same culture conditioning as that bequeathed to the francophone countries by their former metropolitan power. In the independent countries of Asia also, political pressures have forced governments to intervene more positively in the promotion of local cultures through the broadcasting services, largely in order to demonstrate their independence of the cultural imperialism of the United States.

BROADCASTING AND THE ARTS

The introduction of broadcasting into a society affects, and is affected by, a wide range of artistic activities. There are at least three aspects to this interaction. In the first place, broadcasting uses certain arts, and thus the managers of broadcasting must come to terms with their practitioners. Writers, musicians, actors, filmmakers and graphic designers play key roles in the production of radio and television programs; their effect on broadcasting is substantial indeed. Reciprocally, broadcasting affects the arts. The coming of television has everywhere reduced the size of cinema audiences, for example. Radio has stimulated the sale of phonograph records. Broadcasting is regularly blamed for the decline of folk art, as, for example, the art of the storyteller in the Iranian teahouse. There is yet a third sense in which broadcasting and the arts are related, as has already been pointed out in Chapter 1. This is the growing recognition that broadcasting can contribute identity and continuity to national culture by giving expression to the indigenous arts. Incidentally, the concern over cultural identity is as strong in countries such as Canada as it is in Algeria or Peru.

In the following chapters, we deal in some detail with the extent to which broadcasting is fulfilling its promise as an agent of cultural continuity. In this chapter, we deal with organizational aspects of the nature of its alliance with the arts, focusing not only on the types of interaction that contribute to cultural continuity but also on those that contribute to broadcasting itself and to creativity in the broadcast media. Moreover, we discover in this analysis that in some countries broadcasting organizations have become so important as patrons of the arts that they have evolved, in effect, into major instruments of cultural policy.

Iran provides the clearest instance among our case studies of this development. With the establishment of NIRT in 1971, Iran grouped its radio, television, and educational broadcasting facilities within one organization. Over the next few years, we find NIRT establishing a Center for the Preservation of Traditional Music, a Musical Workshop for Youth, an experimental Theater Workshop with its own theater facilities, and a film unit for the production of full-length films. In addition, NIRT organizes the annual Shiraz Festival of Arts with the participation of national and international troupes and artists, the annual Ferdowsi poetry festival at Tus, and other festivals and competitions. NIRT is now considering the establishment of an institute for social and cultural research. These activities are taking on a life of their own; their scope extends beyond the immediate needs of the broadcasting services.

European broadcasting organizations support symphony

orchestras and theater companies, but justification of the existence of these activities lies in their contribution to broadcasting even if they also give public performances. The music, theater, and film groups established by NIRT sometimes contribute to broadcasting, but their primary mission is the cultivation of the arts themselves. NIRT hopes that the workshops will lead to the discovery and development of talent, some of which will be drawn off into broadcasting. It hopes that the theater workshop will stimulate creative writing and experimentation with new forms that might have implications for broadcasting. It wants the film unit to produce more original films than the mass-produced "Easterns" of the commercial filmmakers. Some of these activities provoke ill-feeling in the Ministry of Culture and Arts, but the director-general of NIRT has recently been appointed, together with several other ministers and key personalities, to the ministry's High Council of Culture and Art.

None of the other broadcasting organizations in our studies compares with NIRT in the extent or exclusiveness of its role as patron of the arts. But there are several additional examples worth citing. In Cyprus, the Cyprus Broadcasting Corporation (CBC) established the first professional theater on the island as an expression of "awareness of responsibility vis-à-vis the people who watch television and listen to the radio . . ."[24] The CBC theater is said to have "concentrated, maintained, exhibited and made worthy use of the human potential in the fields of stage direction, acting, designing and costume-designing, which otherwise would either have been scattered outside the country or would have deteriorated in the familiar conditions of the deficient theatrical ambience."[25] The theater has presented works by Molière, Pirandello, Anouilh, Peter Schaffer, Pinter, Max Frisch, Arthur Miller, Beckett, Durenmatt, and Chekhov, as well as by classical Greek authors. Since its establishment, it has performed hundreds of times in

Nicosia, as well as, before the de facto partition of the island, in Morphou and Famagusta. These performances were broadcast by television, thus helping to establish a theatrical library. In the musical field, CBC has founded a string orchestra, which plays at concerts covered by radio and television. It also organizes concerts of choral music, with the participation of choirs from the main cities. CBC founded a film club in 1969 and organizes competitions in creative areas such as radio programs, other writing, and Cypriot song composition in the framework of the Artistic Festival of Limassol. It established a publishing house, issuing titles in areas as varied as sociology, anthropology, literature, philosophy, physics, psychology, and the arts. The expression of these latter activities in the area of broadcasting is, however, rather modest, judging by the program schedules.

In this sense, then, CBC and NIRT resemble each other, although one assumes, taking distance alone into account, that more Greek Cypriots have access to the live performances than Iranians. In both cases, the elite of the capital city are obviously well served by this kind of patronage; the broadcast audience far less so.

NBC in Nigeria has sponsored the Festival of Black Arts, an international gathering, and it also sponsors a theater group that is closely linked to broadcasting. The director-general of NBC is a member of the Arts Council, and through this liaison broadcasting contributes to those activities of the council that are appropriate for transmission.

Patronage of the regional arts is an activity pursued by a number of broadcasting organizations. Thus, Radio-Télévision Algérienne sponsors cultural weeks in the several regional centers. NIRT radio devotes the third week of each month, in an experimental series of "weeks," to the folklore arts, and character of each of Iran's provinces.

The relationship of television to filmmaking and to writing is worthy of special note. No station or network can produce all the film it needs. Certainly, if a broadcasting organization wishes to change the ratio of local to imported film, it must give commissions to independent local filmmakers. In the West and elsewhere this has led to the familiar phenomenon of a decline in the number of movie theaters and in the rate of attendance and a rise in the number of films, both features and shorts, produced. Some of the developing countries have local film industries. A number of Asian countries (India, Turkey, Iran, Vietnam, Thailand, and others) produce large numbers of films each year. So do Egypt and Lebanon in the Middle East and some of the South American countries, particularly Brazil. Film industries of any consequence are, however, rare in Africa south of the Sahara. The relationship between filmmakers and television is obviously of central importance to both. We have not studied this subject systematically, since at present films, as a flexible and mobile medium, still exceed by far the importance of television in most developing countries. But filmmakers tend to regard television, where it exists, as exploiting their industry with very little return to it. The Thai film industry, for example, produces some 80 to 120 films annually. These are widely shown throughout the country, in urban theaters and, by itinerant entrepreneurs, in the villages as well. The television stations broadcast these films at the end of their runs, and several of the Thai series are made by independent producers. But the television organizations take no serious interest in the state or quality of product of the film industry and have not associated themselves with the filmmakers' campaign to persuade the government to relax the very heavy taxes imposed on equipment and film. Similarly, in Senegal, which also has a significant film industry, no agreement on tariffs and royalties has yet been reached between the independent filmmakers and the broadcasting organization. The problems are difficult of solution everywhere, but a strong film industry is a prerequisite for an effective television service that aims to avoid excessive reliance on imported material.

A similar problem exists in the case of writers. Most broadcasting organizations pay only low fees for radio and television writing. Hence the best writers are not attracted to work for these media. Yet the cultivation of writers and the assurance that they are available to the broadcast media is a matter of central concern. Globo, Brazil's largest network, has made a strong effort to attract the best writers in the country, with notable success. Radiodiffusion Télévision Sénégalaise, at the opposite extreme, has yet to come to a satisfactory agreement with the writers' association.

Algeria has rather a different problem. Its writers prefer to write in French, while the Arabization policy of the broadcasting organization requires that broadcasting be in Arabic. As a result, some of the best native writing has to undergo translation, to the displeasure of the creative echelons of the organization.

Finally, it should be recorded that certain broadcasting organizations have experimented with the translation of some of the traditional performing arts into the language of broadcasting. These experiences are recounted in the chapter that follows; it is appropriate here, however, to note that in Senegal and in Thailand, traditional storytellers and singers are employed as regular members of the staff of the broadcasting organizations.

Thus, broadcasting can be an important stimulant to the other arts, not only for their sake but for its own. Governments concerned over indigenous self-expression in the field of culture might be wise to provide broadcasting organizations with substantial additional sums earmarked for subsidies and commissions for creative individuals and organizations in both the traditional and modern sectors of their countries.

Part Three

Performance

5

Programming Patterns

Having looked at the technology and organization of the media and the process of their transfer and institutionalization we now turn to consider their output. In this chapter and the next we consider the extent to which the performance of broadcasting has lived up to its promise. How much as broadcasting contributed to national development?

When we attempt to assess the performance of broadcasting, we do so armed with the observations and data derived by the research methods described in the Preface. In addition, we listened to and viewed broadcasts as best as we could. We tried to see the programs that were most talked about. One can get a fair idea—even without knowledge of the language—of what a television news broadcast is about, of the style in which it is presented. Similarly one can get some inkling of what a variety show or a serial is like. Crossing the linguistic barrier is more difficult in the case of radio, although even sound-only programs in a strange language convey useful impressions. We studied program schedules, where necessary in translation. We obtained detailed descriptions of what was being broadcast and examined both the content and structure of programming. In this way we came to know what is and, equally important, what is not being broadcast.

149

THE UNIFORMITIES OF BROADCASTING SCHEDULES

When comparing broadcasting systems in many countries, one is struck by the important uniformities that characterize them. In all countries radio is pervasive and television, where it exists, is still heavily concentrated in the larger, and richer, centers of population. Radio, therefore, has a tendency toward the local and the regional in accent and in substance; television is more metropolitan and cosmopolitan. Advertising has a share in all the television systems we studied and in most of the radio systems. The media in the developing countries are directly owned or heavily controlled by government, but supervision tends to be restrictive rather than directive. Executives and employees must be native-born; information must be precensored; stations are required, typically, to transmit official news bulletins. In many countries stations must devote part of their time to educational broadcasts, often produced and delivered for transmission by people working under the direction of the ministry of education.

It is notoriously difficult to compare the output of different national broadcasting systems. As has often been pointed out, the categories used for classifying programs vary widely, sometimes from station to station within the same country. Even the BBC and ITV in the United Kingdom, for example, have different category systems.[1] More recently UNESCO has been trying to develop some standardized system to remedy these discrepancies. In radio broadcasting, the situation is complicated by the very large number of low-powered local stations in many countries, the program schedules of which are not available even after the event. Moreover, attempts at averaging output figures where data are available run the risk of ignoring differences among stations in both strength of signal and size of audience.

Bearing in mind these limitations, we attempt nevertheless to compare ten of our case-study countries. Table 5.1

Table 5.1 Radio time allocated for serious and entertainment programs in ten selected countries.[a]

Type of program	Brazil[b]	Indonesia[c]	Tanzania (national service)[d]	Tanzania (commercial service)[e]	Senegal[f]	Algeria[g]	Nigeria[h]	Thailand[i]	Cyprus[j]	Iran[k]	Singapore[l]
Serious	35%	55%	53%	40%	53%	47%	37%	28%	31%	22%	40%
Entertainment	65%	45%	47%	60%	47%	53%	63%	72%	69%	78%	60%

a. Serious programs include news and news magazines, talks, current-affairs programs, school broadcasts, adult-education programs (instructional), and religious programs. Entertainment programs include music, sports, plays, dramatic series and serials, children's programs, light entertainment, and comedy. All figures in this table are for these categories only; advertising or "other" categories are not taken into consideration. Thus for some countries, especially those with commercial services, these figures are not percentages of total output (which may include up to 20 percent advertising) but only of program output in the categories listed. All figures except those for Tanzania are composite.

b. Composite national figure for all stations, estimated by interview respondents.

c. Composite figure for Radio Republik Indonesia only, all stations, 1973.

d. Calculated from the Radio Tanzania program schedule for December 31, 1974 to January 6, 1975.

e. Calculated from the Radio Tanzania program schedule for December 22–28, 1974.

f. Calculated from the ORTS programme schedule for January 6–12, 1975, national channel.

g. Calculated from the RTA programme schedule for April 15–21, 1974, three channels.

h. A composite figure calculated from NBC, Western Nigeria Radiovision Service, and BCNN program schedules for October–December, 1973.

i. From *Directory of Communications Resources in Thailand* (Bangkok: Thammasat University Press, 1971).

j. From Marketing Advisory Services, Ltd., *Survey* (1972), composite for two channels.

k. From *Fourth National Development Plan* (Tehran: Plan Organization, 1968).

l. A composite figure calculated from the Radio Singapore program schedule for 1974, four channels.

compares the proportion of radio time devoted to serious and to light-entertainment programming in ten countries.

Speaking very broadly, about 40 percent of radio time in these countries is taken up by serious programs: news, current affairs, religion, school programs, adult education, and features for special audiences such as farmers, women, or children. But there is considerable variation among countries.

The figures suggest that certain countries are more didactic than others. Tanzania and Senegal are among the best examples: about half of their radio programming falls into the categories of news, current affairs, information, and adult education. Even Tanzania's commercial service devotes 40 percent of its programs to information. Indonesia's RRI programming ranks very high in these categories (55 percent). Thailand and Iran equal the BBC's serious output of about 25 percent of total radio time.

Popular music may be strongly local in flavor or, more exactly, a hybrid of local and international music, much of it performed by local artists. Thus, the popular music category in Indonesia consists of 85 percent Indonesian music and only 15 percent imported music. The same proportions more or less hold true in Iran. Despite its renown in the field of popular music, Brazil broadcasts more imported than home-produced music.

These two categories—serious and entertainment—account for 85 percent or more of total radio time, with a modal ratio of 1 : 2, but with considerable variety, as Table 5.1 shows. For our purposes it is particularly interesting to see the explicit attention given to adult education in countries such as Tanzania, Iran, Indonesia, and Cyprus.

Somewhat more uniformly than those of radio, television schedules in most of the countries we studied are divided into serious programs (25 to 30 percent), (including news, current affairs, documentaries, and talks), and entertainment (70 to 75 percent), (including variety shows, drama, and children's programs).

Overall, the division of television time in ten of our case-study countries for which data are available does not differ dramatically from the composite data for Independent Television in the UK, as the right-hand column of Table 5.2 demonstrates.[2] News and current affairs together are alloted about 20 percent of ITV time. The arts, religion, children's programs, and education of all sorts, including school broadcasts, take up 13 percent, bringing the proportion of serious programming to about one-third of the output.[3] Drama of all kinds—series, serials, plays, and feature films—take up another third, while light entertainment, children's entertainment, and sports take about 10 percent each. Compared with ITV, light entertainment and music get more time in the developing countries, and sports seem to get less.

There does appear to be an underlying pattern of demand around the globe which results in similarities among television schedules. Yet the detailed breakdown in Table 5.2 indicates some important differences. In news and current-affairs programming, Senegal and Algeria are particularly high, while Brazil, Peru, and Thailand are particularly low in programs with informational content. Adding adult education widens the gap between the public-service systems (to which category the systems of Nigeria and Iran also belong) and the private-enterprise (or at least not exclusively government-controlled) systems of Brazil, Peru, and Thailand. But comparisons may be misleading. Consider, for example, that a shortage of money forces most African stations to produce the type of informational talk show that can be produced cheaply in a studio. Indeed, the current-affairs category for Algeria and Senegal includes a disproportionate number of such programs. Or consider that the stations that are on the air for more hours tend to have lower proportions of serious content because the daytime and late-night hours are generally filled with low-cost entertainment. These stations are more likely to be private enterprises, which have to maximize their audiences for finan-

Table 5.2 Television program structure in eleven selected countries (Weekly average percentage).

	Indonesia TVRI	Nigeria NBC	Nigeria WNTV	Nigeria BCNN	Senegal ORTS	Algeria RTA	Thailand (composite)	Iran NIRT (national network)	Cyprus CBC	Brazil Globo	Brazil Tupi	Peru channels 4 & 5 (composite)	Singapore	U.K. ITV [b]
News	⎫ 22	8	9	8	24	14	8	17	10	7	4	11	14	10
Current affairs and documentaries	⎭	12	9	10	15	21	7	5	9	8	13	4	9	10
Adult education	⎫ 33	0	4	7	10	3	2	10	7	2	2	0	0	3
Education (school broadcasts)	⎭	22	8	28	0	7	0	0	0	0	0	0	0 [a]	5
Religion		1	1	2	0	4	1	0	0	0	0	0	0	3
Sports		6	7	4	2	3	4	8	7	1	10	18	1	11
Children's programs	⎫ 45	15	10	9	10	11	2	10	8	9	7	13	9	11
Series and serials		12	26	20	12	10	40	19	26	24	28	25	13	⎫ 24
Plays		2	1	4	0	5	3	1	7	1	0	1	16	⎭
Light entertainment		13	13	8	10	5	12	11	2	16	22	14	9	
Music (international)		0	0	0	10	7	2	2	2	2	0	2	⎫ 10	⎫ 13
Music (local) and folklore		1	6	4	0	0	4	11	2	0	1	0	⎭	⎭
Feature films	⎭	7	4	6	7	11	14	5	20	30	13	12	19	10
Total hours broadcast per week in these categories (hr/min)	38.00 [b]	44.50	36.30	49.25	28.00	52.25	193.25	62.00	33.10	113.45	110.35	171.00	106.30	

a. School broadcasts produced by Singapore Educational Media Service (SEMS).
b. 1974–75, composite.

cial reasons. Note that the government-financed stations of
Africa broadcast relatively few hours, ranging from
twenty-eight hours weekly in Senegal to fifty-two in
Algeria. School broadcasts in Nigeria inflate the total and
thus reduce the proportions of other serious programs as
well as of entertainment.

A different analysis can be undertaken, comparing programming during "prime time," when audiences are greatest. For the major broadcasting service in each of the seven
countries for which we have sufficiently detailed data, this
analysis brings out some additional differences among
countries. Thus Cyprus ranks high in news programs, because it broadcasts the news in English and Turkish as well
as in Greek and its total broadcasting output is low. The
very high proportion of serials in Brazil (34 percent of total
broadcast time) is a reflection of the addiction of South
American viewers to the local style of daytime serial, the
telenovela, which occupies almost all peak time in Brazil. In
Nigeria, "plays" is a category the size of which reflects the
determination of NBC to create an indigenous type of
Nigerian television drama. The high proportion of series
(with the same characters, but a different story each week)
in Singapore, Thailand, and Iran is an indicator of the high
proportion of imported programs broadcast in these countries.

Indeed, buying programs abroad is one of the most important indicators of the character of a television system.[4]
Table 5.3 shows that the proportion of imported programs
ranges from 30 to 75 percent, averaging about 55 percent.
By contrast, the proportion of programs purchased abroad
by either of the British television services is limited by con-
vention to 14 percent. (In fairness one must add that some
of the smaller European countries buy one-third or more of
their television programs abroad.) The content of the imported programs is often alien to the values and imagery of
the importing country. When programs from Europe and

Table 5.3 Percentage of imported and locally produced television programs in ten selected countries, 1973–74.

	Indonesia	Nigeria NBC	WNTV	BCNN	Senegal	Algeria	Thailand	Iran	Cyprus	Brazil	Peru	Singapore
Imported	35	30	55	55	75	50	50	40	65	57	60	58
Locally produced	65	70	45	45	25	50	50	60	35	43	40	42

Source: Information provided by the broadcasting organizations.

the United States are imported by developing countries, the gap in values and imagery can be unbridgeable. It is this consideration that has caused the Nigerian Broadcasting Corporation to raise its own production to 70 percent of its output and Algeria to make similar efforts, raising its home production from 26 to 49 percent in the last few years. The identification of the ideal ratio of imported to locally produced programs requires careful attention, bearing in mind the developmental goals enunciated by most developing countries.

IMPORTED PROGRAMS

The bulk of imported programs in most countries consists of the standard television fare: action adventures, of which "Kojak," "Ironside," and "Hawaii Five-0" were typical during the period of the study, and family-situation series exemplified by "I Love Lucy," "A Family Affair," and the like. Everywhere regardless of type of regime or broadcasting system, American imports outnumber those from all other countries. Even in countries that have cultural ties elsewhere, such as Cyprus with Greece or Algeria with France and other Arabic-speaking countries, United States programs predominate. Culture, even ideology, makes way for "L'Homme de Fer" ("Ironside!") and other imported programs that commanded prime-time positions in most of the countries we studied.

The importance of imported American programs is illustrated by their places in the prime-time program schedules of the major stations of nine countries on summer Saturday and Thursday nights in 1975 (see Tables 5.4 and A.6). Cultural ties, old and new, are on display in Cyprus (Greece), Algeria (France), Thailand (Japan), and Singapore (U.K.). The growing influence of British series is hinted at. But the feature films and dramatic series that dominate the evening are peopled by American detectives, cowboys, and housewives—and their adversaries. During the week for which

Table 5.4 Television schedules, summer Saturday evenings in nine selected countries, 1974–75.

Time	U.K. BBC Channel 1 7/12/75	Brazil Globo Brasília 7/19/75	Nigeria NBC Lagos 7/26/75	Cyprus CBC 7/19/75	Singapore Channel 5 7/26/75	Iran NIRT Channel 7 7/24/75 [a]	Algeria RTA 4/20/74	Thailand Channel 7 7/19/75	Peru Channel 4 7/26/75	Peru Channel 5 7/26/75
5:00		The Waltons (U.S. series)			Special Branch (U.K. series on Scotland Yard)					Peru 74 (variety)
5:30	Tom and Jerry (U.S. cartoon)					Goli and Friends (puppet show)	Arcana (French series on music)	Music Show	Abbot and Costello (U.S. comedy)	
5:45	News; Weather; Jim'll Fix It (personality show)				Manis Manja (children's program)	The Osmond Brothers (U.S. pop music group)	The Affair of the West (U.S. film)			
6:00		Disneyland (U.S. children's film)	International News; Saturday Sports							
6:15					Consumers Guide (in English/Malay)	Sporting Magazine (for the young)				
6:30	Saturday Night at the Movies (U.S. film)			Opening News, weather; Puppet Theater (Greek)	News in Brief; Wheelie & Chopper Bunch (U.S. cartoon)			Documentary		Soccer
6:45						Film on employment				
7:00			National News; The Bar Beach Show (live)	Gunsmoke (U.S. series)	Family Time (magazine series in English)	Sports News	Ivanhoe (U.K. series)	Devil Man (Japanese detective series)	Nichols (U.S. series)	

Time								
7:15		Bravo (Brazilian serial)	entertainment, bands & dancing					News Magazine Pan Americano
7:30				Evening story for children	News (in Malay)	Short Thai Play	El Asnam's Puppet Festival Magazine West (regional program)	News
7:45				Human Stories (Greek series of sentimental stories)	Cilla Black Show (U.K. musical variety)	The Mind & the Senses (quiz)	Local, sports, world News	News in Turkish and English Music Program
8:00		Jornal Nacional (news)	Play of the Week (produced either by NBC or by other Nigerian stations)			Dear Uncle Bill (U.S. series)	Weather Forecast, News	
8:15						Thai Classical Music		
8:30	Cannon (U.S. detective series)	Escalada (Brazilian serial)		News, weather	The Streets of San Francisco (U.S. police series)	News	Press Review (in French)	Theater Play
8:45	Seaside Special (outside variety broadcast)				Carlotta (U.S. serial)	King of Sports (French comedy series)	Thrill-Seeker (U.S. series)	
9:00	Kojak (U.S. series)		News					
9:15	Cannon (U.S. detective series)		Matters of the Moment (current affairs)					
9:30				News & Newsreel (in English)				

Table 5.4 Television schedules, summer Saturday evenings in nine selected countries, 1974–75. (*Continued*)

Time	U.K. BBC Channel 1 7/12/75	Brazil Globo Brasilia 7/19/75	Nigeria NBC Lagos 7/26/75	Cyprus CBC 7/19/75	Singapore Channel 5 7/26/75	Iran NIRT Channel 7 7/24/75 [a]	Algeria RTA 4/20/74	Thailand Channel 7 7/19/75	Peru Channel 4 7/26/75	Peru Channel 5 7/26/75
9:45								Thai feature film	Feature film (*imported*)	
10:00	News Weather That's Life (*chat show*)	Film (*U.S.*)	Saturday Movies (*U.S.*)	Anthology (*U.S. film*)	Gomer Pyle (*U.S. situation comedy*)	On The Way (*political discussion*)				
10:15								World Cup Soccer (*European videotape*)		
10:30					Callan (*U.K. espionage series*)	Movie of the Week	News			
10:45	Easy on the Ice (*ice skating*)						Variety Evening			
11:00			Night Report							
11:15	Eleventh Hour (*series of plays*)			News, weather						
11:30					Midnight Movie (*U.K.*)				Feature film (*imported*)	
11:45	Ghost Story (*series of plays*)						Closedown			Platea Latina (*imported variety show*)
12:00		TV Movie (*U.S.*)								

a. The schedule is for Thursday evening, preceding the Iranian Sabbath.

we have program schedules, two or more of the countries we studied were broadcasting "Gunsmoke," "A Family Affair," "The Streets of San Francisco," and "Kojak."

Nor does competition make much difference. Competing channels usually present the same fare. For example, on Monday, July 15, 1975, at 8.30 p.m. the viewers of Bangkok could choose among three American series: "Manhunt," "The FBI", and "Get Christie Love!" On a Saturday night in Tehran the viewer had a choice of "A Family Affair" and "Days of Our Lives" on one channel and "The Bold Ones" and "Kojak" on the other. The examples are handpicked, of course, for the choice sometimes includes— as in Thailand on Sundays—wrestling, a Disney film, or "Hawaii Five-0." Singapore has a more indigenous Channel 8 and a more cosmopolitan Channel 5. This difference in emphasis also characterizes several other developing countries. On the whole, however, competition leads to sameness, except when the different channels are jointly managed and an explicit effort is made to create choice.

The dependence on the West as a source of supply for television programming has often been commented upon and has too often, perhaps, been oversimplified. Some analysts argue that the use of American, British, or French television programs in the developing countries is further evidence of the neocolonialism that has replaced the classical relationship between the metropolitan nations and their former wards.[5] In this view, Western television programs are imposed by a combination of aggressive salesmanship on the part of the production companies and seductive offers of tied aid and assistance from the exporting countries. They are part of the same package, it is said, that brings the technology and the organizational skills of the West to the developing world only to create further dependence. It is through this same network of relationships, so it is alleged, that television programs and films are diffused, complete with their messages of materialism and the legitimacy of things-as-they-are.[6]

Quite a different view of the cause of the pervasiveness of American programs (and to a lesser extent those of other countries) is stated in terms of their inherent attractiveness. It is argued that the high technical quality of the programs, the simplicity of the story, and the reliance on action and pace, on familiarity of characters, and on predictability of outcome combine to make for their universal appeal.

There is something in both these arguments, of course, but neither is adequate to account for the phenomenon. Even taken together they merely serve to remind us that both supply and demand are necessary to any satisfactory explanation.

We have already seen how the introduction of broadcasting in a developing country takes place. In most countries the basic decision to broadcast even five hours per day is enough to create the need to buy programs abroad. Most developing countries that make a decision of this kind do not, or cannot, budget to spend the money needed to produce 2,000 hours of programs of reasonable quality per year. Even an average cost of no more than $500 per hour would in the mid-1970s have required a production budget of at least a million dollars a year. If this amount is divided equally between direct and indirect costs, only $250 per hour remains for the direct production costs. Few if any stations can function on a budget of this size; twice as much is still extremely constricting. The average BBC cost per hour during the same period was $30,000 (£90 million for 6,000 hours), and it is not unusual for an hour-long drama on either BBC or ITV to cost $100,000.

The money for production actually available to a small television station in a developing country is often barely enough to produce the most rudimentary of talk shows or amateur drama or variety programs. If a viable schedule is to be built up, more programs have to be found elsewhere. Since the price of certain types of imported programs is low and alternative local supply is nonexistent, it is to low-cost imports that program managers turn. In 1974 the price of an installment of an average American series was $300 to $400 per hour in Iran, $250 to $300 in Thailand, and slightly less in Peru; Nigeria could buy for as little as $60. These "country prices" [7] are a function of the number of sets in use and are applicable to programs that other countries in the same geographic or cultural area agree to acquire.[8] Since the price is a negotiated one, it will also reflect the extent of encouragement that the producing and distributing companies want to give to a television station in the hope of expanding the local market for their products.

Thus the cost of producing a program like "Ironside" or "Hawaii Five-0" in Hollywood or New York may be $200,000 or more, but Peru, Thailand, or Iran can buy it for less than the least expensive of their home productions. A more complex program—a variety show or a drama—might cost these countries $10,000 to produce, and they obviously cannot often afford these.

Thus the reliance on imported programs derives from a more complex combination of causes than neocolonialist ambition and the popularity of the programs themselves. It derives from the frame of reference that was imported with the hardware and that conceives of television as a nonstop supply of programs during operating hours. As long as this frame is not broken, only the very poorest countries, which must remain satisfied with one-camera talk shows, or the richest countries, whose "country price" may be so high as to approach the cost of quality production at home, will not rely largely on imports. The only other brake on importing derives from ideology or local pride. Algeria and Nigeria, for example, have in recent years sharply cut back the proportion of programs imported from abroad as a result of decisions deriving from cultural policy. Peru, by contrast, has not succeeded in reducing imports despite the elaborate publicity it has given to the reasons why it ought to.

The exceptions to this general picture are significant for

possible future development. With the decision to cut back sharply on the importation of programs, Nigerian broadcasters began to increase their own production. The direct costs of these local programs in 1975 were estimated at an average of $150 per hour. By Western standards, therefore, the quality of the production is bound to be low. But production quality is only one indicator of program quality. If audience appreciation is taken as another indicator, locally produced programs which are very popular meet the qualitative expectations of their audiences.

The problem of production quality is not only financial. Human resources are as relevant. Even where money is available, the necessary talent often is not. The writers, directors, cameramen, graphic artists, and others needed to produce entertainment of quality have generally been trained in an established infrastructure in the arts of theater and film. In most developing countries there is no such basis for training. Traditional forms of entertainment, where they exist, are not readily transferred to the television studio. Even where a film industry exists, as it does in many Asian countries, the high cost of production, pegged to Western standards, often holds back domestic television production rather than advancing it.

In the United States the film industry has in recent years adapted itself to the production of television films. The never-ending demand for program material in the United States itself has led to the development of assembly-line production of television series and serials following the principles of economy of scale. The "one-off," or special program, in which Britain takes so much pride has disappeared from American screens, giving way to the series of thirteen, twenty-six, or thirty-nine episodes or more. Lately, Britain has also been moving in this direction. The reason is plain: it is only a succession of long-running series that can solve the scheduling problems of the program director of a large network, just as it solves those of his colleague in a small television station. Both need something to broadcast *every Monday night* at eight o'clock. Neither could hope to succeed if he had to find a different program every week. For the overseas buyer, it takes as long to preview a one-of-a-kind drama or variety show as it does to preview a series or serial that runs to hundreds of installments. The buyer cannot risk reliance on the supplier, the price, or the suitability, culturally speaking, of television "specials," nor can he undertake the constant vigil of monitoring and selection. As soon as he decides to buy abroad, very little will answer his requirements apart from the long-running American (and some British and French) series and serials.

In view of the growing export market, many television series are no longer financed so as to cover their costs by transmission in one country alone. They are intended, like films, to be shown worldwide in order to recoup their original outlay and make profits. Hence the need for itinerant salesmen to ensure such worldwide exposure and the tendency to promote a high level of homogeneity of supply. It is this system of supply and demand, rather than the quality of the product or the neocolonialist ambitions of Western countries, which accounts for the transmission of the same series throughout the world. Of course it is possible that other forces are also at work in the diffusion of Western series and serials. We assert only that the phenomenon in question can be explained more parsimoniously, without recourse to such perspectives.

The homogeneity of demand is abetted by the importation of the models of television from the West. The quest for speedy modernization does not allow the new nations much time to create their own symbols or to translate their own identities into the language of the media. It is far easier to buy the symbols of modernization wholesale. This reinforces the demand for the same program patterns and the same programs as those shown everywhere else. This is, of course, convenient for the suppliers and unlikely to be discouraged by them.

GLOBAL VILLAGE?

As a result of the homogeneity of demand—no matter what its source—the content of broadcasting is similar around the world. The same mix of news and entertainment can be seen and heard in the most diverse cultural, ideological, and economic settings. As we have seen, the actual programs are often the same, imported from the United States and, for certain countries, from the U.K., France, Japan, Mexico, and elsewhere.

Even the home-made programs are often based on Western models, and some of the companies that market television films also sell program formats that can be replicated by local producers to make children's programs or quiz shows, for example. The American soap opera is the format with the most widely diffused local versions in the world. It is the staple of South American television.

Thus the flow of entertainment programs and entertainment formats is almost wholly in one direction.[9] The flow of news is even more unidirectional. Radio and television organizations subscribe to the international agencies and the international news-film services that are based in London, Paris, and New York. It is not difficult, against this background, to understand the call by the leaders of the nonaligned countries for their own press agencies that will better serve the needs of these countries to present themselves as they appear in their own eyes.[10] Yet, if the presentation of news—and not only its content—is any indication, the television services of the developing countries have so far been satisfied to imitate the West. The rapid flow of terse, disconnected news items presented with staccato urgency by a team of breathless announcers dressed in the latest London fashions is the predominant format of the evening news. Naturally, it is more difficult for us to judge the presentational style of radio news.[11]

The homogeneity of broadcasting patterns can also be seen in the flow pattern of programs during broadcasting hours or over the course of a week.[12] Looking back at Table 5.4, it is clear that the early evening hours are devoted to children, and that puppets are a favorite medium for addressing children (Cyprus, Iran, Algeria). The family unit is then assembled (Singapore, Iran, Algeria). The news punctuates the evening: it tends to go out at 8:00 p.m. The evening entertainment follows. Home-produced programs tend to be shorter and to be broadcast earlier, while the dramatic programs and entertainment following the news are often imported.

Nevertheless, as we have noted, there remain some differences among countries. On the evenings in question (see Table 5.4), Thailand was an exception. It featured its own play, its own documentary, and a Japanese series. Nigeria presented its own play. Brazil carried on with the *telenovela*. Greek music and stories were featured in Nicosia.

Over the whole of the week there is evident the tendency for the privately owned companies to have a higher proportion of entertainment programming and for the government-owned or publicly controlled companies to have a higher proportion of serious programming. But these latter services also tend, as we have seen, to be on the air for fewer hours and to have lower budgets. The African countries provide good examples of this tendency. They also demonstrate how difficult it is to give relative weight to government control, finance, or cultural policy in accounting for the precise proportion of each ingredient that goes into the making of a program mix.

Moments of change-of-mix provide clues. Indeed, during the period of our study we have seen Nigeria reverse the proportion of its imported programs from 70 percent to 30 percent. Algeria has moved closer to the other Arab countries and has begun to exchange programs in the wake of its determined "Arabizing" policy. We have witnessed the effort of Cyprus to draw closer to Greece by importing Greek programs (although Cyprus itself has more experience and more sophistication in television than has Greece). We see the federal television station in Nigeria trying to develop its own dramatic programs as the country's struggle for national unification becomes more desperate. We see Japan edging out the United States as a program supplier to Thailand, while postrevolution Peru, despite its declared intentions, remains a loyal client of American television series.

On balance, however, the impression of uniformity outweighs the differences among countries. Not the least important reason for this is the similarity of functions that radio and television perform everywhere. These media have to serve the society as a whole and the family as whole. They must be responsive to those common denominators that unite age, sex, and class within the society and within the home. They provide background music and "moving wallpaper" (as Stuart Hood has characterized much of television programming) [13] to accompany the round of daily life and the evenings at home. That these media have come to be associated primarily with entertainment, whatever the other problems of society, is a fact. Even Soviet Russia, we are told, has despaired of television as a medium of indoctrination and has abandoned it to entertainment.[14]

Radio, it seems, is not as closely bound to the image of the urban, nuclear family relaxing together after a hard day's work. Radio is altogether more flexible, and although its program schedule may be no less standardized than that of TV its contents are more familiar: radio programs are more often homemade. One can accept McLuhan's idea that radio is the tribal voice, even if one stops short of his implication that it somehow stirs the racial unconscious. The announcer is local; the names in the news are more familiar; the people of the *radionovela* are old friends; the chanting is authentic; the tunes are singable. Even in radio, however, the lion's share of the programming, the music, may be largely imported.

It is the tension between these functions of radio and television—those familiar functions that accompanied them from the West—and the urgent priorities of the developing nations that we consider in the next chapter.

6

Promise and Performance

When we considered the promise of broadcasting in Chapter 1, we did so from the point of view of the developing nations themselves. We tried to focus on their hopes and expectations, not our own. We noted that social scientists and communications experts have also dealt with this subject, often in close collaboration with governments and international organizations. But it is the policymakers' point of view that we take as our starting point. We ask whether the performance of the broadcast media has approached the promise that the policymakers in the new nations saw in them. It is our evaluation of the fulfillment of the promise these policymakers perceived that is the subject of this chapter.

It should be clear by now that systematic data on the effects of listening or viewing hardly exist on the broad canvas with which we are concerned. We did not have the resources to conduct audience research, and even if we had had them, the answers to some of our questions are not directly accessible to survey research.[1] In what follows, therefore, we draw on the limited data that are available from audience research conducted by others in the case-study countries themselves and on the work of other students of the relationship between communication and development. Foremost, however, are our own impressions of broadcasting policy and performance and of the extent to which these have been brought to bear on development goals. These qualitative data are, as we said at the outset, drawn from the extensive documentation we collected and from discussions with scholars of each society, with broadcasters, with members of the political and cultural elite, and, informally, with ordinary viewers and listeners both in towns and in rural areas.[2]

We now return to the three themes of promise outlined in Chapter 1: the hope that the broadcast media will contribute to the integration of society, that they will accelerate the development process, and that they will provide a new channel of authentic creativity through which the values of the culture and its arts, traditional and modern, might be widely diffused.

In our study we asked ourselves, our data, and our informants whether broadcasting is advancing these goals. Often, we came across *other* goals—some of them in sharp opposition to those proclaimed. Throughout, we tried to bear in mind the major problems of developing societies: the multiplicity of ethnic, regional, or language groups; the instability of governments and their need for legitimation; the great gaps in the distribution of resources among classes; the ancient traditions, sometimes great ones; predominantly agrarian populations, often living as tenants or farming small plots on a subsistence basis; problems of illiteracy and poor education; problems of disease and high mortality. And we asked, What relationship has broadcasting to these problems?

NATIONAL INTEGRATION

Highest among the hopes for the broadcast media in the new nations is the hope that they will contribute to national integration. Integration means a sense of identification with the larger whole that is the nation-state, a feeling of being a Thai or a Nigerian or a Peruvian. In states where loyalties have rarely extended beyond the village or the tribe or the region—as is the case in most developing countries—the achievement of such national awareness would be no mean accomplishment for the broadcasting services.

By national integration, however, the political leaders mean more than that. Their hope is that loyalty will focus on them and on the legitimacy of their rule. Thus, the Shah of Iran wants to underline the unbroken connection between his family and the great Cyrus of 2,500 years ago. He looks to broadcasting and to other myth-making media—festivals, for example—to help him in this.

An understanding and acceptance of the political institutions and their legitimacy is also part of national integration. Regimes concerned with development speak of mobilizing political participation as well, spreading (under clearly defined conditions) responsibility for decisions, and thus initiative, to ever-widening circles. They say they want the media, as in Tanzania, for example, to explain the policies of government and to motivate peasants to take part in elections. They also want the media, within well-defined limits, to be the channels for complaints and criticisms. This feedback role of radio, as employed in Senegal, for example, is the more important the higher the rate of illiteracy.

The first requisite for the fulfillment of this promise of national integration is coverage: the media must reach out to the whole population. In the case of radio, this coverage has been achieved to a considerable extent. In the case of television, it has hardly begun.

Radio networks have been extended in almost every country and have overcome many of the problems of terrain and distance. Where commercial systems left the job undone, as in Brazil, governments have stepped in to complete it. In Algeria, satisfactory networking of radio throughout the Saharan South of the country was completed only in the early 1970s. In both Indonesia and Tanzania, reception is still unsatisfactory in substantial parts of the national territory, despite the grand rhetoric of integration in Indonesia and the centrality attributed to the propagation of indigenous socialism in Tanzania. Both countries are still at the earliest stages of substituting medium-wave for shortwave coverage; Indonesia is only now installing equipment that will extend medium-wave coverage to 25 percent of its population, and Tanzanian medium-wave coverage is limited to the area around the capital. The large majority of their populations must remain with shortwave coverage of questionable effectiveness or, as in the case of half the Tanzanians, with no reliable coverage at all. In Indonesia, as in Thailand and Peru, hundreds of local stations dot towns and villages without, however, contributing much to connecting local populations with the center.

In addition to coverage the promotion of national integration requires the establishment of networks, whereby at least certain broadcasts can be received simultaneously throughout the nation. This possibility exists in about half the countries we studied. In the other half, programs are delivered physically (by recordings) or transmitted from station to station by shortwave or microwave and then rebroadcast.

Special attention is given in certain countries to areas peopled by groups with dual loyalties across frontiers or with insurgent political tendencies. These areas are connected to the national network sooner than others, often at great expense. Independent stations with long-range coverage, such as Radio Voice of the Gospel transmitting from Ethiopia to Africa, the Middle East, and South Asia, are tolerated so long as they do not conflict with local political or cultural patterns. Thus, for example, Tanzania allows RVOG to produce its Swahili programs at Moshi, a town in northern Tanzania. They are then flown to Addis Ababa for transmission.

News broadcasts are often mandatory. All stations, public and private, networked or not, must broadcast the news. News bulletins are often prepared by, or under the control of, the ministry of information or its equivalent. In Algeria, for example, the head of news is answerable not to the director-general of the broadcasting service, but effectively to the head of state. A few countries let local radio news go its way, making certain only that it stays away from politics. In other countries (Algeria, Iran, Senegal), where broadcasting is organized as a single national system and radio networking is complete, the news is broadcast from the center and transmitted simultaneously, as is, for example, the national news from London or Paris.

The national news everywhere is carefully controlled. In many countries even the news announcers are required to be native-born nationals (as are station managers). Emphasis is laid on "official" news: reporting the activities of the leaders and proclaiming their achievements. Authority is treated with deference; friendly nations are praised and enemy nations are vilified; care is taken to alert the population to the dangers of subversion or insurgency and to their penalties. Observers have remarked that the absence of criticism and the ignoring of events outside the capital city may well boomerang as populations become more sophisticated consumers of news. And, indeed, we have one such example in the dramatic drop of credibility of Radio Thailand after the student demonstrations of October 1973. In his report to the Public Relations Department of Thailand, a BBC consultant anticipated this problem, emphasizing the effectiveness of the Voice of Free Thailand, broadcasting from China, which sometimes seemed to know more about what was happening in Bangkok than did Radio Thailand itself. The liberalization of news coverage, allowing for criticism and participation, may be threatening initially, says the report, but may contribute to stability in the long run.[3]

The most important use of radio in the promotion of national integration is its encouragement of the national language. Where there is a reasonable degree of sympathy in a country for a single, unifying language, this task is made easier. Radio has carried Portuguese, and an agreed metropolitan pronunciation of it, to some of the remotest regions of the Brazilian jungle. The new regime in Peru hopes to spread knowledge of Spanish via radio to rural Indians who are said to be eager to learn it. Algeria is using the broadcast media as agents of its Arabization policy, while the spread of radio in Senegal demands the use of Wolof, which is understood by 80 percent of the people, and thus gives de facto support to those who want to substitute Wolof for French as the official language.

On the other hand, in the desire to get through to special language groups, national, and certainly regional, broadcasting systems take special account of pluralism. This is where radio, as compared with television, is at its strongest. Radio is capable of meeting local language needs at low cost. In all multilingual countries, broadcasters struggle with the dilemma caused by linguistic diversity. They recognize that broadcasts in local languages are a good means of mobilizing participation in socioeconomic development, but are also aware that the cause of national integration requires a lingua franca.

The Nigerian case is a good example. The national service of the Nigerian Broadcasting Corporation broadcasts in English in order to overcome the problem of reaching more than a fraction of Nigeria's two hundred language groups; however, English itself is unfamiliar to a majority of the population. The many state and local stations do not have this problem, as they broadcast in the local languages.

Diversity in radio music presents a similar dilemma. In Thailand, for example, there are five kinds of radio music: classical Thai, popular-urban and popular-rural ("country and Western") Thai, classical Western, and popular Western. Thus, official stations of Radio Thailand, like the National Program of Radio Republik Indonesia and the First Program of Radio Iran, emphasize the traditional music of the country. The local stations are much more diversified and often "specialize" in one or another form in order to cater to local taste or to woo a particular segment of the audience. In Thailand, even the local and regional stations emphasize Thai music, but of the more popular sort, rural and urban. This is the music that is best liked in the country, and it is worth noting that it has been influenced by the popular music of the West.[4] Music in Iran is also becoming increasingly westernized. Prima facie, national integration is probably better served by shared than by diverse cultural experience.

Television is a different story, at least so far. If national coverage is a prerequisite to promoting the message of integration, television seems at its present stage of development more divisive and invidious than integrative. It is impossible to reconcile the promise of the role of television in mobilizing popular participation and loyalty and in promoting national integration with the concentration of coverage in the capital and, at most, other big cities. It is useless to announce that television will be a force for overcoming regional and linguistic particularisms when the cost of a television set is out of reach of most of the rural population.

There can be no doubt that the location of television transmitters is determined by political prestige and commercial factors. Receivers and antennae are for the rich and the politically influential. Access to a television signal and ownership of a television set have become a status symbol in societies in which success and wealth are achieved mainly in urban, and particularly in metropolitan, settings.

Only where there exist vigorous programming and very substantial resources for coverage beyond the urban concentrations is there hope that television can fulfill its promise as a medium of unification. Iran is one of the few examples. Although it was slow at first to extend its television network, an aggressive program of national expansion is now under way. Algeria, India, and Indonesia have ambitious plans to extend coverage by satellite, but only the Indian satellite has operated so far, and its achievements remain to be assessed. The governments of Peru, Brazil, and Thailand also have plans for dramatic expansion, but these plans are not linked to realistic implementation schedules. In Brazil the government threatens to create its own television network in view of the procrastination of the commercial system in its expansion beyond the centers of major consumption.

Given the high costs, cumbersomeness, and complexity of program production on the Western model, television as a medium is much less capable of diversity than radio. Program production tends to consist of centralized, ready-made material for relay to the hinterland. If regions do produce their own programs, their resources permit them to fill only a small proportion of potential broadcast time. Occasionally, as in Nigeria, regional output is exchanged among stations; and sometimes, as in Thailand, a program is taped at one of the four provincial stations for broadcast over the network. However, the heavy concentration of production at the center, together with the rarity of hearing the voice of a region or locality presented or relayed from the center, lends weight to the need to strengthen the ties between center and periphery. But obviously, all this awaits the expansion of coverage.

Much more direct efforts at connecting center and periphery are to be seen in Tanzania and Senegal. Leaders in those countries have sought to use radio to encourage a form of dialogue with rural villagers. In Senegal, experimentation with dialogue programs has apparently proved successful in allowing farmers to express their satisfactions and dissatisfactions with government. And in Tanzania experiments in mass education and election campaigns via radio, using a combination of mass media and local field-workers, have also had substantial measures of success.

More conventionally, however, the leaders in the developing countries are only symbolically accessible, even within the range of radio and television. The generals of Peru and Brazil fill the news; the activities of the Shah and his family are the daily lead story in Iran; the ministrations of the king of Thailand are a central focus of Thai television. The role of the king in Thailand is integrative indeed. Traditionally, long before the broadcast media were invented, the role of the king entailed the bringing of bounty to disaster-stricken villages, the introduction of innovation to remote rural areas, and intervention in the resolution of conflict. Television has enhanced this kingly role, portraying the king and his entourage descending from the skies into remote villages to introduce the local health or agricultural worker, to bring relief from disease, to distribute gifts.

A very different sort of integrative activity is the sporting event. Identification with the national team participating in an international contest is a powerful focus of attention and creates strong feelings of solidarity. The same thing is true in national competitions. Regional and local teams and leagues competing for a national prize constitute a kind of map of the unity, as well as of the rivalries, within the population. Sports events of this kind provide opportunities for local and regional stations to originate programs that are networked throughout the nation and thus constitute an additional source of pride for the originating region and its broadcasters while reinforcing the feeling that the country is "connected." Soccer in Brazil is one of the best examples of this phenomenon.

We are tempted to say that the presentation of television news may be achieving the opposite result. Viewing the team of seven or nine announcers in one or the other of the hour-long Peruvian news programs, for example, the observer is struck by the exaggerated transplantation of a Western format. Television news in the West was influenced by the entrenched pattern of radio news and the *March of Times* newsreels. Its staccato message, as McLuhan says about newspapers, is that the world is a nervous place. Vaulting from London to Cairo to Rio and back again, its message is alienating except, perhaps, when it shows the national leader at the airport, coming or going, receiving guests or overseeing their departure. Perhaps it suggests that the national airport is the crossroads of the disconnected world. Broadcast news in the standard form may be all very well for the elite, but even that is unlikely. In its present form it is surely unlikely to be of much use to the emergent or aspiring members of a national or international community. Neither the team of intense Peruvian newsmen nor the Iranian announcer reading at equal speed against the rear-projection of silent film or slides is likely to be of genuine relevance in enhancing political participation and sophistication. It is typical for radio and television to spend 20 percent of its total broadcast time on providing information. But is the information understandable? Is thought given to editing the programs to take account of the image of the world in the minds of the viewers or listeners? The developed countries have their own problems here, but it is ironic that the developing countries have adopted not only the same selection of news but also the same formats for its presentation.[5] Neither seems particularly appropriate.

Do the media broaden horizons? Do they, as Lerner suggests, permit "psychic mobility," creating understanding of remote roles such as cabinet minister or police chief or doctor? [6] Perhaps so. And if so, perhaps even the imported programs on television, showing the doctor and the police chief and the mayor, do some good. Good for whom? one might ask. Granting the effectiveness of broadcasting in creating images and presenting models, Marxist theorists would argue, as the Peruvian revolutionaries do, for example, that these are models of individualist striving, of mobility orientation, of hard work and cash reward and dreams of luxury that serve only to reinforce the dependence of the developing countries on the developed ones.[7] Both these positions share two assumptions: that television programming is an active agent of socialization and that entertainment—perhaps even more than information and education—is the decisive form of television's influence.

In any discussion of the role of broadcasting in the promotion of national integration, therefore, we cannot focus simply on the extent of coverage and on information programs. Entertainment is at least as important. At its most elementary level, the shared experience of viewing any program, even "Hawaii Five-0," is an integrative one: it gives people shared heroes and villains, shared metaphors and common topics of conversation for next morning in the fields or in the factories. At another level, one must ask what the content of these symbols are: Who are the heroes? What are their values? What is the message of the settings in which they appear? At yet a third level, one should ask whether the boundaries of one's self, in Lerner's sense, are extended by the experience. Lerner argues the primacy of the medium, no matter what the message.

While these problems are central to our discussion of imported versus indigenous cultural expression, they also have implications for national integration. If the adoption of new horizons tears people from their traditional roles and substitutes new values for old, the integration of society is directly affected. That, of course, is what modernization is all about. In an extreme form, to use the language of Durkheim, it changes the basis of social integration from "mechanical" to "organic," that is, from a society in which every man and his neighbor experience the solidarity of similar occupational and leisure pursuits to a society based on the interdependence resulting from an elaborate division of labor. Thus, Lerner's idea that the media provide insight into the variegated structure of society and serve as substitutes for physical mobility has important implications for social integration. The shared experience of viewing the same program is reminiscent of the shared experience of partaking of a common ritual.

In his study of adolescents in El Salvador, Robert C. Hornik has data to support Lerner's suggestion that the "psychic mobility" made possible by the media may serve as a substitute for physical mobility. He finds that those adolescents whose parents had recently acquired a television set became *less* interested in moving to the city.[8] This echoes what the manager of a local television station in Iran told us: a highly respected local physician had been intending to leave for Tehran because he longed for the life of the big city, but when television came to his town he felt connected again, felt himself part of the cosmopolitan world, and changed his mind about leaving.

Whatever the potential impact of broadcasting, however, one should not forget that only radio has so far made its way out into the countryside. As a senior executive of Nigerian television has said: "Unfortunately it would appear that broadcasting has not been accorded its rightful place in the country. It has always been given a low priority. This is rather sad because of its real possibilities as a powerful instrument for keeping this great nation together."[9]

SOCIOECONOMIC DEVELOPMENT

The last few paragraphs make clear how close and complex are the connections among social integration, cultural values, and economic modernization. The mass media are heavily involved in these relationships.

Continuing this discussion, we ask here how the media have performed with respect to the promise of modernization. In assessing the performance of the media, we make two related points: first, that the media have a share, but certainly not the only share, in the modernization of attitudes and behavior and, second, that the media are at their most effective as support for agents of change on the ground.

The fact is that social and technical change is not brought

about piecemeal but occurs in packages. Modernization is a message that reaches people from many sources. It is difficult to isolate the share that the media have in the overall message system and even more difficult to isolate their effects. At both the individual and aggregate levels, exposure to mass media is correlated in varying degrees with years of schooling, literacy, size of farm, trips to the city, empathy, innovativeness, achievement motivation, and so on.[10] Just as the study of media effects was confounded by other modern stimuli in the West, so the study of media effects is confounded by other modernizing stimuli in the developing countries. The media have a part in all this, but the extent of their direct contribution and whether they are cause or effect are all but impossible to assess.

At the individual level, the data relating media use to modernizing attitudes and practices of peasants seem consistent and persuasive. There are not very many such studies, but they demonstrate quite strong correlations between media exposure and modernity, even when other variables are taken into account. Literacy is even more strongly related. The most recent evidence comes from Inkeles and Smith who insist that their data, though cross-sectional, should probably be read causally: the mass media induce urban workingmen to hold modern attitudes—to feel efficacious, for example.[11]

To a certain extent, then, it is fair to argue that the mass media have an identifiable share in the modernization of individual attitudes and practices. Indicators of economic and political modernity such as empathy (the ability to take the role of the other), innovativeness in agriculture and in the home, or participation in political affairs can each be shown to be related to mass-media exposure. And the magnitude of the correlations, even when other variables are held constant, is impressive compared with comparable studies in modern societies. But, nevertheless, it is clear that intervening variables, social status, for example, do reduce these relationships substantially and that it is better to speak, as does Frederick Frey, in terms of two sets of variables, one defining "exposure to change" and the other, "cognitive flexibility."[12] The first group includes urbanization, literacy, mass-media exposure, and schooling, and the second group encompasses empathy, innovativeness, tolerance of deviant behavior, open-mindedness, and other elements of individual modernity.

Moreover, those studies that have taken a closer look at the influence of mass communication are at pains to point out what the media do not or cannot do. Thus Hornik and others before him have pointed out that there is no evidence to support the assertion that media glamour is responsible for a "revolution of rising frustrations" or, indeed, for any kind of revolution at all, at either individual or national levels.[13] Societies that have more developed mass media do not appear to have experienced greater instability. Individuals who have access to the media tend to be more satisfied with their lives (although not necessarily because of the media) than those who do not.

At the aggregate level, the influence of the media is even more difficult to assess. Frey reviews several studies that have tried to fit national data to Lerner's causal model of development, which proceeds from rates of urbanism to rates of literacy to mass-media growth to political participation (such as voting rates). The variables are surely related, as all the studies agree, but the sequence of their causal links is not clear; the one that stands up best is the one linking media exposure to political participation.[14]

But, following Philip Elliott and Peter Golding's warning, let us not make the mistake of assuming that the polity emerges only as the denouement in the drama of modernization.[15] The polity is there to receive the electronic media when they arrive at the dock, and its leaders and rulers are careful to put them under tight security. That social integration may be enhanced thereby or that the basis of social solidarity may be affected is the point of our story so far.

It follows that the mass media tend to be closely linked to the sorts of opinions and behavior that are considered modern, but the mass media do not act alone. It is an error to exaggerate the power of radio and television to induce change by themselves.

Attitudes and actions are most influenced by mass communications when the latter are linked with, and reinforced by, agents of change in the field. Thus, the effective teaching of improved farm methods is best accomplished through the combined efforts of radio and, say, a network of agricultural agents. Educational broadcasting, whether intensive or extensive, is more likely to succeed when the teachers have been trained to incorporate the broadcasts into their teaching. When a religious radio message is reinforced by a catechist, it has a chance of sinking in.[16] And so on for messages in the fields of health, family planning, literacy, and the other subjects that have become part of modernizing campaigns.[17]

New information, as distinct from new attitudes and actions, is often acquired directly from the mass media. Thus news of the existence of a new fertilizer or of a new method of birth control is efficiently communicated via the mass media in situations where the media are widely available. Similarly, generalized images and "enriching" content may also be communicated effectively by the media without benefit of intermediaries. But modernizing campaigns aimed at achieving change in the relatively short run depend on a communications system that combines the efficient diffusion of information with opportunities for reinforcement, discussion, and feedback. These opportunities require the use of trusted agents of influence in addition to the mass media. The performance of the broadcast media in the fields of development, as in education, depends on two factors: the amount of attention given to development problems by the mass media and the extent to which these development efforts are linked with agents of change in the field.

Indeed, the same intervening variables that act to speed or retard the flow of mass communication in modern societies have been rediscovered in traditional ones.[18] If it is true that China has been as successful in its use of the media as is sometimes claimed, it is almost certainly because of monopolization.[19] Unlike Russia, which is reached by foreign broadcasts, radio in mainland China is limited, almost without exception, to the national broadcasting service, which is distributed, in large measure, to wired one-channel sets. And where the media are associated with diffusion of change, it is certainly because of canalization, whereby the new is linked symbolically with an already established attitude.[20] Most important of all is the role of supplementation: the media are at their most effective when they are linked with a social infrastructure dedicated to doing a certain job, as when the media reinforce the work of the teacher, the agricultural agent, the "farm forum" type of discussion group, the literacy corps worker, the health worker, or the local influential.

On the whole, the media appear to be responsive to development campaigns. They allocate time to education in agriculture, health, home economics, and the like. But while they may give such campaigns time and attention, the extent to which their professional hearts are in it depends on the lead given by their controlling authorities. We have the impression that this is not always the case.

Sometimes, attention is given in the form of advertising slogans, pointing listeners and viewers to a modernizing campaign by means of brief messages and jingles. Family-planning messages are often presented in this way. A number of countries have pressed their commercial radio channels into the service of campaigns to buy home-produced goods, proceeding on the assumption that if the media stimulate consumption anyway, why not direct the consumer to local products? Indonesia and Tanzania are both following this policy. Sometimes the message is incorporated in regular programs "for the farmer," "for the housewife," or "for the parent." Instructional programs are often of this type, asking the child or adult to set aside a fixed period of time to follow a given subject. The former kind of message can, at best, create "awareness." Systematic instruction can lead to change or learning, to the extent that it links up with a personal agent of change. That is not to say that the housewife or the farmer does not learn the odd trick of the trade or sometimes a more basic skill from such programs; we mean only to emphasize that a campaign aiming at large-scale change cannot be achieved by the mass media alone, even when special programs are set aside for that purpose.[21]

Another form into which messages of modernization are increasingly incorporated is the serial story. Broadcasters in Europe and North America have been doing this since the 1950s. "The Archers," a serialized story about an English family of farmers who discuss the problem of dealing with inflation or of experimenting with a new hybrid seed, is a famous example. A family-planning message in Iran was disseminated in this way.

Other countries have programs built around wise men who dispense advice in street-corner or coffeehouse settings, and often modernizing ideas are incorporated into these. We found considerable thought being given to this sort of thing in South America. There, the *telenovela* has been used as the vehicle for communicating modernizing ideas and values. In Rio an installment series using the *telenovela* form is combined with textbook exercise and leads to a certificate attesting to four years of elementary school. Thousands of workers have taken the course in order to present the necessary academic qualification for factory employment. Also in Brazil, the major television network has created a *novela* around the theme of ecology: a village agent of modernization comes into conflict with traditional leadership and thereby reflects also the generational conflict. The great success of the serial "Simplemente Maria" in Peru is often used as an example of how, even unwittingly, the strong identification with the heroine of many of these stories can lead to change. The effectiveness of this kind of false consciousness is scoffed at by some educational broadcasters and condemned as misleading by moralists. But the idea of making the devil do God's work has for many years been implemented by media planners and other agents of change.

Community viewing centers, such as those set up by the Broadcasting Company of Northern Nigeria (BCNN), besides enabling people in rural areas to gain access to television, are often good reinforcers of such messages. As meeting places they become, in effect, group learning centers that, like group psychotherapy, are often more effective than addressing people as isolated individuals. Traditional gathering places, such as marketplaces, teahouses, pubs, tavernas, and coffeehouses, serve all societies as crucibles for the formation of public opinion. The presence of television sets in such situations enlarges the range of subjects for discussion and informal learning; thus providing sets could be a good investment as part of a wider process of modernization.

Tanzania and Senegal have both conducted successful experiments with the use of community listening and viewing groups. The Senegal experiment, building on a traditional model of village talk sessions, has been highly successful. It consists of a twice-weekly recorded exchange between rural-development experts and a group of villagers, dealing with rural themes. Listeners are encouraged to write, and their letters are usually read during a following program, thus bringing problems to the notice of government officials. Listening groups organized in connection with the program, as well as individual listeners, have the feeling, we are told, that this form of two-way communication is satisfying and effective. Other countries have also used broadcasting in the service of this kind of ombudsman function. Singapore, for example, has done so in connection with consumer prices, but not usually in a setting of organized listening.

The most extensive use of such linkage mechanisms among our cases is that of Tanzania, described earlier. On the other hand, we found little evidence of continuity in the use of radio to aid the development of the Kazvin area in Iran after a UNESCO experiment was concluded there. But successful examples of cooperation between agencies of change and broadcast media may be found in Algeria and, to take a rather different kind of example, in the shortwave links established and maintained by Christian missionaries with Indians in the highlands of Peru.

So there is evidence of success when the media are linked to organized agencies of change or to informal or formal listener forums. The trouble is that this linkage is only seldom achieved. In Iran, for example, there is little or no joint planning between broadcasting and the conscripted members of the elaborately planned health corps or literary corps. Though the nation is justly proud of these field-workers, broadcasting is essentially uninvolved. The experiments one reads and hears about, those collected by ourselves as well as those reported in the literature, are typically not carried out on a large scale. Nor are they institutionalized in continued cooperation between agents of change and broadcasters.

The analogy with the lack of careful planning in the use of school broadcasts is instructive. The problems of coordinating instructional broadcasts with the curriculum, of training teachers to use the broadcasts constructively, of providing sets to the schools have all been described. It is no wonder that both broadcasters and educators tend to prefer "enrichment" to "instruction": this formula commits neither side to effective integration with the other. But we believe that even enrichment programs can be strongly reinforced by being discussed. Sometimes parent and child make up the ideal listening-and-discussion unit, but this arrangement is rarely encouraged. Certain versions of "Sesame Street," a children's program that has been adopted around the world, do seem successfully to promote such interaction.

The need to connect planning for education and development with broadcasting policy is becoming more salient. The UNESCO group that proposed the expansion of educational broadcasting for children and adults in Thailand was extremely sensitive to the need for this kind of linkage. Its plan calls for linking programs of adult education to activities in community centers and teahouses, and it proposes that careful attention be given to the integration of radio broadcasting with the school system, its staff and curriculum. The plan is to emphasize the role of broadcast education in smoothing the transition from tradition to modernity without upsetting the village structure.

The amount of time devoted to specifically developmental themes cannot easily be estimated from the categories of programs, because development may come under a variety of headings ranging from the *telenovela* in Brazil to women's programs in Nigeria. Current affairs and documentaries also are often directly relevant. Using the more restricted category of adult education, the figures vary widely from country to country; the average falls somewhere above 5 percent of total time for each medium. But a recent report from Nigeria suggests that radio is increasingly responsive to development themes.[22]

Within the rules of the game then—those transplanted from the West—broadcasting in most of the new countries is playing a part in development. But do Western rules apply? Why should the allocation of communication resources in countries suffering from illiteracy, poverty, and disease be made in the same way as in the countries of the West? Why should countries struggling with the mobilization of manpower or with the forging of a common language be allocating their time, the scarcest of all resources, according to an imported formula? Tanzania, for one, seems to have broken away from the formula, although the establishment of its new commercial channel raises doubts. Senegal also seemed to be applying its media to developmental problems, at least until the reintroduction of television in 1972, just in time for the Olympic Games.

An intensive campaign of development needs a different kind of broadcasting policy. This means a different kind of programming and a system of linkages to other institutions in the community. These changes, in turn, must be accompanied by a different set of audience expectations of the media. Dr. Estella Garland, an educational television expert in Peru, called this matter to our attention most cogently. If the Indians of the Sierra are to benefit from the massive campaign of change being proposed by the Peruvian planners, she argues, their introduction to television, now that the network is being expanded, should not be to the universal programming formula. Their expectations already appear to be in the realm of development: health, education, agriculture, the Spanish language. These expectations can be met, in some measure, by the broadcast media. Why then not provide a radio and television service that will serve these expectations? Why ask these people to change their expectations, so that they look forward to Saturday nights with "Kojak"? [23]

Indeed, policymakers in the field of development cannot ignore the whole of the program schedule, even if they succeed in planting their message within it. Increasingly, they will have to face the criticism of the committed researchers and ideologues who find values in the prime-time programs that run counter to the goals of modernization.

Fatalism, for example, is a recurrent theme in the *telenovela*, says one researcher, and the underlying message is that place in the social order continues to be ascribed rather than based on achievement.[24] Violence in interpersonal relations is another theme that has come under attack, as have the values of acquisitiveness and materialism. Even "Sesame Street" has been sharply criticized by South American researchers who say that its latent function is to socialize the child to accept television advertising and perhaps even to accept authority unquestioningly. Reformist Peru has refused to allow "Plaza Sesamo" to be shown "because the reality with which the child is put into contact through the program is a reality adjusted to elitism, consumerism, fantasy, unreflexive obedience . . . very modern and attractive, but conceptually traditional and excluding."[25] When broadcasting planners say that it is "alienating" to categorize programs as information or education or entertainment, this is part of what they mean.

CULTURAL CONTINUITY AND CHANGE

The issue of the alien versus the indigenous entered, inevitably, into our discussion of the functions of broadcasting for national integration and socioeconomic development. But cultural continuity and authenticity of self-expression were seen as a promise of broadcasting in their own right. Of the three goals for broadcasting that we have been considering here, the role of broadcasting in cultural development is the most recent.

The goal of authentic cultural self-expression is related, as are the other foci of broadcasting policy, to events both external and internal to broadcasting. It is a particularly complicated area, perhaps because of the dual recognition that (1) there is some contradiction between it and the other goals of development (national integration and socioeconomic growth) and (2) the business of broadcasting, whatever the content of its programs, *is* culture.

These two points need elaboration. The first is an expression of concern by intellectuals and others in the new states who do want modernization but also want the reinforcement of their national identities. They begin to realize that standardization and secularization are side effects of the modernization process. They see people around them adapting their farming to cash crops, only to find their children moving to the city. They see people listening to radio, viewing television, beginning to dress differently, and whistling Western songs. They see people accepting the idea that some part of the future is in their own hands and abandoning some of the ancient arts and crafts. Even those most committed to modernization sometimes ask whether there are no more authentic forms of response to change than the wholesale adoption of Western popular culture. Others go so far as to ask whether improved methods of production really counterbalance the loss of traditional ways of life. These are the people who fear the homogenization of the world by Western popular culture. These are people who fear that the symbols of new nationhood are no subsitutute for the continuity of ancient tradition. When this awakening is accompanied by a nationalist motive to shake off a colonial tradition, as in Algeria, for example, the search for indigenous roots—Geertz's "essentialism"—is the more intense.[26]

On occasion these voices of neotraditionalism are joined by the voices of certain politicians and planners. These may or may not be much concerned with the conflict between modernity and authenticity, but they are concerned with the potential uses of tradition for advancing modernization wherever the two can be linked. "Inca socialism" is an example of the instrumental use of tradition to promote modern Peruvian policy.

These voices converge on broadcasting and elaborate the second of the two points referred to above. In an earlier period, when national planners became interested in broadcasting, their concern tended to focus on its informational and educational potential for promoting political, economic, and social development. Entertainment, the largest quantitative component of broadcasting, tended to be regarded as neutral from a political and developmental point of view, as a useful source of psychological diversion from the strains of society. However, as concern over the fate of indigenous arts and traditional values began to grow, there was a realization that radio and television entertainment is not simply neutral but value-laden. There followed the realization that "the media are American" in Jeremy Tunstall's phrase,[27] or, from a more radical perspective, that the media are an extension of "American empire," as Herbert Schiller argues.[28] What they surely are not, says the neotraditionalist, are Persian, Senegalese, Peruvian, or Nigerian.

There is some truth in these observations although they are not as simple, or as true, as they appear at first glance. Moreover, there is a tendency to use the media as scapegoats for everything that has gone wrong in society. Television has been blamed for the rise in the rate of violence and for changing mores, as well as for the decline in the traditional arts, not just in the new nations but in the older ones as well.

In addressing ourselves to the performance of broadcasting with respect to cultural continuity and change, it is necessary, therefore, to take account of the complexity of the subject.

First of all, the media are by no means uniformly American, at least not in the superficial sense that all the material broadcast is imported from the United States. In radio, the American influence is even less, although radio's two staples—music and news—are heavily influenced by foreign materials and fashions. It is true that American (sometimes Anglo-American) music is popular with young people almost everywhere; the best-liked station in Lima, for example, broadcasts American music almost exclusively. On the other hand, Zairian music is a firm favorite with Tanzanian audiences, and Arab music with Algerian audiences.

Insofar as American music penetrates radio services, it may be because the rhythms of modernization are implicit in it. More important, probably, is that changing fashions in music are a defining mark of each new adolescent generation, and processes of modernization tend to breed peer groups in need of such symbols of demarcation. Most important of all, perhaps, is the American music industry's sheer output of records and tapes which is able to keep pace with the ravenous demand for new material by the hundreds of thousands of radio stations of this world. Researchers are all too aware of the supply side of the equation, but they often seem to ignore the size of the vacuum that creates the voracious demand, as much for films and television programs as for popular music.

The other major component of radio, the news program, is also supplied from sources abroad, most particularly from the Western (largely Anglo-American) news agencies. The process of producing bulletins, however, allows for a large degree of local intervention, and it is by no means self-evident that radio news is dictated overseas. In fact, radio in most countries is experienced as intimate; the disc jockey and announcer manage to make even foreign culture sound familiar. If anything, radio in the developing countries errs on the side of casualness and lack of professionalism—by Western standards.[29]

A more subtle blend of the imported and the indigenous is to be observed in the importation of ideas for doing things rather than the things themselves. Thus we have noted that the favorite music of rural Thais is indigenous, but that the audience researchers call it "country and Western" because it is a local blend of traditional folk music and the American counterpart.[30] Radio seems to have provided this sort of stimulus to local composers everywhere. About Iran, for example, one of our respondents observed that radio has been at the same time the principal patron and conservator of the Persian musical tradition and the most active agent in the vulgarization and hybridization of that tradition. The respondent added that in this sort of activity television had already surpassed radio. Apart from music, radio has had a formidable effect upon popular culture, where its impetus has been toward the acceleration of westernization, and more specifically Americanization, of the more superficial aspects of the life-style of urban society.

As a consequence of the production problems that we have already defined, the content of television tends to be less indigenous than that of radio. We have already noted the high proportion of imported programs in many countries. These programs are, moreover, concentrated during peak viewing hours, so the effective proportion of foreign programming is even higher if it is calculated in terms of audience impact. And much that is not directly imported may be derived from an imported model or stimulus that has been translated into local terms. Salesmen for the international television marketers come equipped not only with packages of film and tape but also with catalogs of ideas for local production which are for sale: quiz number E-46, for example.

The standardization of television around the world is further reflected in the program schedules that we examined in the previous chapter and in the proportional distribution of programs by category. The variations by country are slight: the French tradition (in Algeria and Senegal) includes more talk and current affairs; the South American tradition gives prime time to *novelas*. Cyprus, Algeria, and Senegal make more deliberate selections of foreign material in order to give explicit emphasis to their cultural ties to Greece, the Arab countries, and France respectively, thus symbolically distancing themselves from Anglo-American global culture.

There are, however, important examples both of indigenous programming and of imaginative adaptation of formats in radio and television which must be given if we are to tell the whole story. At least a few examples are to be found in most countries, and we report several of them here in order to bring some central issues into focus. South America is a good place to begin. We have already noted the impact of the thirty- or sixty-minute *telenovela*, shown five days a week, hundreds of episodes long, which is made for television in Mexico, Venezuela, Argentina, Brazil, and elsewhere. Mexican television thrives on the export of its *telenovelas*. But the form is also being used creatively. In Mexico itself, the *telenovela* has been adapted to the presentation of historical drama, to tell the story of Mexico's march to independence. We are interested to note that during our visit to Algeria the broadcasters there were debating the same question: How do we translate Algeria's epic struggle for independence into television terms?

In Brazil, the largest of the networks, Globo-TV, has commissioned some of the country's best writers to create stories in the *novela* form. And they are doing so: the late-evening *novela* (there are three *novelas* each evening) is now a "serious" affair, relating to real-life people (rather than escapist dreams) and contemporary social issues. It is an interesting example of a carefully considered and costly initiative by an oligopoly to improve the quality of the product. That the move is probably a response to the increasingly vocal concern of government with matters of television makes the achievement no less real.

Several lessons are to be learned here. First of all, in its various forms the domestic serial seems to be the most popular genre of television the world over.[31] Locally produced, it is even more widely accepted than the imported action-adventure story, production of which is limited to the U.S., England, France, and Japan.

A second lesson, then, is the challenge to the widespread

assumption that American thrillers and Westerns are necessarily the most popular programs everywhere. It is fascinating, admittedly, to see how easily such programs cross national boundaries. Visual action, not words, is surely a key to the answer, and it would be of great value, now that entertainment is being taken more seriously, to study the meanings these programs carry in different cultures and the functions they serve. But their popularity notwithstanding, the fact is that certain homemade programs—especially the homemade soap opera—almost always outdraw them in popularity, technical sophistication notwithstanding. Thus, Iran's most popular program is colorful "Morad Barghi" 's discourses to his family; the story of a moralizing taxi driver, his clients, and his comrades is one of Senegal's leading programs. The "Village Schoolmaster" in Nigeria provides a continuous vehicle for the confrontation between the modernizing agents and the forces of conservatism. Cyprus and Israel both began their locally produced dramatic presentations with a family soap opera. The characters are familiar, the setting is recognizable, the problems are real, even if exaggerated and sentimentalized.

A third lesson from the Brazilian experience is that the status and authenticity of broadcasting as an art can be considerably enhanced when artists established in other media are used. The broadcast media cannot be genuinely creative unless they cultivate and harness the other creative arts in the society. It is extremely difficult to establish a Western-style television system without a tradition of theater, a local film industry, and experienced craftsmen in the other graphic arts. Most Asian countries have highly productive film industries. The Indian film industry is well known, but other Asian countries are very active as well—much more active, proportionately, than most European countries. In Senegal, we found that the active local theater and film studios were a great asset in the introduction of television, although the lack of formal agreement with the writers' and filmmakers' guilds has impeded the cultivation of these alliances. The introduction of television in Colombia, on the orders of General Rojas when he took office, made early use of a tradition of theater in the country.[32] Thai television immediately employed the dubbing troupes that, for years, have ad-libbed translations of imported foreign films in the movie theaters (and still do). Patronage by broadcasting of these allied arts is of central importance to creativity and authenticity on radio and television.

South American television has another original aspect, the ebullient celebrity presiding over a variety show of great duration, sometimes six or seven hours long. While this format seems to be on the decline, it is interesting to note both the "folksy" quality of these shows and their open-ended character. In this kind of program the format seems to have defeated the tendency of television to be transferred to the new nations complete with the stop-watches so essential to the Western obsession with precise fifteen, thirty-, and sixty-minute segments. It is worth asking whether creativity in broadcasting in the new nations might not benefit from the more widespread assertion of this freedom from the rigidities of Western time frames.

The earliest days of Thai television contained a much higher proportion of indigenous creativity and of televised material based on traditional art forms such as the shadow play, the dance theater, puppeteering, and so on. The decline in the proportion of these original productions in Thailand and elsewhere followed the increase in the number of hours of broadcasting, the easy importation of foreign films and serials, and the invention of the videotape recorder, as well as, perhaps, just plain exhaustion.[33] The fact is that Thailand has several classical dramatic forms that have not yet found their place in television; the national theater is the last preserve of the dance-drama, for example. Instead Thailand is importing gory Japanese thrillers at a very high rate vying with that of the importation of American series. One wonders why the native traditions of theater find so little real expression in the broadcast media? On the other hand, Thailand has a film industry that produces over a hundred films per year; television does show its share of these films, many of which are reminiscent, however, of the *telenovela*. Indeed, one wonders how much these "Easterns," which are rather similar, we are told, to the films produced in Iran, India, Turkey, and the other Asian countries that have substantial film industries, are based on indigenous themes and how much they are influenced by Western models.[34]

One of the traditional Thai forms has been successful on both radio and television. This is the *mau lum* folk opera, or song-story, of which Dr. S. J. Tambiah writes:

> A measure of the contemporary appreciation of it is that wherever the radio has spread into the villages the programme most avidly listened to is *mau lam*. The entertainment appeal of *mau lum* stems from the fact that much of its content is drawn from the pool of north-eastern tales and myths . . . rather flexibly constructed rhyming songs [with] room to improvise and be adept at repartee. The *mau lum* singers not only preserve and propagate religious traditions; they are also the channel through whom certain stories and epics, popularly known and appreciated in northern and central Thailand, are passed on to the north-eastern villagers. They sing stories about the life of the Buddha which are nationally known and in a different form are heard in the temple . . . The repertoire includes courtship and love poetry, burlesque and earthy, bawdy jokes; it echoes and stimulates the romantic sentiments of the young men and women.[35]

Traditionally, the *mau lum* singers travel widely, particularly in the northeast of the country, appearing at all-night sessions of fairs held in the temple grounds. Efforts have been made to expand their repertoire to take account of campaigns of rural development, anticommunist propaganda, and other contemporary and development topics. "To the extent to which the singers take to [the new texts]," writes Dr. Tambiah, "a truly grass-roots propaganda machine will have been harnessed by the government to promote its political and socio-economic policies."

Other broadcasting systems, too, have successfully incorporated traditional media. Some of the *griot* (praise singers) of Senegal, for example, who sing of lineages and history as chroniclers of an oral tradition, are on the regular payroll of the radio and television service.

Here, too, are several important principles for us to consider: (1) The distinction between information, education, and entertainment is of little relevance to these artistic traditions. (2) An art form, such as the *mau lum*, which is associated with festivity and holiday, can be sufficiently secularized and standardized to fit the time slots and production formats of radio and television. (3) The incorporation of contemporary references is well established in many traditional art forms in which entertainment is the essential vehicle of information. (4) Art forms that traditionally take place outdoors have been successfully moved into the studio.

Why is it so difficult, then, to marry the broadcast media to the traditional performing arts?

One reason is that these arts tend to be eclipsed by the pace of modernization. As far as we are able to judge, this is not primarily because of broadcasting. The traditional storyteller of the Iranian teahouse or the Ruhozi theater-on-the-pool (played by an itinerant troupe with a limited repertoire and much audience participation) began to disappear before the rise of television.[36] The Ruhozi, in fact, began to decline even before the rise of radio. To choose another example, the classical dance-drama of Thailand, one of the great achievements of its high artistic traditions, survives only under the patronage of the national theater, and the theater is the only training school for artists. Similarly, the national theater in Japan is the only remaining school for Kabuki actors; the family tradition that passed the art from father to son has been broken by the arrival of occupational mobility.[37]

The causes for this eclipse appear to be the causes of modernization and mobility, both social and geographical. Richard Hoggart blames the tourists for the Westernization, if not the decline, of the dance-drama in Bali.[38] It is not primarily a performing art, he argues. The same is probably true of other art forms deriving from communal celebration or religious traditions: they do not easily survive the intrusion of spectators and the process of secularization.

A second reason for the difficulty in transposing these traditional forms is their limited repertoires and the demand for novelty fostered by the mass media. Many traditions are built on a very small number of classical themes, which are rapidly exhausted by radio or television. Although the themes of broadcast drama—love, death, conflict between good and evil—are no more numerous, the greater resources of the media allow them to be presented in more varied forms, thus rendering the audiences impatient with the traditional limitations on form. Those artistic traditions that do succeed on radio or television tend to have the facility for refreshing and varying their material by means such as the contemporary allusions in the *mau lum* or the *griot* song histories. Where there is a fixed or sacred repertoire, radio and television seem to be inhospitable.

Broadcasters and artists in several countries called to our attention the incompatibility between the traditional location of some of the best-liked of their performing arts (in the open, on the village square) and the constraints of the sometimes very tiny television studio. (Curiously, this constraint is felt less by radio producers.) This problem was emphasized in both Algeria and Nigeria. Part of the problem is the bias imported from less favored climates which leads professionals to think that even in an open-air society the studio is where broadcasting belongs. As a consequence, capital investment in most countries has gone into fixed studios and equipment rather than into mobile broadcast units. But the difference is also of a sociocultural kind. There *is* a certain incompatibility between "inside" and "outside" because an outside location limits the degree of control that broadcasters can exercise over their operations. The participatory and unpredictable nature of the "outside" audience, on the one hand, and the freedom of movement of artists in the open, on the other, create an entirely different production environment. They also create an entirely different "consumption" environment: more casual, more intermittant, and yet possibly more attentive. Communal listening and viewing of this kind could well constitute growing points for the diffusion of radio and television. The communal radio set is already widely available. The communal television set is a necessity in the diffusion of television in developing countries. Perhaps it has advantages over individual viewing. We have already noted the importance of the traditional meeting places. Coffeehouse discussions of the content of the newspaper were, and in some places still are, the breeding place of public opinion. Perhaps television should be oriented much more to being seen in the teahouse or the village square.

Still another difficulty, which Western broadcasters also face in their use of some traditional arts, is the festive and occasional character of many of these arts. They cannot be made into just another program on a Tuesday evening. Here, the broadcast media are caught in a paradox. Some of the best and most authentic of their materials are appropriate to special occasions, yet the imported orthodoxy of broadcasting prescribes "continuous performance." Perhaps television would be better if it were less continuous; perhaps the aim should not be to be on the air every day for as many hours as possible. It is no coincidence that broadcasting is often at its best on feast days and holidays when it has something "special" to say. The media often rise to these occasions with special bursts of creativity. They manage to catch the mood and enhance the celebration of both traditional and modern holidays. In devising new national holidays appropriate to the independent status of their countries, governments often show acute awareness of the potential role of the media.

THE TRANSLATION OF TRADITION

Our entire discussion of the problems of broadcasting and culture turns on the fundamental question of whether the media are capable of contributing to "essentialism," as defined by Geertz, or whether they are its sworn enemy, agents of "epochalism" or worse.[39] It is clear that the media are capable of "opening a window to the world," even if the view can be distorted and, in the opinion of some, demeaning. It is clear that they are natural allies of the forces of modernization and development, however casually or unintentionally they pursue those goals. What is not clear is whether the values and artistic traditions of the society must also make way, along with the methods of subsistence farming, for the homogenized popular culture of the West.

In the last few pages, we have given some examples of successful coping by the broadcast media with the challenge of cultural continuity, and we have said something about the ingredients of these successful efforts: joining forces with the traditional performing arts through cultivation and patronage; drawing on those arts that can handle contemporaneity in the context of tradition; building on special occasions such as holidays; going "outside" for both production and reception. But the problem goes beyond specific programs, even special programs. In the absence of clearly identified standards of their own, new countries find it easiest to adopt the style of Western television and radio programs as if the instructions for presenting a news program or a variety show came wrapped together with instructions for assembling the microphones and cameras. Indeed, we have noted that these formulas are for sale as well and tend further to standardize the broadcast media around the world.

One wonders whether this has to be. Cannot Nigerian or Peruvian or Senegalese television be more indigenous, not just in programming, but in style? What is needed are more radical suggestions for making radio and television relevant for peoples who have more important problems than those that can be solved by Chief Ironside. Tanzania is an example of a country that has tried, and Peru is another that is talking about it. Their ideas are not based only on the content of specific programs but on a different conception of the role of the media. Radio and television need to be "reinvented" in a sense. But how? How can tradition be translated into the language of the broadcast media?

One idea is to make certain that producers have a deeper grounding in their own cultural traditions and not only in the traditions and technology of metropolitan broadcasting. Informants in several countries told us how ill-informed broadcasters are about the traditional arts of their own societies and about ceremonies and values of their own cultures. The techniques of producing and directing are mistakenly thought of as content. Sorting this out may lead to a more creative blending of the old and the new.

This idea perhaps can be further developed. A society concerned over the use of broadcasting for cultural continuity might experiment with the establishment of an "institute for the translation of tradition," whose members would give serious thought to traditional forms and content, on the one hand, and to the language of the media, on the other. Experts in the tradition, scholars and researchers, could sit together with producers and directors in an effort to find solutions to the problem of "domesticating" the broadcast media. What is needed are not programs *about* tradition but a series of creative acts that will take the mood or style of a culture and translate it into broadcasting terms.

For example, broadcasting systems everywhere have to solve the problem of how to mourn: there are holidays of mourning such as punctuate the calendar of Islam, or commemorative mourning on the anniversary of wars, or mourning as on the death of a leader or a great man. All cultures provide conventions for such occasions. There are rituals to be followed and symbols to be displayed, pleasures to be denied, and a variety of enabling means through which people can commune with the living and the dead. These rules are not readily translated into the language of radio and television, yet the more modern a society becomes, the more its broadcasting is expected to take the lead on such occasions. Spontaneously, or by imitating foreign models, broadcasting stations do their best. Often, they simply transmit the rituals and ceremonies as they are enacted outside the studio. The celebration of Shi'ite Islam of the deaths of Ali and Hussein, the death of John Kennedy in the United States, the mourning for the dead of the wars in Europe, the commemoration in Israel of the holocaust that brought death to six million Jews are all improvised by the media. For example, the replacement of scheduled radio programs by the broadcasting of classical music is the accepted form of broadcast mourning in Israel. But little or no systematic effort is given anywhere to finding authentic solutions to the problems of how broadcasting might capture the mood of the tradition. Obviously, the answer is not to be found ready-made in the traditional sources, but rather in a creative welding of the old and the new.

Celebration of Sunday and of the Sabbath are other examples. Christianity and Judaism have a day each week that is not simply a day off but one endowed with spiritual significance. Other cultures have similar days. Islam has an entire month of Ramadan. The challenge to broadcasting is to discover forms that capture the spirit of these occasions, more for the modernizing groups in the society than for the

traditional ones. The standard solution for Sunday is a pre-
scribed amount of air time devoted to religious programs
and other presentations that are a little more highbrow than
usual. Are there no solutions more authentic?

Creativity based on the interaction of research, tradition,
and the media would be the primary charge of the institute.
But within the context of an institute of this kind producers
could also be trained in their own cultures. They could be
sent out into the countryside to observe and record the
traditional performing arts. They could be assigned to listen to the radio and to view television—preferably their
own programs—together with families and groups in traditional settings. They could be asked to analyze the meanings and the functions of different sorts of programs for
these groups. They might study and observe the teahouse
or coffeehouse as forms of community center in which communication goes on. The issue of differentiating information, education, and entertainment in program schedules
could be thrashed out.

The performance of broadcasting in the realm of cultural
continuity has until now fallen short of the promise held
out for it. Indigenous self-expression, which requires initiative and the confidence to experiment, still tends to take
second place to the use of the standardized forms exported
from the metropolitan centers, not just in content but in
style. There is a need to link the media with other arts,
traditional and modern, from which ideas will flow. There
is a need to create programs that will give authentic expression to the culture in the process of its confrontation with
modernity. But more than this, there is the need to try—at
least to try—to employ broadcasting in ways that will better fit the moods and styles of the national heritage and of
its special occasions. Perhaps the luxury of immersing producers in their own cultures and forming creative groups of
broadcasters, scholars, and carriers of the tradition, who
will plan schedules and invent programs together, holds out

a fragile hope that broadcasting might live up to its promise of contributing to cultural continuity.

It is all too easy, of course, to suppress free expression in the name of culturally authentic creativity. But even for men of good will, the commitment to authenticity in the media poses a dilemma: how does one reconcile this commitment with the equally compelling commitment to promote mass communication that permits the exchange of ideas among individuals and among nations? The dilemma is a genuine one and therefore cannot be perfectly resolved. Rather, rapidly developing societies must steer a practical course that refuses to sacrifice authenticity to modernity and refuses to sacrifice freedom to authenticity.

Part Four

Prospect

7

Are There Other Ways?

BROADCASTING ORGANIZATIONS AND GOVERNMENT

The evidence presented in the preceding chapters indicates that the situation of broadcasting in many developing countries is a matter for concern. We recognize that our work has been in the nature of a spot check at one particular period of the history of broadcasting in the countries concerned. Thus, although we have sometimes been tempted to regard our viewpoint as terminal, it is nothing of the kind. Nonetheless, the period of our intervention was not wholly insignificant. In most of the countries that we studied the initial phases of the introduction or consolidation of broadcasting had been completed. In addition, governments in all countries were found to be grappling with the consequences of a quarter century of unprecedented effort to increase among their populations the will and the ability to develop. The consequences of these efforts have been more ambivalent than governments expected. The growing awareness of the world beyond their immediate neighborhoods has made the vast underprivileged populations aware that there are many people whose lives are less nasty, brutish, and short than their own, and that much of the wealth of the prosperous section of the community derives from the deprivation of the masses. More important even, there has been spread abroad an awareness of the possibility of a change for the better.

While colonial rule continued, those countries under

such rule hoped that the solution of the inequities articulated by this new awareness lay in the achievement of political independence. Those countries already independent, or that became independent soon after the end of the war, found that political independence as such did not solve their socioeconomic problems. Varying degrees of political instability followed independence in most of the countries we have studied.

Broadcasting has played a significant part in these developments. The pattern whereby the broadcasting station, together with the airport and the presidential palace (or its equivalent), has come to be the first location to be attacked and, if possible, occupied when a coup or revolution occurs indicates the central importance that has come to be attached to the control of the broadcasting media. In countries where the organization of broadcasting is too diverse to allow insurgents to achieve control of the broadcasting system by the occupation of one or two key broadcasting installations, a combination of two factors tends to operate. The government, or possibly different sections of government and the armed forces, maintain their own stations, so as to have direct access to a broadcasting station when necessary; and the tolerance shown to independent stations depends on their abstention from the transmission of controversial political material, as well as on their compliance with instructions from whatever arm of government happens to be in effective control.

For this reason the most striking fact to emerge from our study is the virtual abandonment, throughout the developing world, of Western patterns of broadcasting in which, however defined, the broadcasting system has some element of autonomy from the government of the day. We have discussed the variations on this theme that exist in different parts of Europe and North America.

Newly independent, or postrevolutionary, or radical reformist governments have found it difficult to allow broadcasting organizations their heads. In the first place they are rarely more inclined than their predecessors to open themselves to criticism. In the second place, confronted with the formidable task of modernization these governments are often motivated by a sense of mission and wish to avoid a situation in which this mission might be cut short. The fear of broadcasting as a potentially disruptive factor seems to occupy policymakers even more than its potentially positive role, but in either case it is rare for broadcasting to be left outside the direct control of government.

It may be asked what difference the development of political parties makes to a situation of this kind. If there were genuine multiparty government, we would expect the demand by all shades of opinion for access to the broadcast media to inject an element of independence into the activities of the broadcasters. But whereas we have found situations in which room is allowed for criticism of government or, more often, of the bureaucracy in a one-party state, we cannot say that any one of our case-study countries has effective machinery for peaceful political change, such as is provided by a genuine multiparty system. The majority of countries in our sample have monopoly parties, usually arising from the unifying circumstances of the struggle for independence. This phenomenon of one-party government in the developing countries has been explained by David Apter: "Modernizing political parties can go much further than their Western counterparts because they, in effect, serve as microcosms of the new societies. Even when the parties are monopolistic (that is, when the party's ideology is the foundation of legitimate authority in the state), their structures incorporate such diversity that the real instruments of bargaining and debate in the country, the 'legislatures,' are the party congresses, the presidium, or the national party executive rather than the formal governmental organisation." [1] Since Apter wrote these words the predominance of one-party states has increased, but the point about the inclusive character of many of these parties remains valid.

Moreover, the relationship of party to government in a one-party state is essentially different from the relationship that prevails in a multiparty state. And whether in this context one speaks of a single party or of the army that has, usually for the time being, taken control of the country's affairs does not really matter. There is a substantial element of concurrence in situations of this kind. The party certainly (the army to a much lesser extent) assumes, or is assigned, responsibilities that would elsewhere be undertaken by direct agents of government. In Tanzania, and to some extent in Senegal, the local party cadres at area and village levels are essential links in the relationship between government and people. The party provides these links through its organizational, educational, and hortative functions in addition to its conventional electoral and parliamentary activities. These wider functions derive from the role of the party during the colonial regime, which tended to attribute to it the characteristics of a parallel or "shadow" administration during the final period of colonialism. As and when these countries achieved independence the party became the driving force of government, pushing the government along to achieve its objectives. In such a situation there is bound to be "a blurring of the distinction between the functions and responsibilities of the party on one hand and those of the government and administration on the other." [2] Although, for reasons of constitutional propriety that have usually also been transferred from a Western model, the distinction between the party and the government is as yet maintained in most of the countries in our sample, one cannot be certain that this distinction will continue indefinitely. In a situation in which, as in Tanzania, the minister of information and broadcasting is at the same time the public relations secretary of the TANU party, the line between the two organizations becomes extremely blurred.

Justified though much of this type of arrangement may be in a society whose leaders espouse a single all-embracing objective that is shared by the major sections of that society, one cannot help wondering what will happen as and when the objectives of the different sections begin to diverge in significant ways. It may be argued that when that happens, not even a multiparty structure will save the country from bloodshed. Events in some developing countries suggest that this may already be the case. Moreover, recent trends in Europe indicate that not all multiparty systems there are immune from the attacks of those who wish to achieve change at a faster rate than such a system makes possible.

Nonetheless the need for constitutional devices that will permit politicians to survive the point at which by one means or another they are stripped of their power should encourage political leaders to seek to establish machinery for peaceful change. It is reasonable to suppose that intelligent politicians will do so at the point at which they come to recognize the inevitability of such change, if not on doctrinal then on personal grounds. Similarly, as the socioeconomic role of government develops and grows more sophisticated, the need becomes obvious for continuity of government, whatever the political changes. The more people come to rely on government for the management of their affairs, the less can a country afford a breakdown of the government machine. Hence the need for a means of changing political control which will not interrupt the day-to-day conduct of a country's business.

In the achievement of such objectives, the role of the broadcast media is important. It is in the interests of the ruling circles of today, as well as of the ruling circles of tomorrow, that the processes of change should be explained as dispassionately and as objectively as possible through the mass media. If the media are prevented from doing this, their loss of credibility will render their work self-defeating and reduce their usefulness. The loss of credibility of the news broadcasts of the government Public Relations Department in Thailand after the events of October 1973 shows how a system that is too tightly controlled can defeat its own ends.

We consider therefore that it is in the interests of governments of all developing countries to encourage an element of what may be described as "responsible distance" between themselves and their broadcasting organizations. Such a concept can be developed only on the basis of a common recognition on the part of the community that a broadcasting organization that exercises responsibly an element of autonomy will best serve the interests of the community as a whole. How can such a recognition be achieved? In the last resort, only by a conscious cultivation of an understanding of the relationship between government and the governed and of the relationship between power and responsibility. These phrases are well worn, yet we believe that they are not for that reason meaningless. At present the training, insofar as it exists at all, of both politicians and broadcasters rarely includes any systematic education in these matters. We think that in the interests of good government and good broadcasting more attention should be given to ensuring that those concerned understand these fundamental issues. Training of course is valueless unless it can be put into practice. Hence the political conditions must exist for broadcasters to practice what they have learned. It should be emphasized that this type of understanding is needed not only by broadcasters and politicians but also by administrators, soldiers, and others active in the diagram of forces that determines national politics in a fast-developing country.

BROADCASTING IN THE HIERARCHY OF NATIONAL DEVELOPMENT PRIORITIES

A certain level of broadcasting development is regarded as politically expedient in all but a few developing countries, whatever its social, economic, or cultural justification. No developing country, for example, has decided to do without a radio system. Most countries, moreover, claim that their radio systems provide coverage of the whole of their territory, at least for one service. In practice, we have found, this is by no means always the case. Only one country among our case studies, Tanzania, has deliberately held back from the introduction of television in the context of a review of its development priorities. In a number of other countries not in our sample this is also the case. In the remaining countries television has been introduced, but in the majority of these the television service is effectively little more than a token presence. Coverage tends to be confined to the capital and its immediate hinterland, the cost of receivers limits the audience effectively to the elite, and the developmental usefulness of the medium is minimal. The exceptions are countries that export oil or other primary products in short supply elsewhere and can afford the expansion of television on a national scale.

While, in the case of radio, communications planners must take into account established systems of one kind or another, the field of television is sufficiently unformed in most countries for them to exercise choice in shaping its development and to avoid at least some of the mistakes to which we draw attention in this book.

In our experience the analysis of the need for broadcasting is only now beginning to be given serious attention in national development plans. Algeria is one of the countries in whose plan a fairly explicit statement occurs.[3] The Algerian prospectus of the high developmental priority given to broadcasting is capable of realization owing to the country's new-found wealth deriving from natural gas and oil deposits in the Sahara. But the situation is much different in countries without such natural resources. Indeed the division of the world into developed and developing countries now needs to be refined so as to take account of the countries that, although underdeveloped, have disposable resources on a scale that effectively moves them into an entirely different league. Algeria, Brazil, and Iran are the countries in our sample that belong to this new group. It is likely that Indonesia, Nigeria, and Peru will join them, although they are not as yet as far along the road of realizing their economic potential as the other three.

Another respect in which the classification of countries for purposes of assessing their development priorities requires to be refined is the identification of a distinct group of countries where economic expansion has gone on for a substantial number of years without much regard to the distribution of its fruits. As a consequence, substantial wealth, usually concentrated in the urban areas, runs parallel with poverty in a largely undeveloped hinterland. In these countries the problem of development funding is therefore one of the allocation and distribution of national resources rather than of the absence of such resources. In our sample Iran and Brazil fall into this group.

When the countries falling into these two categories have been removed, there remains the hard core of countries whose level of development is low and which lack the natural or other resources for effectively breaking through the cycle of underdevelopment and deprivation. Many of these are in Africa south of the Sahara, on the Indian subcontinent, in the Pacific, and in the Caribbean. The most recent statistics indicate that about 658 million people now live on incomes of less than fifty dollars a year. Another 100 million are only marginally better off. The World Bank estimates that some 1,000 million people in the poorest countries obtained no increase in real income during 1974 and that the rate of growth of real incomes for this section of the world population will be under 1 percent a year for the rest of the decade.[4] Even in these countries the gap between the rich and the poor is relatively large, and expenditure on social infrastructure comparatively small. Public spending on health care, for example, in many developing countries is less than one dollar per person per year, and the growth in population coupled with little or no growth in educational expenditure will mean that the number of illiterates over fifteen years will actually rise in the next decade by anywhere from 100 million to 850 million.

This widespread lack of the basic conditions for a tolerable life is the most important context within which the argument for the expansion of broadcasting in the affected countries must be conducted. We have thus far assembled the evidence available about the role of broadcasting in the national development process and have offered our assessment of it. Some of the evidence is positive. Much is either negative or inconclusive.

THE USES OF RADIO

Given the social, economic, and political realities of modern statehood, all countries have need of an instrument whereby they can communicate effectively with their citizens. Radio provides such an instrument at transmission and production costs that are lower than those for any other mass medium with comparable penetration. Radio has the advantage over television that it is independent of rural electrification and disproportionately cheaper. It has the advantage over newspapers that it is independent of the quality of surface communications. As this quotation from an Egyptian study shows, radio tends to retain the advantage even where newspapers penetrate into the rural areas:

> In creating an audience receptive to news of non-local significance, radio is the most effective medium for reaching villagers, even literate ones. Therefore, for some time to come, even as literacy rates improve in the rural areas, one must depend chiefly on radio to get a message across. The newspaper in the village, while important, addresses a rather specialized set of consumers who are actually marginal to the rural community. It constitutes a link between the urban centres and the urbanised individuals who

serve as government officials in rural areas, but is not particularly effective in reaching the indigenous members of the rural community.[5]

Similar considerations apply to the cost of reception equipment. Although the ownership of a transistor radio is still beyond the reach of many people in countries at the lower end of the development scale, access to a receiver is widespread and could probably be extended at reasonable cost if governments so desired. One study of possible government action to extend access to radio is that reported in a World Bank study of education in Malawi, which included a section on the use of broadcasting in this context:

> In an attempt to make radio accessible to all sections, particularly the rural community, the provision of community reception facilities is currently being investigated by the Ministry of Information and Broadcasting. The proposal is to provide a receiver for each of the estimated 13,000 villages in the country. The receiver would be in the care of the village headman who would be expected to make it available to general and specific listening groups. Discussion about the supply of such receivers had not in September 1972 been concluded. The possibility of importing receivers from Hong Kong at K5 (= $7.50) per set appears to have been discarded since the receivers are thought to be too flimsy. An alternative now being explored is the production of receivers [locally]. A prototype has been produced at an estimated cost of K16 (= $24). This receiver, which has substantial built-in amplification for use outdoors and with large audiences, is powered by a battery costing K3 (= $4.50), giving 72 hours of service provided it is not used for more than two hours at a time. This makes the receiver unsuitable for storage in a private dwelling, such as the headman's, where the temptation to use it continually could not easily be resisted.[6]

This quotation illustrates that, although the cost of ensuring community radio reception can be relatively low, substantial logistical problems arise in the course of planning and executing even a relatively unsophisticated project of this kind. Thus the effective coverage of a low-income country even by radio is unlikely to be assured except by careful planning and by close cooperation between the various government agencies concerned and the broadcasters. Such planning and cooperation are as yet rare in developing countries. The returns derived from an investment in radio coverage and reception should, however, justify it even in countries at the lower end of the development scale, particularly if radio is used, as in the Tanzanian and Senegalese examples cited earlier, for extensive community education activities. In the Malawi case the proposal made by the World Bank team is that the radio should be housed in the "village college," a type of multipurpose educational unit available for a wide range of rural development activities connected with health, agriculture, housekeeping, and producer and consumer cooperatives, as well as other village activities. In this context the radio receiver would form part of the standard equipment of the village college, which would be the obvious venue for group listening activities based on radio programs.

Besides its economy, radio is also, in some respects, more supportive of the traditional culture pattern of the local community. As indicated earlier, there is evidence that even imported radio formats are more easily adapted to local folk cultures.

THE USES OF TELEVISION

The case for giving high priority to the expansion of television is much less strong, particularly given the existence of radio as an alternative. The disproportionately greater cost of obtaining television coverage has limited both the extension of television signals and the multiplication of receivers in most developing countries. The clustering of television coverage around the big cities has the effect of accentuating the gap between urban and rural standards of life. Instead of promoting national integration as radio does, television tends to divide a nation into those who have access, for good or ill, to the international television "culture" and those whose range of media experience is limited to their traditional setting, at most enlarged by the impact of radio and possibly by the occasional newspaper for those who are literate.

Only if governments decide to give the expansion of television coverage priority in the allocation of development resources will television transmission penetrate the hinterland of the majority of developing countries. Private-enterprise interests are unlikely to undertake this expansion, even where advertising revenue is used to finance television services, since the disposable cash incomes of most rural populations are far too low to make directing advertising to them worthwhile. The disincentive is compounded by the low level of purchasing power that makes it impossible for the majority of the population to afford receivers.

The problems of television reception are enormously greater than those of radio reception. The hopes for a substantial lowering in the cost of receivers have not so far been realized, nor is there much prospect that they will be in the near future. Thus the only practical alternative is the development of group viewing. And this is feasible only where the pattern of settlement is such that people are concentrated in towns or villages. The only rural area among our case studies where group viewing was regarded as a potentially significant development was the North Central State of Nigeria. In countries with more developed urban lifestyles such as Cyprus, Singapore, and Iran, where there is, in consequence, a tradition of gregariousness and where natural foci for assembly exist, group viewing occurs spontaneously. In the Cypriot coffeehouses (where, incidentally, gregariousness is confined to men) and in the outdoor eating halls of Singapore, the provision of a television receiver is seen by the owner of the establishment as an additional attraction for his customers. (Similarly, in Iran, radio and television are often provided in teahouses.) But in the majority of countries where no such point of assembly exists conditions for group viewing have to be specially created.

This is the case in Nigeria. Even here, although television is available in a number of states, only in the area served by the Broadcasting Corporation of Northern Nigeria (BCNN) has any effort at all begun to be made to extend facilities for television viewing to the vast majority of the population who are too poor to buy a receiver or who are without the electricity necessary to operate one. The beginning made in the North is quite small, but in view of the widespread neglect of reception conditions in the broadcasting policies of developing countries, it deserves attention.

The initiative for the creation of viewing centers was taken by the Broadcasting Corporation of Northern Nigeria. At the time of our study twenty-two television viewing centers had been built in villages and in the suburban areas of some towns within easy reach of Kaduna. The centers are open to all without charge, and we were impressed with the functional approach to their design and operation. The design specifications provide that the centers must

1. have a low capital cost
2. provide accommodation for the maximum audience capable of viewing a standard 22-inch receiver
3. provide separate accommodation (the area being Muslim) for men and for women and children
4. house the receivers in such a way as to minimize the possibility of theft or damage
5. be usable in both the dry and the rainy seasons
6. be capable of operation by an unskilled caretaker.

These specifications appear to be proving satisfactory. The centers that we visited were clearly popular. In areas with electrification, power is no problem. In other areas power is supplied by small generators. These have to be housed far enough from the centers for the noise not to drown out the sound of the program. Maintenance of both receivers and generators was, at the time of our visit, undertaken by the BCNN. Since at that time the number of centers was small and all were within reasonable reach of Kaduna, the operational base of the corporation, maintenance could be carried out without the creation of a separate unit for the purpose. Any substantial expansion in the number of viewing centers would of course make a maintenance unit necessary.

It is arguable that, apart from the economic necessity for the development of viewing centers, there is benefit to be derived from the common experience that group viewing provides. Thus it may well not be merely a second best to the more usual Western pattern of a television receiver in each household. If group viewing transforms the viewing experience from an individualistic to a collective act and both contributes to increasing participation by citizens in the resolution of the social issues that are brought to their attention by the medium and enhances the impact of extensive education in such areas as literacy, health, and agricultural development, then this type of activity deserves to be encouraged in its own right. Our experience indicates quite strikingly that informal education through the media is rarely successful unless there is a link between the media and the field workers of the agencies of social change. The logistic problems which have been discussed at some length earlier have in many countries left these links undeveloped. Broadcasting organizations and development agencies have tended to give up their effort of coordination at the first hurdle and to revert to their separate ways. Since most countries are poor, such wasteful dispersion of resources should not be tolerated. If television is to justify its role in the low-income countries, it can do so only if it is used as an instrument of development; and it can be an effective instrument only if it forms part of a coordinated and integrated development effort.

A NEW STYLE OF TELEVISION?

Although lip service has been given to the developmental role of television in almost all countries where it has been established, in practice the entertainment ethos that pervades so much of it in its countries of origin has been imported along with other irrelevant facets of its structure. In Western countries, education, culture, and other so-called minority programs have always had a hard struggle even in the most directive of public-service organizations. This attitude is reproduced in many television stations of the developing world. The self-evident argument that television needs viewers and that what viewers want is to be entertained is absorbed by trainees who are sent to Europe and North America. It is then used on their return to justify the imposition of entertainment programs on viewers who have had little or no opportunity to make a choice on the formats or content of Western programs. It is inevitable, given the traditional attitude toward innovations transferred from the developed countries, that viewers should be eager to try to like what people in Europe and North America are said to like. It is therefore worthwhile to repeat here the argument for giving viewers a choice which was outlined in the *Report of the Committee on Broadcasting* in the United Kingdom in 1962. We think this report is applicable *a fortiori* to countries in which television has been introduced as an alien medium:

> No one can say he is giving the public what it wants, unless the public knows the whole range of possibilities which television can offer and, from this range, chooses what it wants to see. For a choice is only free if the field of choice is not unnecessarily restricted. The subject matter of television is to be found in the whole scope and variety of human awareness and experience. If viewers, the "public," are thought of

as the "mass audience," or "the majority," they will be offered only the average of common experience and awareness; the "ordinary"; the commonplace, for what all know and do is, by definition, commonplace. They will be kept unaware of what lies beyond the average of experience; their field of choice will be limited. In time they may come to like only what they know. But it will always be true that, had they been offered a wider range from which to choose, they might and often would have chosen otherwise, and with greater enjoyment.[7]

Clearly, unlimited choice is impossible in a medium with as narrow a range of outlets as television. Those who control the channels control the choice. For this reason it is the more important that they should be aware of the range of choices to which their audience should be exposed. Having in the main been trained abroad in countries whose arrangements they admire, and having been urged to adopt the formats and styles to which these countries are accustomed, it is not surprising that the program-makers in the developing countries should find it hard to battle against the orthodoxies established in the West. But there are many reasons, some of which have already been set out, why they should not take conformity for granted.

One reason is that because life in northern climates largely goes on indoors, in its countries of origin television was developed as an "indoor" activity. In most developing countries, however, life goes on outdoors. Hence to impose upon these developing countries an indoor model of television is to do violence to the life-style of the people whom television should exist to serve. In planning production facilities it needs to be borne in mind that a studio is an alien environment and that it is better (and may be cheaper) to invest in outside broadcast equipment than in expensive studios. Another reason why Western formats should not be adopted wholesale is that in many developing countries the role differentiation between the citizen as viewer or listener and the citizen as performer does not exist. Drama, story-telling, music-making, and dancing are what villagers and their families do in their spare time and on feast days. It is therefore inappropriate to strain the social structure of a developing country so as to reproduce the division that exists in the West between the citizen as consumer of entertainment and the citizen as entertainer.

The growth of local programming that is documented in Chapter 5 shows that countries *are* aware of the need to innovate and draw on their own talent. This is not to say that total autarky in the production of programs is a desirable objective. By its nature television is an international medium and should be given a chance to act as cross-fertilizer in the realm of ideas and standards. But when a country is able to produce itself most of the programs it needs, it is able to become more selective in its import policy. Greater discrimination on the part of a substantial group of purchasing countries should also have a stimulating effect on the program-makers in North America and Europe. As and when they can no longer sell to a developing country whatever they have left over, they will begin to take the market more seriously and take more trouble to cater to it.

Local initiative should extend beyond the production of programs to the area of program formats. The adaptation of the soap-opera formula for local use, as in "The Village Headmaster" (Nigeria) or the *telenovela* in Brazil and other South American countries is an example. But deriving a format from the culture of the local community is the real challenge. This does of course happen from time to time, but the point of reference remains the imported article, both as to style and to content. This appears to be due, in some countries at least, to the fact that authors, musicians, producers, and directors are often too little acquainted with their own culture to be able to draw from it the material for indigenous programming. This is not surprising, given the assumption of the cultural superiority of the West that was current until recently, particularly in former colonial territories. The role of the broadcasting organization as a patron of the arts tends to be dominant, because it is here that major cultural expenditure is incurred. Such expenditure could in our view be used to even better effect than it already is. Where, as in Thailand, the local culture has been maintained throughout the centuries, there should be little difficulty in incorporating it in broadcasting. Where, as in Algeria, it has been buried under the weight of French culture and tied closely to French linguistic imperialism, the process of rediscovery takes longer, and broadcasting has a major role in this process.

From what has been said it is apparent that we see the role of broadcasting as crucial in the cultural renaissance of developing countries. When it fulfills this role it is doing more than merely supplying television images; it begins to justify its existence also as a major agency of sociocultural development. But if it is to do so, it must take entertainment as seriously as information and education. Indeed, it should seek to overcome the artificial division, which itself reflects the atomized view of culture current in the West. If it can maintain the more integrative view of life that is typical of much African and Asian culture, it should be able to arouse a different level of expectations about the nature and functions of the medium.

How is this to be done? The low expectation that broadcasters tend to have of their own potential reflects the "package" character of the introduction of television. Whether introduced by a national broadcasting service or by a commercial entrepreneur, the transfer has generally been effected en bloc. The "customer," that is, the developing country concerned, had little notion about what was involved and thus displayed all the characteristics of the buyer in the durable-goods market, who wants the effects provided by a car or a washing machine or a television receiver without the bother of learning how they are achieved. In the case of a television system, as we have already pointed out, the package includes production facilities, transmission equipment, receivers and, above all, programs. It also includes a choice of organizational and financial structures. Although the customer may have views about the latter, he rarely expresses them about the former. Thus the package that is delivered rarely if ever meets the customer's precise requirements.

If television could be seen as a collection of components instead of as a package, this would give the countries establishing their systems much greater choice and flexibility. They could decide whether to engage in highly capitalized operations such as those of the West or to take advantage of the technological advances that have been made in, for example, camera techniques, to concentrate on low-cost outside broadcast material. They could decide to launch their television operation in the most backward parts of the country rather than in the capital and to link it with their rural and social development campaigns. They could decide to put their efforts into the creation of community viewing facilities, thus strengthening the structures of local community life. In this way they might obviate the seemingly irreversible trek to the towns, which in turn makes heavy demands on capital investment in urban infrastructure. Although it is assumed in the West that television, because of its high cost, is essentially a metropolitan and centripetal medium, there is no reason why developing countries should accept this received wisdom.

Again, television in Europe has been seen as an instrument of national, as distinct from international, mass communication. The relatively short range of television signals has enabled the larger countries to limit the impact of their signals to their own territories. Thus television has been used to reinforce national particularisms rather than to transcend them. Where there has been an overlap, as between Britain and Ireland, it has been politely ignored, and

by mutual consent coverage areas have been assumed to co-
incide with national boundaries. In northwest continental
Europe this national limitation has in practice long since
broken down. As a result the viewer's range of choices has
been enlarged. Most viewers in Belgium, for example, are
now able to receive ten channels of television from France,
Germany, and the Netherlands, as well as from Belgium itself. This change breaks down the practical effect of national barriers and moves ahead of political events. It is unfortunate that the nationalism that has been exported at the
political level to the rest of the world is being reproduced in
broadcasting terms. There is no reason, for example, why
adjacent African countries should not share their broadcasting systems in the same way that some of them now share
their railway and airline systems. Similarly, the proposed
communications satellite for Indonesia could be used by
Malaysia and Singapore and in this way act as an integrative force in the region. We recognize of course that the
supranational use of television presupposes agreement between the countries covered about the means and ends of
broadcasting. Where this agreement is absent, individual
states will do their best to limit the exposure of their citizens to broadcasting signals from abroad. The Canadian
government, for example, objects to the smothering of the
most populous part of the country, not far from its border
with the United States, by television signals from the
American networks. Thailand is not anxious to receive
broadcasts from neighboring countries. Evidently, very
formidable obstacles stand in the way of the use of television as an instrument of international communication. But
perhaps countries will someday look beyond the short
term, in which the establishment of national identity seems
to be of paramount importance, to the medium term in
which regional cooperation will prove to be essential to
maintain the pace of development.

HUMAN RESOURCES FOR INNOVATION

Broadcasting is not a particularly esteemed profession in most of the developing countries. As has already been noted, where broadcasting systems are controlled and largely financed by government, they are in most cases operated as government departments. Salaries and conditions of employment in broadcasting are therefore in most countries aligned with, if not identical to, those in the civil service.

Staff members now in the upper echelons of government broadcasting systems do not see their role in primarily professional terms. As J. F. Scotton has pointed out, when colonial governments opened broadcasting stations in their dependencies in Africa

> . . . the recruitment of both technical and production personnel continued to be from among those who had done well in their final examinations at secondary school, the British "O-levels" or the French "Brevet." Recruitment was carried on under civil service procedures, in many cases by the Civil Service itself. Little attention was paid to such vital qualifications as talent, aptitude, or even interest: in consequence, individuals with imaginations and creativity were rarely attracted. After surveying some of those who had risen through the ranks to reach executive positions in African broadcasting, a UNESCO team commented "It makes little difference to them whether they are in broadcasting or in the Public Works Department and they will have no hesitation about transferring at any time for a slightly higher salary. These are men and women meant for civil service careers and can never look on broadcasting as a profession.[8]

In Nigeria, for example, where the Nigerian Broadcasting Corporation has progressively adopted civil service management practices since the military takeover in 1966, there are severe problems with staff morale and job turnover. Where there are highly developed sectors in the economy, as there are at the present time in oil-rich Nigeria, staff members at all levels in the organization are tempted to leave broadcasting in favor of industry or the blossoming public relations businesses in which they can earn many times their civil service salaries.

As governments also control information and news, news and current affairs staffs have no opportunity to use their own judgment or to work independently of government. Where journalists and reporters have been trained abroad according to the highest standards of the Fourth Estate, there is understandably on their part a feeling that their professional standards are being eroded.

Where the broadcasting system is based on the American commercial model, there is often a very casual approach to broadcasting, especially in commercial radio stations. Sometimes staff members neglect to service expensive equipment or change jobs many times. There are so many stations and so little creative energy is involved in producing the sort of programming that is provided (mainly record shows) that standards of work are inevitably affected. Although "stars" are very highly paid, the ordinary station manager, who will typically be employed by a large company with many other broadcasting outlets, does not earn much more than the average worker in the commercial sector. As there are so many stations operating, entrance standards to broadcasting are low.

We have referred from time to time to the need of the broadcasting organizations for people capable of being developers and innovators, rather than imitators of foreign models and ways of doing things. This need exists at all levels in the broadcasting organizations, from the director-general to the studio manager and cameraman. Indeed, the need is felt in the political arena where, as we have found, the wish is too often to reestablish locally a model that the leaders of a country have seen elsewhere and that they regard as prestigious, irrespective of its suitability for transfer. The "cycle of deprivation" that operates in many contexts has been operative also in the field of broadcasting training. A country unable to afford its own training institution sends some of its best people for training to a country with a well-established broadcasting system. That country does the best it can according to its understanding—that is, to train the trainees from overseas to reproduce its own system in their home countries. It is in this way that many systems in the Third World have come to be developed, systems that now appear to be incapable of responding to their country's developmental needs.

Sydney Head has described the disadvantages of continued overseas training of African broadcasters:

> The innumerable overseas scholarship, training, attachment and orientation programs which siphon off African broadcasting personnel and keep their organizations in a state of disruption constitute an unconscionable abuse of foreign technical-aid programs. Embassies appear to compete on a "body count" basis—the more host-country personnel they ship home for training programs the higher their efficiency ratings, irrespective of the qualifications of the trainees or the quality and relevance of their overseas experience. Some embassy officials are not above a little arm twisting—"After all we've done for your broadcasting system the least you can do is to give us one or two trainees." The fact is, there are far more offers than suitable candidates. Broadcasting organizations, often already handicapped by essential leaves-of-absence of key men, have to scrape the bottom of the barrel and recommend totally unqualified personnel. In other cases, as Quarmyne and Bebey put it, "training programs are looked upon as rewards for seniority" [A.T. Quarmyne and F. Bebey, "Training for Radio and Television in Africa," com/WS/64 (Paris: UNESCO, 1964)]. As for on-the-job training with foreign broadcasting organizations: "In their present form most attachments . . . give officers a holiday and return them

home confused while their organizations suffer by losing their
services during the period of attachment."

Some overseas training programs, so-called, put the
trainee at the mercy of instructors no more advanced in
broadcasting expertise than the trainee's own colleagues at
home. Often he has to waste much of his training period
trying to learn a new language which has no probable future
value to him and which in any event he never masters sufficiently to allow it to become the vehicle of anything but
the most elementary ideas.[9]

In the overseas training of broadcasting staffs the best
often is the enemy of the good. Standards of engineering,
production, and managment are set which may be excellent
but which are unnecessarily expensive and applicable only
to prosperous countries where financial and technical resources are plentiful. The training of people not only for
competence at their assigned tasks but above all as intelligent improvisers and innovators has been neglected. In
consequence, trainees all too often return home from their
course discouraged by the gap between the amplitude of
resources in their place of training and the poverty of resources available on the spot. Having, as they see it, no
hope of achieving the standards set during their training,
they often give up altogether and do not even try to apply
their experience within the limitations of the resources at
their disposal.

Training for the exercise of initiative is one thing. The
provision of scope to exercise initiative is another. It is a
well-known phenomenon in the field of management training that senior managers are quite willing to send bright
young men to be trained, but are most reluctant on their return to allow them to practice what they have learned. It
has been found that if training is to lead to an improvement
of performance in an organization, it is essential to engage
in a comprehensive staff development program that in-

cludes the whole line of command of the organization. Such comprehensive training for innovators is particularly important in national administrations where officials have for generations been discouraged from taking initiative. Personnel at all levels are reluctant to take responsibility and prefer to work within the limit of clearly defined rules behind which they can take cover in case of criticism.

These observations on the need in developing countries to train for initiative and innovation are, of course, neither original nor relevant only to broadcasting. They apply across the whole range of public and private enterprise in such countries. The delicately poised political situation in many of them accentuates the reluctance of officials to take chances that may cost them their jobs in a country where unemployment in the modern sector of the economy tends to be high.

In broadcasting, the variety of staff positions complicates staff development. The controllers and senior administrators have to be trained to recognize the developmental character of their roles. As we have already indicated, indigenous training tends to concentrate at the base of a staff pyramid but really needs to begin at the apex. At present there are no indigenous institutional resources for advanced training of senior people in the broadcasting organizations in the developing countries. In any one country the number of senior officials is too small to warrant the creation of formal arrangements. Moreover, reasons of prestige make it important that training of this kind should be given in a form and a context acceptable to those concerned. For this reason the form should emphasize the autonomy of the official and the content encourage him to translate the traditions of his country into broadcasting terms, to reflect on his own experience, and to discuss his concerns with his peers. It is likely that such a facility might best be provided on an international scale, preferably in a developing country, although some countries might well wish to establish their own "institutes for the translation of tradition" on the lines suggested above.

Other staff categories include the engineers and other technicians, and the program production staff generally employed full-time in the organization. The problem of encouraging the talents of the creative people in music, drama, design (in the case of television), and writing of all kinds (including especially the radio and television journalists) is of a different order. Similarly the selection and training of commentators, anchormen, and others, all of whom are crucial to the success of a broadcasting operation, pose different problems.

This variety of needs, together with the wide range of circumstances obtaining in the countries that we studied, makes it difficult to make specific recommendations about the structure of training, except in relation to each group and country. In Thailand, for example, the number of people employed in broadcasting is thought to be about 3,000, of whom the five television channels employ 1,000, and the 200 to 300 radio stations, 2,000. If each radio station has, on the average, a staff of between six and ten people and the stations operate very casually, the staff development problem is very different from that of an organization with a large concentration of workers in each of the groups we have identified. In Brazil, for example, about 16,500 people are employed in the broadcasting industry, of whom as many as 4,500 are employed in the larger commercial broadcasting organizations. Nevertheless, there is no attempt to systematize training in institutional form in Brazil. In Thailand, however, a training school for radio broadcasters has been established under Colombo Plan auspices in Bangkok.

The case studies confirm that training and opportunities to use training must be linked more closely if the quality of broadcasting is to improve. The expert sent to launch the Thai training school noted the high potential talent of Thai broadcasters but commented on the difficulty of developing this talent in the face of organizational restrictions on creativity and the free expression of views.[10] Similarly a UNESCO team sent to study educational broadcasting in Brazil noted the need for training educational broadcasters, but did not agree that this was the major obstacle to raising the low level of performance in the Brazilian ETV stations. The team identified this obstacle as the lack of a clear policy, the absence of defined objectives and standards, and the multitude of differing orientations among the stations.[11] These examples could be multiplied throughout the broadcasting systems of the developing world.

The development of human resources for innovation in broadcasting thus requires more than training courses and more than technical and professional upgrading. It requires the development among broadcasters of an understanding of their job in relation to the development process of the country, and in particular in relation to its cultural development. This view of cultural development must be based on an understanding of the cultural history of the country. Only against this background is it reasonable to expect broadcasters to map out the contribution that the broadcasting organization can make to the development of the cultural tradition of the country in terms of the twentieth century. There is some hope that the self-confidence needed to undertake this task is beginning to return to a number of developing countries, with the lessening of the cultural shock suffered during attempts to compress centuries of Western development into the decade or so following the achievement of independence. Then the emphasis was wholly on the adoption of patterns established elsewhere. Now enough political and psychological elbowroom has been gained in many countries to allow a more critical appraisal of what has been gained and lost and a longer view ahead to ensure that the cultural heritage is not only preserved but developed.

THE PROFESSIONAL STATUS OF BROADCASTERS

The status of broadcasters is an important ingredient of their view of themselves, which in turn reflects on their actions. Most broadcasters are employees. The dependent relationship of an employee detracts from that sense of responsibility for one's actions that is a hallmark of a professional. If broadcasters are to play a responsible part in the establishment and maintenance of high standards in the broadcasting services, they should be encouraged to establish these standards for themselves and, at least in some measure, to enforce them in regard to their professional colleagues. Being able to establish agreed-upon standards of conduct would, moreover, put them in a stronger position than at present to defend themselves and their colleagues against unreasonable conduct on the part of their employers. This is particularly important in situations where the conditions of employment are precarious. In the countries in our sample, conditions of employment, as we have seen, range from the wholly casual, with employees subject to minimal notice of dismissal, to the status of established civil servants assured in the absence of serious misdemeanor of a career for life.

The developmental approach to broadcasting that we have tried to describe requires the broadcasters to keep close to the needs of their audience. Broadcasting in the developed countries has a strong metropolitan aura: broadcasters do not easily move away from the capital; they tend to mix with one another and to develop what Richard Hoggart has called a self-defining tendency.[12] The transfer of models has, in some countries, included the transfer of this attitude. The type of training we have sketched out would reverse this trend. The establishment of close links between broadcasters and those in other disciplines or with other skills would do much to break down the occupational self-sufficiency of both. Some interesting types of collaboration have already been established in those countries in which, for example, agricultural extension work by radio is well developed. In the United States similar interdisciplinary teams were set up to develop the "Sesame Street" programs, and in the Open University course teams in Britain, producers, designers, academics, and educational technologists have learned to work together effectively.

By the same token it is important for broadcasters to get out into the areas that their broadcasts are intended to serve. Where there are regional or local stations, staffs from headquarters should be assigned periods of duty in them; they should also take all available opportunities to hear or view programs in the company of ordinary viewers or listeners. Promotion and recognition procedures should be so designed as to encourage excursions into the field. All too often it is still the case that promotion comes most easily to those who sit tight at the headquarters of the organization.

The proposals and suggestions that we make in this section for the raising of the level of developmental awareness of the people working in the broadcasting organizations can of course be implemented only over time. Apart from their intrinsic merit the proposals do, however, have the advantage of involving only minimal additional expenditure. Indeed, raising the level of staff effectiveness and morale should reduce the unit cost of staff, the total expenditure on which tends to account for the major part of the revenue expenditure of broadcasting organizations. These proposals can be accomplished if those responsible for the broadcasting organizations regard the implications of the proposals as a matter of priority and if international initiative is taken to help individual countries with staff development programs.

THE INTEGRATION OF BROADCASTING
INTO DEVELOPMENT POLICY

A great deal has been said and written in the last twenty years about the usefulness of broadcasting in accelerating and encouraging the development process in the Third World. As we have pursued our research we have become conscious of the wide gap between promise and performance in this respect. We think that the reason for the limited concurrence between what people expected broadcasting to do and what it has actually achieved arises from an analysis of the potential of broadcasting that was faulty in origin and from an underestimate of the social, cultural, economic, and political constraints that combine to limit the potential of broadcasting.

In the light of the evidence now available it is disturbing that exaggerated claims for broadcasting continue to be made. Such claims lead to the raising of hopes that can only be disappointed and to investment in the media that will not yield the expected return. We hope that this study will contribute to a more sober assessment of the place of broadcasting in the national development process and will help more modest and cost-effective objectives to be identified and achieved.

As we have seen, broadcasting in one form or another has come to stay in the developing world. However unproven the intrinsic necessity for electronic communication may be, governments have persuaded themselves and their constituencies that this type of mass communication is necessary for modernization. Having been so persuaded, the governments of the developing countries are anxious to lead their people into membership in the "global village." This being so, we have wished to identify ways and means by which they can do so with a minimum of danger to the achievement of their objective of national development. Our concern has been timely. As we have pointed out, the timing of our study, although fortuitous, has in the event not been insignificant. The natural-resources crisis has opened a new divide in the world: that between countries owning increasingly scarce natural resources and those without them. It is now apparent that this divide may in the future be more significant than the divide separating the developing world from Europe and North America. It remains to be revealed whether the newly prosperous countries will, in their policies of aid to those less fortunate than themselves, be more or less farsighted than the traditionally wealthy countries of the West. However this may be, the total volume of the world's natural resources will remain the same while the demands made on them will increase.

We have therefore considered the role of broadcasting both within the spectrum of developmental ambitions that have been roused and disappointed in the last quarter century and in the context of the outlook as it has been disclosed in the period from 1973 to 1976. It has become quite clear that this role will certainly be more modest than that claimed for it in the past, if only for the practical reasons that have emerged strikingly in the course of this study. But this more modest role could yet be of crucial significance in helping developing countries, and indeed the countries of the West, to understand their changed circumstances and to learn to live with them. Broadcasting could be used to promote self-reliance, to help citizens to understand the limitations of current development policies, and to encourage a new, more anthropocentric understanding of development.

There is little indication as yet that broadcasters or those who determine broadcasting policy are aware of the urgent need for a change of direction, toward a simplification of communications systems. The indications are that the wish to exploit commercially and militarily the investment made in space technology is putting developing countries under pressure to buy more sophisticated and more expensive communications systems at a time when their existing systems are far from fully exploited. The rapid growth of satellite systems is a case in point. Satellite communications systems have become the status symbols of the 1970s in the same way that television was the status symbol of the 1960s. Although there are situations in which communications satellites are likely to enlarge the scope of communication and to lower the unit cost, there is as yet no reliable evidence on which the cost-effective application of these techniques can be based. Studies by the Indonesian authorities with the assistance of the Hughes Aircraft Company of the United States suggest that in a country with terrestrial communications problems on the scale of those in Indonesia "a satellite system could provide a national telecommunications service sooner and cheaper than any other system." [13] But we know of at least one Indonesian government radio station that had to close down its transmitter because it could not even obtain a replacement valve.

The integration of broadcasting into development policy has therefore to be seen not merely in instrumental terms. Broadcasting needs to contribute to the formation of development policy as well as to its implementation. The broadcasting organizations have to assess their own performance, the cost-effectiveness of alternative development plans, and the impact of their program patterns on the development of particular regions in their areas of responsibility. This assessment may lead them to discourage governments from adopting for reasons of prestige communications innovations characterized by unproven claims for the improvement of the system.

Conversely, governments need to ensure that their broadcasting services operate at high levels of efficiency, that they exploit fully the potential of the resources they have before demanding the installation of additional resources. They need to integrate the role of the broadcasting services more fully with those of the other government agencies responsible for development. It is, for example, arguable that, where such a person exists, the minister for national development rather than the minister of information should take charge of the broadcasting services. Decisions of this kind can be made only in full knowledge of the network of responsibilities in each particular country, but governments cannot expect good value for the substantial investment that they make in the human and material resources of their broadcasting services if they do not think carefully about their points of impact.

In view of the relatively high costs of broadcasting production, especially in television, the arguments for the regional pooling of television production facilities by groups of governments is worthy of careful study. At present the only regional center of this kind in operation is the Centre for Production and Training for Adult Education Television (CEPTA), which is located in Singapore and is intended to serve the production needs of Indonesia, the Khmer Republic, Korea, Laos, the Philippines, Singapore, Thailand, and Vietnam. It is a nonprofit venture funded jointly by the government of Singapore and the Friedrich Ebert Foundation of West Germany. Since its establishment in 1973 CEPTA appears to have begun to be used by the member states to supplement the staffs and equipment they have available for the production of adult education programs related to development. It is not yet clear whether the material produced can be used in the member states without substantial modification, or whether one-country programs can be produced more economically at CEPTA than in the country concerned.

If either of these potential achievements proves to be the case, there is no reason why what is applicable to adult education programs could not also be applied to a wider range of programs. It would therefore be well worthwhile for an external assessment of CEPTA to be undertaken nearer the end of the decade in order to obtain a clear appreciation of the wider applicability of this model. Other forms of regional cooperation should be developed and, as we have reported at appropriate points in this book, are being developed among the countries flanking the Andes in South America and among the Maghreb countries of North Africa. We have, however, been struck throughout our work by the reluctance of most of these countries to enter into any international commitments that might remove the broadcasting institutions, or any parts of them, from their own effective control. This form of chauvinism often contrasts sharply with the readiness of countries to rely on foreign programs, although this reliance also is lessening under the pressures for domestic and authentically local programming. The sustained pressure for the achievement of cultural autarky that characterizes so much of the cultural policies of the developing countries at present must be recognized as but one aspect of the need that these countries feel for the legitimation of their political independence. It would be sad, however, if it were to lead to a further increase of cultural chauvinism.

Throughout this volume we have been concerned to identify those things that make broadcasting an essential ingredient of the life of countries all of which are undergoing fundamental sociocultural change at a rate unprecedented in their history. We have tried to put ourselves in the position of broadcasters and policymakers in these countries and to ask ourselves what we would do in their place, bearing in mind the difficulties of harnessing media technology to a country's social and cultural priorities. We have found that an impressive volume of professional dedication goes into broadcasting in many of the places we have visited. We have found also that in many countries inherited models are being applied with too little questioning of their origins or their usefulness to the life of the people. In spite of growing political nonalignment, in the field of broadcasting far too much is taken on trust. "What is good enough for the West is good enough for us" remains the unjustified motto in too many instances. But North America and Europe also face profound underlying problems relating to the role of broadcasting in society. Broadcasting in the Third World would be better served if its managers were to be more independent in their judgments; were not to take for granted the suitability of solutions devised elsewhere; and were to think imaginatively about the potential contribution of the resources they command to the development of their countries.

Supplementary Tables

Table A.1 Dates of introduction and organizational form of broadcasting systems in ninety-one developing countries.

Area and country	Date of independence and former colonial power	Introduction of Radio	Introduction of TV	Model for system	Organization of broadcasting system
Africa					
Algeria	1962 (France)	1925	1956	French	Public authority: Radiodiffusion Télévision Algérienne.
Botswana	1966 (U.K.)	1966	N/A	British	Government agency: Radio Botswana.
Burundi	1962 (Belgium)	1960	N/A	Belgian	Government agency: La Voix de la Révolution.
Cameroon	1960 (France)	1940	N/A	French	Government agency: Radiodiffusion du Cameroun.
Central African Republic	1960 (France)	1958	1974	French	Government agency: Radiodiffusion Nationale Centrafricaine.
Chad	1960 (France)	1955	N/A	French	Government agency: Radiodiffusion Nationale Tchadienne.
Congo	1960 (France)	1946	1962	French	Public authority: Radiodiffusion Télévision Congolaise.
Dahomey	1960 (France)	1953	N/A	French	Government agency: Radiodiffusion du Dahomey.
Egypt	N/A (U.K.)	1926	1960	N/A	Public authority: Egyptian Radio and TV.
Equatorial Guinea	1968 (Spain)	pre-1968	1968	Spanish	Government agencies (2): Radio Malabo and Radio Equatorial.
Ethiopia	N/A	1941	1964	N/A	Public authority: Ethiopian Broadcasting Service. Private (nonprofit): Radio Voice of the Gospel.
Gabon	1960 (France)	1959	1963	French	Public authority: Radiodiffusion Télévision Gabonaise. French government relay.

Table A.1 (*continued*) Dates of introduction and organizational form of broadcasting systems in ninety-one developing countries.

Area and Country	Date of Independence and former colonial power	Introduction of Radio	TV	Model for system	Organization of broadcasting system
Gambia	1965 (U.K.)	1942	N/A	British	Government agency: Radio Gambia. Private (commercial): Radio Syd.
Ghana	1957 (U.K.)	1935	1965	British	Public authority: Ghana Broadcasting Corporation.
Guinea	1958 (France)	1958	N/A	French	Government agency: Radiodiffusion Nationale.
Ivory Coast	1960 (France)	1949	1963	French	Public authority: Radiodiffusion Télévision Ivoirienne.
Kenya	1963 (U.K.)	1928	1963	British	Government agency: Voice of Kenya.
Lesotho	1966 (U.K.)	1964	N/A	British	Government agency: Lesotho National Broadcasting Service.
Liberia	1822 (U.S.)	1959	1964	N/A	Public authority: Liberian Broadcasting Corporation. Private (nonprofit) (3): Lamco Broadcasting Station (radio), Radio ELWA, Voice of America Radio Station in Liberia.
Libya	1951 (Italy)	1957	1968	N/A	Government agency: People's Revolution Broadcasting.
Malagasy	1960 (France)	1931	1967	French	Public authority: Radio Television Malagasy.
Malawi	1964 (U.K.)	1963	N/A	British	Public authority: Malawi Broadcasting Corporation.
Mali	1960 (France)	1957	N/A	French	Government agency: Radio Mali.
Mauritania	1960 (France)	1957	N/A	French	Government agency: Radiodiffusion Nationale de Mauritanie.

Table A.1 (*continued*)

Mauritius	1968 (U.K.)	1944	1965	British	Public authority: Mauritius Broadcasting Corporation.
Morocco	1956 (France)	1956	1962	French	Public authority: Radiodiffusion Télévision Marocaine. Private (nonprofit): Voice of America Radio Station in Tangier. Spanish government stations (2) in Spanish territories: Radio Ceuta and Radio Melilla.
Niger	1960 (France)	1958	1967	French	Public authority: Office de Radiodiffusion Télévision du Niger.
Nigeria	1960 (U.K.)	1932	1959	British	Public authorities (5): Nigerian Broadcasting Corporation, Western Nigeria Radiovision Service, Radio Television Kaduna, East Central State Broadcasting Service, Midwest State Broadcasting Corporation.
Rwanda	1962 (Belgium)	1962	N/A	Belgian	Government agency: Radiodiffusion de la République Rwandaise. German government relay: Deutsche Welle.
Senegal	1960 (France)	1939	1964	French	Public authority: Office de Radiodiffusion Télévision Sénégalaise.
Sierra Leone	1961 (U.K.)	1934	1963	British	Government agency: Sierra Leone Broadcasting Service.
Somalia	1960 (Italy-U.K.)	1943	N/A	Italian/British	Government agency: Somali Broadcasting Service.
Sudan	1956 (U.K.)	1940	1963	British	Government agency: Broadcasting Service of the Democratic Republic of the Sudan.
Swaziland	1968 (U.K.)	1966	N/A	British	Government agency: Swaziland Broadcasting Service. Private (commercial): Swazi Music Radio. Private (nonprofit): Trans-World Radio.

Table A.1 (*continued*) Dates of introduction and organizational form of broadcasting systems in ninety-one developing countries.

Area and Country	Date of Independence and former colonial power	Introduction of Radio	Introduction of TV	Model for system	Organization of broadcasting system
Tanzania	1961 (U.K.)	1951	1974 (Zanzibar)	British	Government agency: Radio Tanzania. (Also Zanzibar Television Service.)
Togo	1960 (France)	1953	N/A	French	Government agency: Radiodiffusion du Togo.
Tunisia	1955 (France)	1936	1966	French	Public authority: Radiodiffusion Télévision Tunisienne.
Uganda	1962 (U.K.)	1953	1963	British	Government agencies (2): Uganda Radio and Uganda Television.
Upper Volta	1960 (France)	1959	1963	French	Public authority: Radiodiffusion Télévision Voltaique.
Zaire	1960 (Belgium)	1940	1966	Belgian	Government agencies (2): La Voix du Zaïre and Zaïre Télévision.
Zambia	1964 (U.K.)	1941	1966	British	Government agencies (2): Zambia Broadcasting Service and Television Zambia.
Asia					
Afghanistan	N/A	1925	N/A	N/A	Government agency: Radio Afghanistan.
Burma	1948 (U.K.)	pre-1945	N/A	British	Government agency: Burma Broadcasting Service.
Cyprus	1960 (U.K.)	1948	1957	British	Public authority: Cyprus Broadcasting Corporation. Government agency (Turkish): Radio Bayrak.

Table A.1 (*continued*)

India	1947 (U.K.)	1927	1959	British	Government agency: All India Radio-Television.
Indonesia	1949 (Netherlands)	1924	1962	Dutch	Government agencies (2): Radio Republik Indonesia and Television Republik Indonesia. Private (commercial): 288 radio stations. Private (nonprofit) 800 radio stations.
Iran	N/A	1940	1958	N/A	Public authority: National Iranian Radio and Television.
Iraq	1932 (U.K.)	1936	1954	N/A	Government agencies (2): Broadcasting Service of the Republic of Iraq and Baghdad Television.
Jordan	1946 (U.K.)	1948	1968	N/A	Government agencies (2): Hashemite Kingdom Broadcasting Service and Jordan Television.
Khmer Republic	1953 (France)	—	1962	French	Government agencies (2): Radiodiffusion Nationale Khmère and Republique Khmère Télévision.
South Korea	N/A	—	—	N/A	Public authority: Korean Broadcasting Corporation. Private (commercial): 7 radio stations. Private (nonprofit): 3 radio stations and American Forces Korea Network.
Laos	1949 (France)	1947	N/A	French	Government agency: Radiodiffusion Nationale Lao.
Lebanon	1941 (France)	1938	1959	French	Government agency (radio): Radio Lebanon. Private (commercial) (2): Compagnie Libanaise de Télévision and Télé Orient.
Malaysia	1957 (U.K.)	1946	1963	British	Government agency: Radio Television Malaysia.
Nepal	N/A	1951	N/A	N/A	Government agency: Radio Nepal.
Pakistan	1947 (U.K.)	1947	1962	British	Public authority: Pakistan Broadcasting Corporation. Also public company: Pakistan Television Corporation Ltd.

Table A.1 (*continued*) Dates of introduction and organizational form of broadcasting systems in ninety-one developing countries.

Area and Country	Date of Independence and former colonial power	Introduction of		Model for system	Organization of broadcasting system
		Radio	TV		
Philippines	1946 (Spain/ U.S.)	1924	1951	U.S.	Government agencies (2): Radio Voice of the Philippines and DZKB-TV, Quezon City (both operated by National Media Production Center, Solana). Private (commercial): 87 radio stations and 5 television stations. Private (nonprofit): 13 radio stations, Voice of America (radio), and American Forces television.
Saudi Arabia	N/A	1949	1965	N/A	Government agency: Broadcasting Service of the Kingdom of Saudi Arabia. Private (nonprofit): Aramco Radio and TV.
Singapore	1963 (U.K.)	1935	1963	British	Government agency: Radio Television Singapore. Private (commercial) wired radio and television: Rediffusion Singapore Ltd. Private (nonprofit): British Forces Broadcasting Service.
Sri Lanka	1948 (U.K.)	1925	N/A	British	Public authority: Sri Lanka Broadcasting Corporation.
Syria	1941 (France)	1945	1960	N/A	Government agency: Syrian Broadcasting and Television Organization.
Thailand	N/A	1931	1954	N/A	Government agencies with private (commercial) and private

Table A.1 (*continued*)

(nonprofit) partners: approximately 200 radio stations and 3 television organizations: Television of Thailand, Thai Television Company Ltd., and Army Television HSA TV.

Country					
Turkey	N/A	1926	1968	N/A	Public authority: Turkish Radio Television Corporation.
South Vietnam	1954 (France)	1949	1966	French	Government agency: Voice of Vietnam (pre-1975, Radio Vietnam).
Yemen Arab Republic	N/A	N/A	N/A	N/A	Government agency: Radio Sanaa.
People's Democratic Republic of Yemen	N/A	—	—	N/A	Government agencies (2): Democratic Yemen Broadcasting Service (radio) and People's Democratic Republic of Yemen Television Service.
South America					
Argentina	1816 (Spain)	1922	1951	U.S.	Government agencies: 20 radio stations and 8 television stations. Private (commercial): 90 radio stations and 23 television stations.
Bolivia	1825 (Spain)	—	—	U.S.	Government agencies (2): Radio Illimani and Empresa Nacional de Televisión Boliviana. Private (commercial): over 100 radio stations.
Brazil	1822 (Portugal)	1922	1950	U.S.	Government agencies: 6 radio stations. Private (commercial): 1,200 radio stations and 59 television stations. Private (nonprofit): 4 radio stations and 7 television stations.

Table A.1 (*continued*) Dates of introduction and organizational form of broadcasting systems in ninety-one developing countries.

Area and Country	Date of Independence and former colonial power	Introduction of		Model for system	Organization of broadcasting system
		Radio	TV		
Chile	1818 (Spain)	1922	1958	U.S.	Government agencies: 1 radio station and 1 television station. Private (commercial): 162 radio stations. Private (nonprofit): 4 radio stations and 5 television stations.
Colombia	1810 (Spain)	1928	1957	U.S.	Government agencies: Inravisión and Telebogotá (television broadcasting organizations, with programs produced by private [commercial] organizations). Private (commercial): 307 radio stations.
Ecuador	1830 (Spain)	1937	1959	U.S.	Government agencies: 2 radio stations. Private (commercial): 269 radio stations and 12 television stations. Private (nonprofit): 2 radio stations and 1 television station.
Guyana	1966 (U.K.)	—	N/A	British	Government agency: Guyana Broadcasting Service. Private (commercial): Guyana Broadcasting Co. Ltd.
Paraguay	1811 (Spain)	—	—	U.S.	Government agency: Radio Nacional (1 station). Private (commercial): 23 radio stations and 1 television station: TV Cerro Cora.
Peru	1823 (Spain)	1932	1958	U.S.	Government agencies: 31 radio stations. Government agencies with commercial partners: 31 radio stations and 2 television networks. Private (commercial): 138 radio stations.

Table A.1 (*continued*)

Uruguay	1825 (Spain)	—	U.S.	Government agencies: 1 radio station and 1 television station (SODRE). Private (commercial): 68 radio stations and 8 television stations. Private (nonprofit): 2 radio stations.
Venezuela	1811 (Spain)	1930	U.S.	Government agencies: Radio Nacional (1 station) and Televisora Nacional (1 station). Private (commercial): 143 radio stations and 6 television networks. Private (nonprofit): 1 radio station.
Central America and the Caribbean				
Barbados	1966 (U.K.)	1937	British	Public authority: Caribbean Broadcasting Corporation. Private (commercial) (wired service): Barbados Rediffusion Service Ltd.
Costa Rica	1848 (Spain)	1924	U.S.	Private (commercial): 23 radio stations and 4 television networks. Private (nonprofit): 4 radio stations.
Cuba	1898 (Spain)	1925	N/A	Government agencies: Instituto Cubano de Radiodifusión and TV service. Also U.S. Navy radio and TV station.
Dominican Republic	1821 (Spain)	—	U.S.	Private (commercial): 99 radio stations and 4 television stations.
El Salvador	1841 (Spain)	—	U.S.	Government agencies: 1 radio station (Radio Nacional) and 1 television station. Private (commercial): 36 radio stations and 3 television stations. Private (nonprofit): 1 radio station, Radio Teatro.

Table A.1 (*continued*) Dates of introduction and organizational form of broadcasting systems in ninety-one developing countries.

Area and Country	Date of Independence and former colonial power	Introduction of Radio	Introduction of TV	Model for system	Organization of broadcasting system
Guatemala	1821 (Spain)	—	—	U.S.	Government agencies: Radio Nacional and Radio Cultural. Private (commercial): 96 radio stations and 3 television stations.
Haiti	1804 (France)	—	—	U.S.	Private (commercial): 24 radio stations and 1 television station, Telé Haiti. Private (nonprofit): 4 radio stations.
Honduras	1838 (Spain)	—	—	U.S.	Private (commercial): 71 radio stations and 1 television station, Compania Televisora Hondureña, SA.
Jamaica	1962 (U.K.)	1942	1963	British	Public authority: Jamaica Broadcasting Corporation (radio and television). Private (commercial): Radio Jamaica Ltd.
Mexico	1821 (Spain)	1929	1951	U.S.	Government agencies: 3 radio stations and 1 television station. Private (commercial): 335 radio stations and 95 television stations. Private (nonprofit): 6 radio stations and 1 television station.
Nicaragua	1838 (Spain)	—	—	U.S.	Government agency: 1 radio station. Private (commercial): 50 radio stations and 4 television stations. Private (nonprofit): 2 radio stations.

Table A.1 (*continued*)

Panama	1903 (Spain)	—	—	U.S.	Private (commercial): 56 radio stations and 2 television stations.
Trinidad & Tobago	1962 (U.K.)	1947	1962	British	Government agency: National Broadcasting Service (radio). Private (commercial): Trinidad Broadcasting Co. (radio) and Trinidad & Tobago Television Co. Ltd.
Oceania					
Western Samoa	1962 (New Zealand)	1948	N/A	New Zealand	Government agency: Samoa Broadcasting Service.

Source: See Appendix B.

Table A.2 Sources of financial support of broadcasting systems in ninety-one countries, 1975.

Area and country	Sources of revenues (with percentage where known)	Annual radio license fee [a]	Number issued	Annual television license fee [a]	Number issued
Africa					
Algeria	Government (subvention) (55%); license fees (42%); commercials (3%)	$6.65–$11.44	720,000	$19,00 [b]	300,000
Botswana	Government; license fees	$2.50	8,500	N/A	N/A
Burundi	Government; license fees	—	50,000	N/A	N/A
Cameroon	Government; commercials	none	none	N/A	N/A
Central African Republic	Government (subvention); license fees; commercials	—	—	—	—
Chad	Government (subvention); commercials	none	none	N/A	N/A
Congo	Government (subvention); license fees; commercials	—	80,000	$26.60 [b]	2,600
Dahomey	Government (subvention); license fees; commercials	$2.00	85,000	N/A	N/A
Egypt	Government (subvention); commercials (10%); TV license fees; tax on electricity	none	none	$16.00	610,000
Equatorial Guinea	Government; commercials	none	none	N/A	N/A
Ethiopia	Government (subvention); commercials, TV license fees	none	none	$20.00	2,500
Gabon	Government (subvention); commercials	none	none	none	none

Table A.2 (continued)

Country	Source of revenue				
Gambia	Government; commercials	none	none	N/A	N/A
Ghana	Government (subvention); commercials; relay service; revenue license fees	$3.60	—	$ 6.00 [b]	—
Guinea	Government	none	none	N/A	N/A
Ivory Coast	Government (subvention); commercials	none	none	none	none
Kenya	Government (subvention); commercials; permits	none	none	$ 8.00	37,000
Lesotho	Government; commercials; license fees	$2.00	—	N/A	N/A
Liberia	Government (subvention); commercials	none	none	none	none
Libya	Government	none	none	none	none
Malagasy	Government (subvention); commercials; TV license fees	none	none	—	—
Malawi	Government (subvention); dealer license fees; commercials	—	—	N/A	N/A
Mali	Government; commercials	none	none	N/A	N/A
Mauritania	Government (subvention); commercials; license fees	$2.00	—	N/A	N/A
Mauritius	Government (subvention); commercials; license fees	$1.50–$3.00	80,260	$ 7.50	23,394 / 2,195 [b]
Morocco	Government (subvention); commercials; license fees	$3.00	1,500,000	$ 6.00	225,000
Niger	Government (subvention)	none	none	none	none
Nigeria	Government (subvention); commercials; license fees	$1.20	—	$ 6.00	—
Rwanda	Government	none	none	N/A	N/A
Senegal	Government (subvention) (90%); commercials (10%)	none	none	none	none
Sierra Leone	Government; commercials; license fees	$6.00	61,000	$20.00	—

Table A.2 (*continued*) Sources of financial support of broadcasting systems in ninety-one countries, 1975.

Area and country	Sources of revenues (with percentage where known)	Annual radio license fee [a]	Number issued	Annual television license fee [a]	Number issued
Somalia	Government	none	none	N/A	N/A
Sudan	Government; commercials	none	none	none	none
Swaziland	Government; commercials; license fees	$1.50	—	N/A	N/A
Tanzania	Government; commercials	none	none	none	none
Togo	Government	none	none	N/A	N/A
Tunisia	Government; license fees	$4.00	—	$10.00	—
Uganda	Government; license fees	none	none	$ 0.50	—
Upper Volta	Government; commercials; license fees; French government aid	—	—	—	—
Zaire	Government	none	none	none	none
Zambia	Government; commercials; license fees; grants; foreign sources	$2.00	75,000	$10.00 [b]	—
Asia					
Afghanistan	Government (import tax on sets); commercials; foreign sources	none	none	N/A	N/A
Burma	Government; license fees	$0.50	400,000	N/A	N/A

Table A.2 (*continued*)

	Sources of income				
Cyprus	Government (subvention) (5%); commercials (45%); license fees (50%)	$4.00	135,000	$10.00	66,200
India	Government (subvention); commercials; license fees	—	12,772,297	$ 3.00	56,868
Indonesia	Government (subvention) (84%); commercials (11%); license fees (4%)	$0.20	—	$20.00	293,071
Iran	Government; commercials	none	none	none	none
Iraq	Government (subvention) (90%); commercials (10%)	none	none	none	none
Jordan	Government; commercials; TV license fees	none	none	$14.00	—
Khmer Republic	Government; commercials	none	none	none	none
South Korea	Government; commercials; license fees	—	—	—	N/A
Laos	Government (subvention); foreign aid	none	none	N/A	none
Lebanon	Government; commercials	none	none	none	none
Malaysia	Government (subvention); commercials; license fees	$1.00	456,307	—b	—b
Nepal	Government (subvention); license fees	$1.00	—	N/A	N/A
Pakistan	Government (subvention); commercials; license fees	none	1,680,000	$ 5.00	98,699
Philippines	Government; commercials	none	none	none	none
Saudi Arabia	Government; commercials (TV)	$5.00	none	none	none
Singapore	Government; commercials; license fees	—	313,909	$14.50 b	243,003
Sri Lanka	Government; commercials; license fees	none	500,000	N/A	N/A
Syria	Government; license fees	none	none	$10.00	137,000
Thailand	Government (subvention); commercials	none	none	none	none
Turkey	Government; commercials; license fees	$2.50 c	4,033,577 d	$ 6.00–$15.00 c	261,868 d

Table A.2 (*continued*) Sources of financial support of broadcasting systems in ninety-one countries, 1975.

Area and country	Sources of revenues (with percentage where known)	Annual radio license fee [a]	Number issued	Annual television license fee [a]	Number issued
South Vietnam	Government	none	none	none	none
Yemen Arab Republic	Government	none	none	none	none
People's Democratic Republic of Yemen	Government; commercials; TV license fees	none	none	—	—
South America					
Argentina	Government; commercials	none	none	none	none
Bolivia	Government; commercials	none	none	none	none
Brazil	Government; commercials	none	none	none	none
Chile	Government; commercials	none	none	none	none
Colombia	Government; commercials	none	none	none	none
Ecuador	Government; commercials	none	none	none	none
Guyana	Government; commercials; license fees	$0.70	60,000	N/A	N/A
Paraguay	Government; commercials	none	none	none	none
Peru	Government; commercials	none	none	none	none
Uruguay	Government; commercials	none	none	none	none
Venezuela	Government; commercials	none	none	none	none

Table A.2 (*continued*)

Central America and the Caribbean

Barbados	Government (subvention); commercials; license fees	—	—	$ 6.00	—
Costa Rica	Commercials	none	none	none	none
Cuba	Government	none	none	none	none
Dominican Republic	Government; commercials	none	none	none	none
El Salvador	Government; commercials	none	none	none	none
Guatemala	Government; commercials	none	none	none	none
Haiti	Commercials	none	none	none	none
Honduras	Government; commercials	none	none	none	none
Jamaica	Government; commercials	none	none	none	none
Mexico	Government; commercials	none	none	none	none
Nicaragua	Government; commercials	none	none	none	none
Panama	Government (subvention); commercials	none	none	none	none
Trinidad & Tobago	Government; commercials	none	none	none	none

Oceania

Western Samoa	Government (subvention); commercials	none	none	none	none

Source: See Appendix B.

a. In U.S. dollars.

b. Combined radio and television license fee.

c. The license fee varies according to whether the receiver is located in a rural or an urban area.

d. Only nonportable sets require a license.

Table A.3 Distribution of broadcasting: transmission facilities and coverage in ninety-one countries.

Area and country	Radio							Television			
	Number of shortwave transmitters [a]	Number of medium-wave transmitters [a]	Number of long-wave transmitters [a]	Number of FM transmitters [a]	Total kw	Coverage of land area (%)	Coverage of population (%)	Number of television transmitters	Total kw	Coverage of land area (%)	Coverage of population (%)
Africa											
Algeria	8 (640)	17 (2,212)	1 (1,500)	0	4,352	100	100	7	740	25	80
Botswana	1 (50)	5 (50)	0	1 (0.25)	100.25	100	100	0	0	0	0
Burundi	4 (62.5)	2 (1.25)	0	1 (0.5)	64.25	80	90	0	0	0	0
Cameroon	7 (136)	4 (22)	0	0	158	100	100	0	0	0	0
Central African Republic	1 (100)	1 (1)	0	1 (0.5)	101.5	100	100	0	0	0	0
Chad	2 (130)	2 (21)	0	0	151	30	75	0	0	0	0
Congo	6 (229)	2 (80)	0	0	309	80	95	1	2	1	70
Dahomey	2 (34)	3 (50)	0	0	84	—	—	0	0	0	0
Egypt	1 (1,000)	19 (2,820)	0	0	3,820	100	100	27	682	25	60
Equatorial Guinea	2 (15)	0	0	0	15	80–90	100	0	0	0	0
Ethiopia	3 (300) [b]	1 (100)	0	0	400	—	40	1	0.5	0.01	15
Gabon	6 (184)	4 (42)	0	0	226	100	100	3	0.13	10	65
Gambia	1 (3.1)	1 (5)	0	1 (0.1)	8.2	100	100	0	0	0	0
Ghana	12 (985)	0	0	0	985	100	100	4	46.5	50	70

Table A.3 (*continued*)

Guinea	4 (236)	2 (110)	0	0	346	—	—	0	0	0	0
Ivory Coast	4 (235)	3 (10)	0	4 (1.5)	246.5	100	100	6	60	—	70
Kenya	6 (230)	9 (277)	0	2 (2)	509	100	100	4	20.5	10	40
Lesotho	0	1 (10)	0	1 (0.5)	10.05	—	—	0	0	0	0
Liberia	5 (120) [c]	4 (20.2)	0	0	140.2	100	100	2	12.5	10	35
Libya	2 (200)	8 (2,205)	0	0	2,405	80–90	100	10	80.4	5	15
Malagasy	10 (226)	2 (8)	0	4 (2)	234	100	100	1	0.5	5.6	12
Malawi	2 (120)	6 (15)	0	0	137	70	90	0	0	0	0
Mali	6 (236)	2 (64)	0	0	300	—	—	0	0	0	0
Mauritania	3 (230)	1 (20)	0	3 (1.6)	250	30	70	0	0	0	0
Mauritius	2 (20)	1 (10)	0	0	30	100	100	1	15	100	100
Morocco	7 (320)	23 (1186)	1 (800)	0	1,907.60	100	100	15	562	20	60
Niger	6 (47)	8 (1.7)	0	0	48.7	80	—	1	0.05	—	35
Nigeria	17 (351)	22 (339.75)	0	0	690.75	100	100	8	346	3	5
Rwanda	2 (55) [d]	0	0	1 (10)	65	—	—	0	0	0	0
Senegal	4 (118)	9 (258)	0	0	376	—	—	1	0.1	0.1	15
Sierra Leone	2 (20)	1 (10)	0	0	30	80	95	1	1	0.04	5
Somalia	5 (120)	0	0	0	120	80	95	0	0	0	0
Sudan	4 (310)	2 (160)	0	0	470	60–70	73	2	10.6	1	10
Swaziland	2 (110) [e]	2 (20)	0	2 (0.22)	130.22	50	60–75	0	0	0	0
Tanzania	9 (253)	7 (310)	0	0	563	85	50	2	8	0	0
Togo	5 (310)	2 (20)	0	0	330	30	50	1	1	5	10
Tunisia	4 (175)	4 (805)	0	0	980	100	100	10	1,283.30	0.28, 5	2.67, 10
Uganda	5 (30)	7 (453)	0	0	483	100	100	6	330	90, 50	98, 70
Upper Volta	2 (140)	1 (100)	0	0	140	75	80	2	2	0.02	2

Table A.3 (*continued*) Distribution of broadcasting: transmission facilities and coverage in ninety-one countries.

Area and country	Radio							Television			
	Number of shortwave transmitters [a]	Number of medium-wave transmitters [a]	Number of long-wave transmitters [a]	Number of FM transmitters [a]	Total kw	Coverage of land area (%)	Coverage of population (%)	Number of television transmitters	Total kw	Coverage of land area (%)	Coverage of population (%)
Zaire	17 (286.1)	6 (952)	0	1 (1)	1,239.1	—	—	2	—	—	—
Zambia	10 (512.5)	8 (306)	0	1 (5)	823.5	80	90	3	40.16	0.1	20
Asia											
Afghanistan	4 (300)	2 (125)	0	0	425	—	—	0	0	0	0
Burma	4 (200)	1 (50)	0	1 (0.25)	250.25	—	70	0	0	0	0
Cyprus	0	4 (42.5)	0	2 (20)	62.5	100	100	5	146	60	80
India	32 (1,620.50)	106 (4,105.15)	0	0	5,725	67.5	80.3	3	11	0.003	0.1
Indonesia	216 (1,104)	27 (20.35)	0	2 (0.6)	1,124	100	95	13	292	0.01	0.1
Iran	9 (1,210)	54 (5,472)	0	2 (20)	6,702	100	100	27	130	50	57.6
Iraq	8 (852)	5 (1,941)	0	0	2,793	100	100	4	598	100	100
Jordan	4 (212.5)	2 (210)	0	0	422.5	100	100	3	230	100	100
Khmer Republic	2 (65)	6 (160)	0	0	225	—	—	2	40.8	—	—
South Korea	10 (215)	90 (2,351.25)	0	47 (63)	2,629	65	90	19	870	251	70
Laos	6 (41.1)	9 (119)	0	0	160.1	50	90	0	0	0	0
Lebanon	2 (110)	2 (200)	0	3 (27)	337	100	100	8	289.1	100	100
Malaysia	15 (760)	25 (1,035)	0	3 (3.5)	1,798.5	65	80	30	1,907.50	50	70

Table A.3 (*continued*)

Nepal	2 (105)	1 (10)	0	0	115	—	—	0	0	0	0
Pakistan	65 (8,170)	20 (2,310)	0	0	10,480	70	80	6	561	—	70
Philippines	26 (1,160)	262 (1,891)	0	0	3,051	100	100	28	533	35	60
Saudi Arabia	17 (1,950)	4 (1,351) [f]	0	0 [g]	3,301	100	100	7	130	15	50
Singapore	8 (207.5)	5 (180)	0	4 (40)	427.5 [h]	100	100	1	80	100	100
Sri Lanka	0	10 (240.25) [i]	0	0	240.25	100	100	0	0	0	0
Syria	3 (90)	8 (740)	0	0	830	100	100	4	390	—	—
Thailand	14 (175)	136 (1,687)	0	40 (—)	1,862	100	100	7	184	30	65
Turkey	8 (356)	10 (1,467)	2 (1,300)	2 (1.5)	3,124.50	80	98	13	22.25	5	30
South Vietnam	6 (640)	4 (330)	0	0	970	100	100	1	240	—	—
Yemen Arab Republic	3 (135)	3 (1,070)	0	0	1,205	—	—	0	0	0	0
People's Democratic Republic of Yemen	2 (107.5)	1 (50)	0	0	157.5	—	—	3	1	5	16
South America											
Argentina	6 (327)	127 (1,450)	0	12 (—)	1,777	100	100	31	1,100	—	80
Bolivia	38 (88)	54 (62)	0	0	150	—	50	2	10	—	6.5
Brazil	350 (—)	850 (—)	0	—	—	70	100	189	—	80	65
Chile	26 (333.25)	153 (771)	0	—	179	70	80	31	306	—	75
Colombia	48 (253)	247 (896)	0	91 (—)	1,149	100	100	17	3,740	45	85
Ecuador	96 (252)	231 (544)	0	20 (21)	817	100	100	14	55	—	—
Guyana	3 (22.5)	4 (40)	0	1 (0.1)	62.6	—	100	0	0	0	0

Table A.3 (*continued*) Distribution of broadcasting: transmission facilities and coverage in ninety-one countries.

Area and country	Radio							Television			
	Number of shortwave transmitters [a]	Number of medium-wave transmitters [a]	Number of long-wave transmitters [a]	Number of FM transmitters [a]	Total kw	Coverage of land area (%)	Coverage of population (%)	Number of television transmitters	Total kw	Coverage of land area (%)	Coverage of population (%)
Paraguay	8 (119)	23 (193.5)	0	6 (—)	312.5	—	58	1	60	—	—
Peru	100 (—)	121 (130)	0	0	—	85	100	18	—	35	40
Uruguay	16 (97)	29 (601)	0	4 (4)	702	100	100	17	113	100	100
Venezuela	103 (400)	155 (1,500)	0	23 (—)	1,900	—	80	40	1,687	—	50
Central America and the Caribbean											
Barbados	0	2 (11)	0	1 (0.02)	11.02	100	100	1	60	—	85
Costa Rica	7 (9)	41 (65)	0	0	74	100	100	8	176.8	100	100
Cuba	3 (20)	116 (312)	0	23 (5)	437	100	100	25	—	—	—
Dominican Republic	12 (60)	99 (174)	0	26 (16)	250	100	100	6	30	—	—
El Salvador	3 (11)	50 (158)	0	8 (—)	169	100	100	5	72.5	100	100
Guatemala	4 (20)	85 (350)	0	0	370	100	100	3	30.5	—	—
Haiti	20 (85)	31 (29)	0	5 (—)	114	—	—	2	—	—	—
Honduras	37 (30)	79 (158)	0	10 (0.7)	188.7	100	100	5	30	—	—
Jamaica	0	8 (40)	0	7 (19)	59	75	100	1	0.14	60	—
Mexico	27 (—)	335 (—)	0	51 (—)	(—)	100	100	96	—	—	—

Table A.3 (*continued*)

Nicaragua	13 (110)	67 (350)	0	59 (—)	460	100	100	2	11	40	90
Panama	4 (3.2)	73 (128)	0	37 (9.4)	140.6	100	100	13	78.6	100	100
Trinidad & Tobago	0	5 (41)	0	12 (1.74)	72.74	100	100	6	33.2	—	95
Oceania											
Western Samoa	0	1 (10)	0	0	10	45	55	0	0	0	0

Source: See Appendix B.

a. Figures in parentheses are total kilowatts.
b. In addition, Radio Voice of the Gospel operates two 100 kw shortwave transmitters.
c. The Voice of America operates seven 250 kw and two 50 kw transmitters.
d. In addition, Deutsche Welle operates two 250 kw shortwave transmitters.
e. In addition, Trans-World Radio (a religious organization) operates four 30 kw shortwave transmitters.
f. In addition, Aramco Radio operates one 0.1 kw medium-wave transmitter.
g. In addition, Aramco Radio operates three stereo 86 kw FM transmitters.
h. In addition, British Forces Broadcasting Service operates one 5 kw FM transmitter.
i. In addition, the Voice of America (Colombo) operates three 35 kw shortwave transmitters.

Table A.4 Number of radio and television receivers in use in ninety-one countries, per 1,000 population.

Area and country	Population	Estimated number of radio sets in use	Radio sets per 1,000 population	Estimated number of television sets in use	Television sets per 1,000 population
Africa					
Algeria	14,600,000	1,000,000	68	450,000	31
Botswana	630,400	50,000	79	0	0
Burundi	3,500,000	150,000	43	0	0
Cameroon	5,700,000	220,000	38	0	0
Central African Republic	2,255,500	75,000	33	0	0
Chad	3,500,000	60,000	17	0	0
Congo	1,250,000	150,000	120	2,600	3
Dahomey	2,370,000	100,000	42	0	0
Egypt	35,000,000	5,000,000	143	650,000	19
Equatorial Guinea	310,000	72,000	232	1,000	3
Ethiopia	24,319,000	550,000	23	20,000	1
Gabon	630,000	80,000	127	5,100	8
Gambia	494,300	68,000	138	0	0
Ghana	8,700,000	1,000,000	115	28,000	3
Guinea	4,500,000	100,000	22	0	0
Ivory Coast	4,560,000	500,000	110	100,000	22
Kenya	11,100,000	1,100,000	99	38,000	3

Table A.4 (continued)

Lesotho	1,053,000	10,000	10	0	0
Liberia	2,500,000	160,000	64	8,500	3
Libya	1,900,000	90,000	47	5,000	3
Malagasy	7,200,000	600,000	83	7,000	1
Malawi	4,596,000	111,000	24	0	0
Mali	4,810,000	110,000	23	0	0
Mauritania	1,800,000	260,000	173	0	0
Mauritius	885,000	120,000	147	25,336	0
Morocco	15,520,000	1,502,000	97	335,689	22
Niger	3,810,000	100,000	26	50 [a]	N/A
Nigeria	66,174,000	5,000,000	76	90,000	1
Rwanda	3,900,000	60,000	15	0	0
Senegal	3,950,000	286,000	72	20,000	5
Sierra Leone	2,490,000	200,000	80	6,000	2
Somalia	2,930,000	150,000	51	0	0
Sudan	20,000,000	1,000,000	50	30,000	2
Swaziland	450,000	60,000	133	0	0
Tanzania	15,000,000	1,000,000	67	600 [b]	0
Togo	2,089,900	100,000	48	400	0
Tunisia	5,200,000	300,000	58	175,000	34
Uganda	9,800,000	360,000	37	70,000	7
Upper Volta	5,500,000	500,000	91	500	0

Table A.4 (continued) Number of radio and television receivers in use in ninety-one countries, per 1,000 population.

Area and country	Population	Estimated number of radio sets in use	Radio sets per 1,000 population	Estimated number of television sets in use	Television sets per 1,000 population
Zaire	22,860,000	100,000	4	12,000	1
Zambia	4,515,000	300,000	66	22,000	5
Asia					
Afghanistan	17,125,000	350,000	20	0	0
Burma	30,000,000	650,000	22	0	0
Cyprus	650,500	205,000	315	85,000	131
India	570,000,000	14,033,919	25	75,000	0
Indonesia	124,900,000	5,000,000	40	300,000	2
Iran	31,000,000	3,000,000	97	1,000,000	32
Iraq	10,070,000	1,000,000	99	300,000	30
Jordan	2,467,000	521,000	211	105,000	43
Khmer Republic	7,250,000	1,000,000	138	50,000	7
South Korea	32,900,000	6,000,000	182	1,500,000	46
Laos	3,100,000	400,000	129	0	0
Lebanon	3,150,000	1,321,000	419	375,000	119
Malaysia	9,460,000	425,000 [c]	45	352,235 [c]	37
Nepal	11,500,000	98,000	9	0	0

Table A.4 (*continued*)

Pakistan	64,892,000	1,700,000	26	126,000	2
Philippines	39,420,000	1,825,000	46	450,000	11
Saudi Arabia	8,000,000	1,000,000	125	250,000	31
Singapore	2,203,000	313,900	136	243,003	110
Sri Lanka	13,030,000	800,000	61	0	0
Syria	6,650,000	355,000	53	223,700	34
Thailand	37,410,000	3,000,000	80	650,000	17
Turkey	37,500,000	4,033,600	108	261,868	7
South Vietnam	19,000,000	4,500,000	237	500,000	26
Yemen Arab Republic	6,000,000	100,000	17	0	0
People's Democratic Republic of Yemen	1,510,000	95,000	63	30,000	20
South America					
Argentina	23,364,400	9,000,000	385	4,000,000	171
Bolivia	5,190,000	500,000	96	50,000	10
Brazil	104,500,000	32,000,000	306	10,000,000	96
Chile	10,000,000	4,500,000	450	458,000	46
Colombia	24,000,000	4,000,000	167	1,500,000	63
Ecuador	6,600,000	707,000	107	250,000	38
Guyana	750,000	275,000	367	0	0
Paraguay	2,560,000	175,000	68	57,000	22

Table A.4 (*continued*) Number of radio and television receivers in use in ninety-one countries, per 1,000 population.

Area and country	Population	Estimated number of radio sets in use	Radio sets per 1,000 population	Estimated number of television sets in use	Television sets per 1,000 population
Peru	15,000,000	2,000,000	133	700,000	47
Uruguay	2,956,000	1,500,000	507	300,000	101
Venezuela	11,000,000	2,000,000	182	980,000	89
Central America and the Caribbean					
Barbados	243,000	90,000	370	35,000	144
Costa Rica	1,843,000	230,000	125	150,400	82
Cuba	8,750,000	2,000,000	229	555,000	63
Dominican Republic	4,300,000	185,000	43	156,000	36
El Salvador	3,760,000	940,000	250	111,000	30
Guatemala	5,600,000	261,000	47	106,000	19
Haiti	5,000,000	91,000	18	13,100	3
Honduras	2,650,000	157,500	59	46,100	17
Jamaica	1,997,900	590,000	295	97,000	49
Mexico	52,700,000	15,841,100	301	3,821,170	73
Nicaragua	1,991,000	126,000	63	75,000	38
Panama	1,520,000	260,000	171	200,000	132
Trinidad & Tobago	1,040,000	300,000	288	93,000	89

Table A.4 (*continued*)

Oceania

Western Samoa	150,000	10,000	67	0	0

Source: See Appendix B.
a. Educational television project.
b. In Zanzibar.
c. Number of licenses issued.

Table A.5 Transfer of broadcasting systems to ninety-one countries, by type of transfer.

1. Transfer to independent countries: the U.S. model. (*Minimal state involvement in operation of broadcasting; supervision of airwaves by state; licensing of private operators.*)

Area	Countries
Africa	None
Asia	Philippines
South America	Argentina, Bolivia, *Brazil*,[a] Chile, Colombia, Cuba (prerevolution), Ecuador, Paraguay, *Peru*,[a] Uruguay, Venezuela
Central America and the Caribbean	Costa Rica, Dominican Republic, El Salvador, Guatemala, Haiti, Honduras, Mexico, Nicaragua, Panama
Oceania	None

2. Transfer to dependent territories: the British model. (*Colonial phase: unitary government service; postindependence: either continuation of unitary government service or establishment of public authority modeled on the BBC in unitary system, with state allocating airwaves.*)

Area	Countries
Africa	Botswana,[b] Gambia,[b] Ghana, Kenya,[b] Lesotho,[b] Malawi, Mauritius, *Nigeria*,[a] Sierra Leone,[b] Sudan,[b] Swaziland,[b] *Tanzania*,[a,c] Uganda,[b] Zambia [b]
Asia	Burma,[b] *Cyprus*,[a] India,[b] Malaysia,[b] Pakistan, Singapore,[b] Sri Lanka
South America	Guyana [b]
Central America and the Carribean	Barbados, Jamaica, Trinidad & Tobago [b]
Oceania	None

3. Transfer to dependent territories: the French model. (*Colonial phase: unitary government service; postindependence: either continuation of unitary government service or establishment of public authority in unitary system, with state allocating airwaves.*)

Area	Countries
Africa	*Algeria*,[a] Cameroon,[b] Central African Republic,[b] Chad,[b] Congo, Dahomey,[b] Gabon,

Area	Countries
	Guinea,[b] Ivory Coast, Malagasy, Mali,[b] Mauritania,[b] Morocco, Niger, *Senegal*,[a] Togo, Tunisia, Upper Volta
Asia	Khmer Republic,[b] Laos,[b] Lebanon,[b] South Vietnam [b]
South America	None
Central America and the Caribbean	None
Oceania	None

4. Transfer to dependent territories: other models.

Area	Countries
Africa	Burundi (Belgium), Equatorial Guinea (Spain), Rwanda (Belgium), Somalia (Italy/ U.K.), Zaire (Belgium)
Asia	*Indonesia* [a] (Dutch)
Central America and the Caribbean	None
Oceania	Western Samoa (New Zealand)

5. Transfer: hybrid models in independent countries.

Area	Countries
Africa	Ethiopia, Liberia, Egypt, Libya
Asia	Afghanistan, *Iran*,[a] South Korea, Nepal, Saudi Arabia, *Thailand*,[a] Turkey, Iraq, Jordan, Syria, Yemen Arab Republic, People's Democratic Republic of Yemen
South America	None
Central America and the Caribbean	None
Oceania	None

---

a. A case-study country.

b. Remained a government service.

c. Tanzania did introduce a public authority at independence (the Tanganyika Broadcasting Corporation), but this was dissolved in 1965. Radio Tanzania is now a government service within the control of the Ministry of Information and Broadcasting.

Table A.6 Television schedules, summer Thursday evenings in nine selected countries, 1974–75.

Time	U.K. BBC Channel 1 7/17/75	Brazil Globo Brasília 7/24/75	Nigeria NBC Lagos 7/24/75	Cyprus CBC 7/17/75	Singapore Channel 5 7/24/75	Iran NIRT Channel 7 7/22/75	Algeria RTA 4/18/74	Thailand Channel 7 7/19/75	Peru Channel 4 7/24/75	Peru Channel 5 7/24/75
5:30	Apollo/Soyuz Sir Prancelot (cartoon)	Hanna Barbera 75: Devlin, ó montequeiro (U.S. cartoon)				Cartoons	Philosophy (educational TV)		Gilligan's Island (U.S. series)	Variety show
5:45	National news Weather						Ivanhoe (U.K. serial)			
6:00	Nationwide (regional news)		International news		Opening Adventures of Rupert Bear (U.K. puppets)	Persian Literature (stories from the Shahnameh)	History (educational TV)		Comedy	Soccer
6:15		Senhora (Brazilian serial)	Children's Hour		Consumer's Guide (English and Malay)	The Seven Obstacles (game for children)		Western music show (Thai)		
6:30				Opening News, weather Cartoons (U.S.) On We Go (U.K. teaching English)	News in Brief Manis Manja (children's program)	Educational Program	Interschool Quiz	Supernatural Power (Japanese series)	Feature film (U.S.)	
6:45	A Question of Sport (quiz program)									
7:00		Bravo (Brazilian serial)	National news Family Quiz	Survival (U.K. series on the environment)	Wonderful World of Brother Buzz (U.S. educational film series for children)	Sports News		A Little Boy and His Elephant (Thai series)		
7:15	Top of the Pops (pop music)			Star Soccer		Evening Story for Children	Survival			

Time									
7:30	Apollo/Soyuz		(U.K.)	News (in Malay)	Women's Program (magazine format)	(U.K. documentary series on the environment)	Live show		Mellaman Gorion (Telenovela)
7:45				Six-Million-Dollar Man (U.S. series)					
8:00	Jornal Nacional (news)	Soccer/international table tennis				Weather News	Local, sports, and world news	Hoy (news)	
8:15	Escalada (Brazilian serial)		The Court Is in Session (Greek comedy)						
8:30		News, weather			News		Short Thai play		
8:45				Science Report (U.S.)					
9:00	Chico City (comedy feature film)	Nine O'clock News	News in Turkish News in English Discussion program	Tune-Inn (musical variety)	Bitter and Sweet (Iranian serial)	Television Viewers Club	Ray Anthony Show (U.S. music program)	Mujer (Venezuelan telenovela)	
9:15		News Highlights							
9:30	War and Peace (serial from Russian novel)			News and Newsreel (in English)					
9:45	Editorial (news) program	Bookstand (book review)	Western Festival	Harry-O (U.S. detective)			Chinese feature film (Hong Kong)		

Table A.6 (*continued*) Television schedules, summer Thursday evenings in nine selected countries, 1974–75.

Time	U.K. BBC Channel 1 7/17/75	Brazil Globo Brasilia 7/24/75	Nigeria NBC Lagos 7/24/75	Cyprus CBC 7/17/75	Singapore Channel 5 7/24/75	Iran NIRT Channel 7 7/22/75	Algeria RTA 4/18/75	Thailand Channel 7 7/19/75	Peru Channel 4 7/24/75	Peru Channel 5 7/24/75
10:00		Gabriela (*Brazilian serial*)	Village Headmaster (*repeat*)	(*U.S. films*)	series)	Mister Know It All (*Iranian comedy*)			Hawaii Five-0 (*U.S. series*)	24 Hours (*news*)
10:15										
10:30						Cannon (*U.S. detective series*)				
10:45	Apollo/Soyuz	Tomorrow (*news*)								
11:00		Kojak (*U.S. series*)	Night Report		Only a Scream Away (*U.K. suspense series*)		News		Medical Center (*U.S. series*)	Feature film (*U.S.*)
11:15										
11:30	Weather, regional news			News, weather			Closedown			
11:45										
12:00	Feature film (*U.S.*)				Closedown					

Methodology

According to the United Nations there were 207 "territorial units" within de facto boundaries in October 1971 (*UN Statistical Yearbook, 1971*). When we came to study the "developing" countries we faced the problem of defining which of these 207 territories should be categorized as such. There were several alternative strategies that we could have adopted. Most international agencies use straightforward criteria such as GNP per capita, but we wanted to incorporate social criteria as well as economic criteria. A paper prepared for UNCTAD outlined a method that satisfied these criteria in many respects.[1] The "I-distance" method of defining the less-developed countries (developed by B. Ivanovič) provides a means of overcoming the usual problems inherent in constructing global development indicators. Using a sophisticated factor analytical and correlational design, Ivanovič has incorporated five economic indicators and five social indicators into one global indicator of relative development.

As the I-distance method depends for its value on economic and social statistics that are reasonably recent and accurate, it was not possible to include in our group those territories for which data are lacking, incomplete, or known to be inaccurate. After excluding such countries there remain 118 territories to which the I-distance method was applied. Using this method we selected a group of countries that shared a relatively low level of development.[2] This reduced the number to 98, but this included five European countries (Spain, Greece, Malta, Yugoslavia, and Portugal) and South Africa. These six countries were excluded because they were not generally regarded as Third World countries. There then remained 92 countries. Because of the ambivalent political status of Taiwan, this country also came to be excluded. Thus our final group of 91 countries all fall below a certain level of development relative to the "developed" countries, are all Third World countries, and were all at the time of selection independent states for which UNCTAD had social and economic data (see Appendix C).

The limitations of time and budget were such as to enable us to visit not more than eleven countries of our total of 91, so we endeavored to select a small sample of countries that could be said to be in some way representative of the wide range of conditions and circumstances of all 91 countries. We started once more using the I-distance method, as this supplies five groups of countries, each group sharing a broad level of development. Each of the five socioeconomic groups was divided into nine geographical areas or regions (West Africa, East Africa, Central Africa, North Africa, the Middle East, the Far East, South America, Central America, and Oceania), creating a matrix or sampling frame of 45 cells, each cell representing a group of countries whose geographical position and socioeconomic profiles were similar. These 45 cells were further classified according to four criteria based on colonial or linguistic affiliations (British, French, other, inapplicable). At this stage a sample was taken that broadly reflected the distribution of these three main parameters in the group of 91 countries. Where it was necessary to choose between several countries in any cell, a "media development" index was used to differentiate countries into high, medium, and low levels of media development (see Table B.1).

Our primary sources of information were of course, the case studies that we carried out in 11 of the 91 developing countries. We arranged many of our meetings in advance and were usually able to extend the range of respondents through the individuals with whom we had originally been in touch. We relied heavily on the broadcasting organizations in the first instance, but we were fortunate enough to be able to draw upon the expertise and knowledge of nationals in all walks of life who were known to one or another of us through previous visits or because they were alumni of our universities. Thus we met a wide range of individuals from most sectors of each country. We usually recruited local associates who helped us both during and after our visits. Reports of the eleven case studies have been produced and are available at

Table B.1   Media development indicators.

Radio (sets per thousand population)		Television (sets per thousand population)	
Low	0–50	Low	0–10
Medium	51–150	Medium	11–50
High	151+	High	51+

Coding matrix

		Radio		
		High	Medium	Low
Television	High	1	2	3
	Medium	4	5	6
	Low	7	8	9
	No TV	10	11	12

cost from the Department of Adult and Higher Education, University of Manchester, Manchester M13 9PL, United Kingdom.

In addition to the case studies we relied upon mailed questionnaires that were sent to the 80 countries that we did not visit. There were two types of questionnaire: one for broadcasting organizations (222 sent, 39 completed and returned from 28 countries, a 17.7 percent response) and one for government ministries (91 sent, 25 completed and returned from 25 countries, a 27.4 percent response).

These response rates are usual for mailed questionnaire surveys. The questionnaires were available in French, Spanish, and English. In addition we wrote to hundreds of former students of our universities, members of the International Institute of Communications (IIC), and persons known to us or whose names were provided by other respondents. We eventually obtained good primary source material from 59 countries.

For the remaining 32 countries we had to rely on secondary source material. To this end a 1,500-item bibliography was compiled, and files were built up for each country from a wide variety of sources. Many "fugitive" papers were supplied by the Asian Mass Communication Research and Information Centre (AMIC) in Singapore and by several other research institutions and universities throughout the world. A major problem with these data was that they very often conflicted. We tried to overcome this problem in a pragmatic manner. Thus in the tables in Chapter 2 all the figures are taken from more than one source. Where two sources gave the same figures we relied on these; where there was no corroboration of figures we relied on our judgments of which figures were the most accurate—for example, if one knows that country X has only a Y kilowatt television transmitter and a total area of Z square miles, one can judge the validity of an estimate of broadcast coverage with a fair degree of accuracy.

Thus we have in many cases selected figures from a wide range of conflicting data on the basis of our own judgment of their validity. For this reason we have not provided detailed references to sources for this type of information, but these sources include, in order of our reliance on them:

1. case studies
2. statements and estimates from individuals with knowledge of a country's broadcasting system.
3. questionnaire responses
4. secondary source materials (articles, books, the Office de Radio-Télévision Française, the British Broadcasting Corporation, and Independent Broadcasting Authority documents)
5. *World Radio-TV Handbook*
6. UNESCO, *World Communication*, 1975, and other reports and papers.

As far as we are aware, the data we present are the most accurate available at the present time. It should be noted, however, that data in this field are notoriously inaccurate, and informed estimates are often more reliable than official statistics.

Levels of Development of Ninety-one Selected Countries

Within each group, countries are listed in order of their level of development.

GROUP A
(LEAST DEVELOPED)

Burundi
Rwanda
Yemen Arab Republic
Upper Volta
Niger
Mali
Nigeria * (West Africa, British affiliation, media development: 7)
Chad
Ethiopia
Nepal
Dahomey
Somalia
Laos
Tanzania * (East Africa, British affiliation, media development: 9)
Malawi
Gambia
Afghanistan
Sudan
Botswana

Mauritania
Guinea
Togo
Central African Republic
Haiti
Madagascar
Uganda
Burma
Zaire
Lesotho

GROUP B

Ivory Coast
Senegal * (West Africa, French affiliation, media development: 8)
Ghana
Vietnam
Bolivia
Thailand * (Far East, no colonial history, media development: 8)
Morocco

* A case-study country. The figures for "media development" are calculated using the matrix set out in Table B.1.

Swaziland
Tunisia
Sierra Leone
Khmer Republic
Cameroon
Pakistan
Kenya
Indonesia * (Far East, Dutch
  affiliation, media
  development: 8)
Congo
Equatorial Guinea
India

GROUP C
Iraq
Iran * (Middle East, no
  colonial history, media
  development: 8)
Syria
Algeria * (North Africa,
  French affiliation, media
  development: 5)
Liberia
Zambia
Gabon
Saudi Arabia

GROUP D
Guyana
Western Samoa
Sri Lanka
Mauritius
Jordan
Ecuador
Guatemala
Honduras
El Salvador

Malaysia
Dominican Republic
Paraguay
Philippines
Nicaragua
Turkey
Brazil * (South America, no
  recent colonial history,
  media development: 2)
Peru * (South America, no
  recent colonial history,
  media development: 5)
Colombia
Egypt
People's Democratic Republic
  of Yemen
South Korea

GROUP E
(MOST DEVELOPED)
Libya
Argentina
Uruguay
Cyprus * (Middle East, British
  affiliation, media
  development: 1)
Panama
Mexico
Chile
Jamaica
Lebanon
Cuba
Barbados
Costa Rica
Singapore * (Far East, British
  affiliation, media
  development: 3)
Venezuela
Trinidad & Tobago

* A case-study country.

Notes

1. THE PROBLEM OF DEVELOPMENT AND THE PROMISE OF BROADCASTING

1. Throughout we use the terms "new" and "developing" almost interchangeably in relation to the countries with which we are concerned, as does Clifford Geertz. Geertz also refers to certain countries as "least favored" (C. Geertz, *The Interpretation of Cultures* [New York: Basic Books, 1975], p. 234).

2. We include even Tanzania in this statement since Zanzibar, which has introduced television, forms part of the Republic of Tanzania, in the whole of the mainland of which, however, it has been decided not to introduce television.

3. "Symposium on Colour Television in Zanzibar," *Combroad*, April-June 1975.

4. It is interesting that the development of the technology of wireless telegraphy—the earliest radio—was connected with the simultaneous reporting of sporting events from the field to the newspapers. See E. Barnouw, *A Tower in Babel* (New York: Oxford University Press, 1966), p. 23.

5. The Colombian case has been extensively documented by Elizabeth Fox de Cardona in a paper presented to the meeting of the International Broadcast Institute in Mexico City in 1974. We draw on it frequently. See E. Fox de Cardona, *Broadcasting in Colombia: Communication Structures and Regulatory Frames* (Bogotá: 1975), mimeographed, and the same author's "Multinational Television," *Journal of Communication* 25 (1975): 122–127.

6. In 1976, the federal government nationalized the six existing television stations to operate them as a federal service, Television of Nigeria. Our discussion here is generally based on data from 1973–1975, when we conducted and analyzed the case studies. Rather than attempting to keep up with changing events, we report the situation as it was then.

7. *Interpretation of Cultures*, p. 270.

8. Ibid., p. 240.

9. Ibid.

10. D. Lerner, *The Passing of Traditional Society* (New York: Free Press, 1955).

11. This is the crux of the problem: even where exposure to the media has been found to correlate with empathy and other measures of "cognitive flexibility," it is difficult to say which came first. See, for example, E. M. Rogers with L. Svenning, *Modernization among Peasants: The Impact of Communication* (New York: Holt, Rinehart and Winston, 1969), p. 203. Indeed, Lerner himself treats empathy sometimes as cause, sometimes as consequence. See F. Frey, "Communication and Development," in I. de Sola Pool and W. Schramm, eds., *Handbook of Communication* (Chicago: Rand McNally, 1973), p. 402.

12. A. Inkeles and D. H. Smith, *Becoming Modern: Individual Change in Six Developing Countries* (Cambridge, Mass.: Harvard University Press, 1974).

13. J. N. Mosel, "Communication Patterns and Political Socialization in Transitional Thailand," in L. W. Pye, ed., *Communications and Political Development* (Princeton: Princeton University Press, 1963).

14. See, for example, L. R. Beltran, "TV Etchings in the Minds of Latin Americans: Conservatism, Materialism and Conformism," a paper presented to the International Association for Mass Communication Research Conference, University of Leicester, 1976. See also G. Gerbner, ed., *Mass Media in Changing Cultures* (New York: Wiley, in press).

15. W. Schramm, *Mass Media and National Development* (Stanford: Stanford University Press, 1964).

16. E. M. Rogers, *The Diffusion of Innovations* (New York: Free Press, 1962), and Rogers and Svenning, *Modernization among Peasants*.

17. See the brilliant review by T. McCormack, "Folk Culture and the Mass Media," *European Journal of Sociology* 10 (1969): 220–227.

18. See Beltran, "TV Etchings."

19. N. Bennett, "Planning for the Development of Educational Media in Thailand," *Educational Broadcasting International*, 1974, pp. 176–179.

20. D. W. Smythe, "Mass Communications and Cultural Revolution: The Experience of China," in G. Gerbner, L. P. Gross, and W. H. Melody, eds., *Communications Technology and Social Policy* (New York: Wiley, 1973).

21. A. Mattelart, "Mass Media and the Socialist Revolution: The Experience of Chile," in Gerbner and others, eds., *Communications Technology and Social Policy*. See aso K. Nordenstreng and T. Varis, "Television Traffic: A One-Way Street?" *Reports and Papers on Mass Communication*, no. 70 (Paris: UNESCO, 1974).

22. W. Dizard, *Television: A World View* (Syracuse: Syracuse University Press, 1966).

23. See Rogers, *Diffusion of Innovations*, and Rogers and Svenning, *Modernization among Peasants.*

24. Lerner, *Passing of Traditional Society.*

25. Algerian Democratic People's Republic, *Plan Quadriennal 1970–73* (Algiers: Secretariat au Plan, 1970), p. 77, translated from the French.

26. The Hon. Daudi Mwakawago, Minister of Information and Broadcasting, Republic of Tanzania, *Financial Estimates, 1973/4* (Dar es Salaam: Government Printer, 1973).

27. "Symposium on Colour Television in Zanzibar."

28. Thailand's draft *Regulations Governing Official Radio Broadcasts, 1968* continue: "(5) To be a good mass medium [by providing] general news and official news from the government to the people with accuracy and speed in order to promote understanding; (6) to support activities concerned with national education; (7) to encourage people in helping to safeguard the culture, tradition and language of the Thai nation and to ensure that these may continue to exist in a satisfactory manner; (8) to provide knowledge and entertainment (pleasure) to the people in accord with its culture, tradition and morality; (9) to co-operate with nations that are friendly to Thailand, through exchange of views and programmes which are of common interest in order to create good mutual understanding." Of equal interest from the point of view of goals is what may *not* be broadcast. The same regulations ban the reporting of "the loss of officials in the suppression of bandits, terrorists or rebels; reports of movements of crime suppression officials; news reports that adversely affect public morale or cause panic to the people; news reports that will put merchants on the alert, resulting in prices of goods being increased; and news reports that are in the interests of the enemy or that will strengthen the status of the enemy, unless they are official reports." Stations must also "broadcast anti-communist programmes and programmes supporting government policy" (Article 21).

29. S. Olusola, *NBC and Nigerian Culture* a Paper presented to the Nigerian Broadcasting Corporation Management Seminar, Lagos, July 26, 1973, mimeographed.

30. E. Quandt de Oliveira, Minister of Communications, Brazil, addressing the Fourth Southern States of Brazil Congress on Broadcasting, 1974, as reported in *Abert em Noticias*, October 1974, p. 1.

31. E. Quandt de Oliveira, "Television as a Medium of Mass Communication," address to the Anhembi Faculty of Social Communication, São Paulo, November 19, 1974.

2. BROADCASTING STRUCTURES IN THE DEVELOPING COUNTRIES

1. In some countries (Ethiopia, Gambia, Liberia, Morocco, and Swaziland) there are broadcasting stations that are not operated by government, such as Radio Voice of the Gospel in Addis Ababa, but all these are operated in addition to a national government service.

2. J. Hale, *Radio Power* (London: Paul Elek, 1975), p. 98.

3. B. Young, "How Should Broadcasting Be Financed?" *Independent Broadcasting* (London) August 5, 1975.

4. S. Head, ed., *Broadcasting in Africa* (Philadelphia: Temple University Press, 1974).

3. THE TRANSFER OF BROADCASTING

1. E. G. Wedell, *Broadcasting and Public Policy* (London, Michael Joseph, 1968), p. 51.

2. T. Green, *The Universal Eye* (London: Bodley Head, 1972), p. 63.

3. J. F. Wilkinson, "The BBC and Africa," *African Affairs* 71 (April 1972): 176–185.

4. Ibid.

5. G. Mytton, "Tanzania: The Problems of Media Development," *Gazette*, 14, no. 2 (1968): 91.

6. Ibid.

7. Nigerian Broadcasting Corporation, *Ten Years of Service* (Lagos: NBC, 1967).

8. Wilkinson, "The BBC and Africa," p. 179.

9. Speech in the National Assembly, Dar es Salaam, March 16, 1965.

10. Leslie Diamond, interview, September 10, 1973.

11. I. K. McKay, *Broadcasting in Nigeria* (Ibadan, University Press, 1964).

12. *House of Representatives Debates, August 1–15, 1961* (Lagos: Federal Government Printer, 1961), p. 11.

13. UNESCO/ED/190, May 18, 1962.

14. See UNESCO, "Mass Media in an African Context," *Reports and Papers on Mass Communication*, no. 69 (Paris: UNESCO, 1973), and also UNESCO, "Television and the Social Education of Women," ibid., no. 50 (Paris: UNESCO, 1967).

15. A. Fall, *La Radiodiffusion en Afrique* (Dakar: Radiodiffusion Sénégalaise, 1968), mimeographed.

16. Radio Republik Indonesia, *Broadcasting in Indonesia* (Jakarta: RRI, 1972).

17. "Deputy Prime Minister Orders Radio Thailand to Improve News Format," *The Nation* (Bangkok), October 30, 1973.

18. K. Nordenstreng and T. Varis, "Television Traffic: A One-Way Street?" *Reports and Papers on Mass Communication,* no. 70 (Paris: UNESCO, 1974).

4. THE INTERACTION OF BROADCASTING AND ESTABLISHED INSTITUTIONS

1. W. A. Lewis, "Beyond African Dictatorships," *Encounter* 25 (August 2, 1965): 3–25.

2. "Where there is one party, and that party is identified with the nation as a whole, the foundations of democracy are firmer than they can ever be when you have two or more parties, each representing only a section of the community." President Nyerere at the Annual Conference of the TANU party, 1963.

3. Although the United States was not a colonial power its economic and trading position in South America has been of comparable predominance (see Chapter 3).

4. B. Maddox, "The Beam in India's Eye," *The Guardian* (London), August 5, 1975.

5. E. Faure, *Learning to Be* (Paris: UNESCO, 1972), p. 122.

6. *Survey of Educational Broadcasting in Commonwealth Countries* (London: Centre for Educational Development Overseas, 1972–73).

7. P. Fougeyrollas, "Television and the Social Education of Women," *Reports and Papers on Mass Communication,* no. 50 (Paris: UNESCO, 1967).

8. For a review of these projects see "Mass Media in an African Context: An Evaluation of Senegal's Pilot Project," ibid., no. 69 (Paris: UNESCO, 1973).

9. See Richmond Postgate's interesting analysis, "The Coordination of Educational and Communications Development," a paper presented to the Annual Members' Meeting of the International Broadcast Institute, Cologne, 1975.

10. September 26, 1970, p. 68.

11. W. Schramm, *Mass Media and National Development* (Stanford: Stanford University Press, 1964), p. 164.

12. "Coordination of Educational and Communications Development."

13. P. H. Coombs, *The World Educational Crisis: A Systems Analysis* (Oxford: Oxford University Press, 1968).

14. I. Illich, *Celebration of Awareness* and *Deschooling Society* (London: Penguin Books, 1973).

15. J. Nyerere, "Education for Self-Reliance," in Nyerere, *Ujamaa: Essays on Socialism* (Oxford: Oxford University Press, 1968).

16. W. S. Kajubi, "Is the School an Obsolete Institution?" in *Educat-*

ing the Young People of the World (Washington, D.C.: National Education Association, 1970).

17. P. Freire, *Pedagogy of the Oppressed* and *Cultural Action for Freedom* (London: Penguin Books, 1972).

18. E. G. Wedell et al., *Education and the Development of Malawi* (Manchester: Centre for Overseas Educational Development of the University of Manchester, 1973), pp. 10–12.

19. *Report of the Sixth Commonwealth Education Conference* (London: The Commonwealth Secretariat, 1975), p. 49.

20. Ibid.

21. B. L. Hall and C. Zikambona, *Mtu ni Afya: An Evaluation of the 1973 Mass Health Education Campaign in Tanzania* (Dar es Salaam: Institute of Adult Education, 1974), pp. 12–13.

22. A. Curle, *Educational Strategy for Developing Countries* (London: Tavistock, 1963), pp. 11–12.

23. Radio Republik Indonesia, *Broadcasting in Indonesia* (Jakarta: RRI, 1972), p. 7.

24. Public Information Office, Nicosia, *Cyprus Today* 10 (September–December 1972): 21.

25. Ibid.

5. PROGRAMMING PATTERNS

1. See E. G. Wedell, *Broadcasting and Public Policy* (London: Michael Joseph, 1968), pp. 166–167, for a discussion of the problems raised by these incompatibilities.

2. Independent Broadcasting Authority, *TV and Radio, 1976* (London: 1976), p. 11.

3. Ibid., pp. 11–15.

4. The pioneering study of this subject is K. Nordenstreng and T. Varis, "Television Traffic: A One-Way Street?" *Reports and Papers on Mass Communication*, no. 70 (Paris: UNESCO, 1974). Unfortunately, most of our case studies are not among the countries for which data are provided in their study.

5. For leading views on this subject, see H. I. Schiller, *Mass Communication and American Empire* (New York: Kelley, 1969); P. Elliott and P. Golding, "Mass Communication and Social Change: The Imagery of Development and the Development of Imagery," in E. de Kadt and G. Williams, eds., *Sociology and Development* (London: Tavistock, 1974); and J. Tunstall, *The Media Are American* (London: Constable, 1977).

6. Cf. L. R. Beltran, "TV Etchings in the Minds of Latin Americans: Conservatism, Materialism and Conformism," a paper presented to the

International Association for Mass Communication Research Conference, University of Leicester, 1976. Professor George Gerbner suggests that the local elites are actively in favor of these programs; see G. Gerbner, ed., *Mass Media in Changing Cultures* (New York: Wiley, forthcoming).

7. Figures are from our own respondents and from *Variety*, January 1974.

8. The requirement that other countries agree to acquire the same program reflects the contractual relationship between the producers and the associations representing the artists. Contracts stipulate that royalties are to be paid when a program is first exhibited in a particular geographical region. Thus a small Asian country, for example, can obtain a program at its regular country price only if, say, Australia—which pays a high country price—also adopts it. If the large countries do not wish to acquire the program, the small country has to cover the entire cost of the regional royalties by itself.

9. The question of multidirectional flow—not only between developed and developing nations but between Eastern and Western Europe—is being raised in international forums such as UNESCO, the International Institute of Communications, and the International Association for Mass Communication Research and in ad hoc groups at MIT and the University of Pennsylvania. See Nordenstreng and Varis, "Television Traffic," for further discussion.

10. In his analysis of Reuter's West Africa service, Phil Harris demonstrates that only a third of the reports are about African affairs despite the promise that 60 percent would be. Although sympathetic to the call for a press service for and of nonaligned countries, Harris's analysis shows how difficult such a service would be to implement. Harris also notes the difficulty of changing the present balance of wire-service coverage so as to include more information from the developing world. See P. Harris, "Selective Images: An Analysis of the West African Wire Services of an International News Agency," a paper presented to the International Association for Mass Communication Research Conference, University of Leicester, 1976.

11. See E. Katz, "Television as a Horseless Carriage," in G. Gerbner, L. P. Gross, and W. H. Melody, eds., *Communications Technology and Social Policy* (New York: Wiley, 1973).

12. In his *Television: Technology and Cultural Form* (London: Fontana, 1974), Raymond Williams attempts this kind of analysis for British television. We do so only very superficially here, but the problem, as illustrated in Williams' analysis, is intriguing.

13. *A Survey of Television* (London: Heinemann, 1967).

14. D. E. Powell, "Television in the USSR," *Public Opinion Quarterly* 34 (1975): 287–300.

6. PROMISE AND PERFORMANCE

1. See the notes on methodology in the Preface and in Appendix B.

2. Documentary sources and names of interviewees and others who assisted us are cited in the case-study reports that we produced for each country we visited.

3. Jack Thompson, Colombo Plan consultant to the Thai Public Relations Department, as cited by Claudia Ross, "Do We Really Need 192 Radio Stations?" *Bangkok Post*, August 5, 1973.

4. The term "country and Western" is enough to suggest this. Nor should one overlook the presence in Thailand until recently of a large number of American military personnel.

5. The debate over the selection and presentation of news has assumed considerable intensity in recent years. See, for example, E. Epstein, *News from Nowhere* (New York: Random House, 1973); Glasgow University Media Group, *Bad News* (London: Routledge, 1976); G. Tuchman, "Objectivity as Strategic Ritual: An Examination of Newsmen's Notions of Objectivity," *American Journal of Sociology* 77 (1972): 660–679; H. Molotch, "News as Purposive Behavior: On the Strategic Use of Routine Events, Accidents, and Scandals," *American Sociological Review* 39 (1974): 101–112; and the controversial articles by J. Birt and P. Jay in the *Times* (London), September 2–3, 1976.

6. D. Lerner, *The Passing of Traditional Society* (New York: Free Press, 1955).

7. L. R. Beltran, "TV Etchings in the Minds of Latin Americans: Conservatism, Materialism and Conformism," a paper presented to the International Association for Mass Communication Research Conference, University of Leicester, 1976; and P. Golding, "Media Role in National Development: Critique of a Theoretical Orthodoxy," *Journal of Communication* 24 (1974): 39–53.

8. R. C. Hornik, "Mass Media Use and the Revolution of Rising Frustrations: A Reconsideration of the Theory," Papers of the East-West Communications Institute (Honolulu), no. 11, 1975.

9. M. Olumide, "Television in Africa—Nigeria," *Combroad*, July–September 1973, pp. 6–9.

10. For an extensive review of empirical studies, see F. Frey, "Communication and Development," in I. de Sola Pool and W. Schramm, eds., *Handbook of Communication* (Chicago: Rand McNally, 1973), pp. 337–461.

11. A. Inkeles and D. H. Smith, *Becoming Modern: Individual Change in*

Six Developing Countries (Cambridge, Mass.: Harvard University Press, 1974). But others argue that television is a conservative influence: See J. Cazeneuve, "Television as a Functional Alternative to Traditional Sources of Need Satisfaction," in E. Katz and J. Blumler, eds., *The Uses of Mass Communication* (Beverly Hills: Sage, 1974).

12. Frey, "Communication and Development."

13. Hornik, "Mass Media Use."

14. Frey, "Communication and Development."

15. Elliott and Golding, "Mass Communication and Social Change."

16. As the Maryknoll Fathers tried to do among the Sierra indians of Peru.

17. See the review in E. M. Rogers with L. Svenning, *Modernization among Peasants: The Impact of Communication* (New York: Holt, Rinehart and Winston, 1969).

18. The three concepts are from the classic paper by P. F. Lazarsfeld and R. K. Merton, "Mass Communication, Popular Taste, and Organized Social Action," in L. Bryson, ed., *Communication of Ideas* (New York: Harper, 1948), pp. 95–118.

19. I. de Sola Pool, "Communication in Totalitarian Societies," in Pool and Schramm, eds., *Handbook of Communication*, pp. 491–500.

20. See E. Katz, "On the Use of the Concept of Compatibility in Research on the Diffusion of Innovation," *Proceedings of the Israel Academy of Sciences* 5, no. 5 (1976): 126–145.

21. The more professional a listener (a skilled farmer, for example), the more likely he is to act on his own after weighing the advice of a fellow expert in a broadcast. Less skilled farmers will ask their neighbors, or their agricultural agent if they have one.

22. F. O. Ugboajah, "Nigerian Mass Media Behaviour on Development Issues of Conflict," a paper presented to the International Association for Mass Communication Research Conference, University of Leicester, 1976, mimeographed.

23. That most people, even the uninitiated, expect television to entertain more than to inform or to educate is the finding of a survey in Iran: A. Banani, "The Role of the Mass Media," in E. Yar-shater, ed., *Iran Faces the Seventies* (New York: Praeger, 1971), p. 328. A pretelevision survey in Israel arrived at the same conclusion. See E. Katz and M. Gurevitch, *The Secularization of Leisure: Culture and Communication in Israel* (Cambridge, Mass.: Harvard University Press, 1976). Again, when television broadcasting was extended to a remote part of Algeria by sending recorded material for broadcasting locally, the television executives in Algiers decided to cut out all Western programs and sent only indigenously produced cultural and information programs. There was a huge

outcry from the new audience members, who felt that they had been tricked. Eventually all the output from Algiers was sent uncut, and the protests ceased.

24. These and the references that follow are from a survey of broadcasting research in South America by Beltran ("TV Etchings").

25. S. P. Barreto, "El Caso Plaza Sesamo en el Peru," *Textual: Revista del Instituto Nacional de Cultura* (Peru) 8 (1973): 22–31. See also A. Mattelart, "El Imperialismo en Busca de la Contrarevolución Cultural–Plaza Sesamo: Prologa a la Telerepresion del Ano 2000," *Comunicacion y Cultura* (Chile), no. 1 (July 1973), pp. 146–223.

26. C. Geertz, *The Interpretation of Cultures* (New York: Basic Books, 1975).

27. J. Tunstall, *The Media Are American* (London: Constable, 1977).

28. H. I. Schiller, *Mass Communication and American Empire* (Boston: Beacon Press, 1969).

29. C. Ross, "Do We Really Need 192 Radio Stations?" *Bangkok Post*, August 5, 1973.

30. In commenting on these observations, the Norwegian sociologist Arild Boman remarked that we are understating the reciprocal influence of African and Asian music on the popular music of the West. Such influence naturally makes Western music more familiar to Africans and Asians when it returns to them.

31. For an analytic account of the content of soap opera see H. Newcomb, *TV: The Most Popular Art* (New York: Anchor, 1974). See also N. Katzman, "TV Soap Operas: What's Been Going On Anyway?" *Public Opinion Quarterly* 36 (1972–73): 200–212, for an up-to-date report on changes in the U.S. genre.

32. E. Fox de Cardona, *Broadcasting in Colombia: Communication Structures and Regulatory Frames* (Bogotá: 1975), mimeographed.

33. Commenting on the ravenousness of the medium, James Carey has estimated that one week of television time would be sufficient to broadcast all Shakespeare's plays.

34. Here again is an interesting subject for study. The productivity of the Asian film industry has been little noticed, except for India.

35. S. J. Tambiah, "Literacy in North-East Thailand," in J. Goody, ed., *Literacy in Traditional Societies* (Cambridge: Cambridge University Press, 1968), pp. 113–117.

36. Some of our informants thought that the success of the Iranian television series *Morad Barghi* is partly related to its roots in the *Ruhozi*. All agree that the television form is vulgar and inauthentic. The *Ruhozi* reached its climax of creativity and popularity during the nineteenth century.

37. Thelma McCormack argues that models of the relationships between folk culture and popular culture fall into three patterns: in the *evolutionary* models, folk culture is seen as coming to a natural end when folk society disappears; *additive* hypotheses argue that folk culture is a universal and is ahistoric, a dynamic factor in modern societies and coexisting with popular culture; *conflict* hypotheses explain the death of folk culture through conflict with the sirens of popular culture. See T. McCormack, "Folk Culture and the Mass Media," *European Journal of Sociology* 10 (1969): 220–237.

38. R. Hoggart, "Economic Growth and the Quality of Life," a paper presented to the Rehovoth Conference, Israel, September 5–11, 1973, p. 4.

39. Geertz, *Interpretation of Cultures.*

7. ARE THERE OTHER WAYS?

1. D. E. Apter, *The Politics of Modernization* (Chicago and London: University of Chicago Press, 1965), p. 186.

2. T. L. Hodgkin, *African Political Parties* (London: Penguin, 1961), p. 167.

3. Algerian Democratic People's Republic, *Plan Quadriennal 1970–73* (Algiers: Secretariat au Plan, 1970), p. 77.

4. See World Bank, *Annual Report for 1974* (Washington, D.C.: IBRD, 1975).

5. I. Abu-Lughod, "The Mass Media and Egyptian Village Life," in J. Tunstall, ed., *Media Sociology* (London: Constable, 1970), p. 333.

6. E. G. Wedell et al., *Education and the Development of Malawi* (Manchester: Centre for Overseas Educational Development, University of Manchester, 1973), pp. 211–212.

7. *Report of the Committee on Broadcasting 1960* (London: Her Majesty's Stationery Office, June 1962), p. 17.

8. J. F. Scotton, "Training in Africa," in S. Head, ed., *Broadcasting in Africa* (Philadelphia: Temple University Press, 1974), p. 282.

9. Head, *Broadcasting in Africa*, p. 359.

10. See the report summarized in C. Ross, "Do We Really Need 192 Radio Stations?" *Bangkok Post*, August 5, 1973.

11. See R. Bretz and D. Shinar, *Brazil: Educational Television*, report no. 2775/RMO.RD/MC (Paris: UNESCO, October 1972).

12. R. Hoggart, "The BBC's Duty to Society—VII," *The Listener*, August 5, 1965.

13. "Indonesia: Proposals for a National Satellite System," *Intermedia* (London), August 1975, p. 15.

APPENDIX B. METHODOLOGY

1. B. Ivanovič, "Problème de l'identification des pays les moins avancés parmi les pays en voie de développement," UNCTAD Research Division, memo no. 41, November 5, 1970.

2. All 98 countries selected in this way had an "I-distance" relative to each other of less than I-20.

Index

Advertising, 48, 49-51, 52-53, 117-119, 185-186

Afghanistan, 51

Africa, 101, 102, 144, 155, 167, 218, 244; development of broadcasting, 78-79, 231; finance of broadcasting, 48, 52; license systems, 51; organization of broadcasting, 42-43; reception technology, 60, 61; transmission difficulties, 58. *See also* West Africa

Afro-Shirazi party, 81

Algeria, 20, 85, 112, 120, 188, 192, 195, 196, 228; Arabization, 30, 145, 168, 175; finance of broadcasting, 52, 53; goals of broadcasting, 29-30, 217-218; introduction of radio, 8, 85; introduction of television, 85-86; policy changes, 17, 18, 88; programs, 153, 155, 157, 163, 167, 174, 201-202; transmission difficulties, 12, 172, 176-177

Apter, David, 213

Argentina, 70, 196

Arts, 140-145

Asia, 94, 101, 102, 105, 144; finance of broadcasting, 52; license systems, 52; organization of broadcasting, 43-44; reception technology, 60, 61

Bebey, F., *see* Quarmyne, Alex T., and F. Bebey

Belgian colonies, 89, 90

Bennett, Nicholas, 23

Brazil, 72, 94, 117, 138, 144, 172, 196; educational broadcasting, 125-126, 237; goals of broadcasting, 34, 218; introduction of radio, 7, 8, 46, 70, 71; introduction of television, 72; National Commission on Space Activities (INPE), 126; national communications policy, 76; National Program for Educational Television (PRONTEL), 126-127; organization of broadcasting, 44, 45, 236; policy changes, 73, 75, 105; programs, 152, 153, 155, 167, 186-187, 197, 227; Superintendency for the Development of the North East (SUDENE), 126; transmission difficulties, 12, 177

British Broadcasting Corporation (BBC), 49, 66, 97; and British colonies, 77, 78, 79, 80

Broadcasting Company of North-